Successful IT
project delivery

learning the lessons of project failure

David Yardley

 Addison-Wesley

An imprint of **Pearson Education**

London ■ Boston ■ Indianapolis ■ New York ■ Mexico City ■ Toronto ■ Sydney ■ Tokyo ■ Singapore
Hong Kong ■ Cape Town ■ New Delhi ■ Madrid ■ Paris ■ Amsterdam ■ Munich ■ Milan ■ Stockholm

PEARSON EDUCATION LIMITED

Head Office:
Edinburgh Gate
Harlow CM20 2JE
Tel: +44 (0)1279 623623
Fax: +44 (0)1279 431059

London Office:
128 Long Acre
London WC2E 9AN
Tel: +44 (0)20 7447 2000
Fax: +44 (0)20 7447 2170
www.it-minds.com
www.awprofessional.com

First published in Great Britain in 2002
© Pearson Education Ltd 2002

The right of David Yardley to be identified as the Author of this Work has been asserted by him in accordance
with the Copyright, Designs and Patents Act 1988.

ISBN 0-201-75606-4

British Library Cataloguing in Publication Data
A CIP catalogue record for this book can be obtained from the British Library

Library of Congress Cataloging in Publication Data
Applied for.

All rights reserved; no part of this publication may be reproduced, stored in a retrieval system, or transmitted
in any form or by any means, electronic, mechanical, photocopying, recording, or otherwise without either the
prior written permission of the Publishers or a licence permitting restricted copying in the United Kingdom
issued by the Copyright Licensing Agency Ltd, 90 Tottenham Court Road, London W1P 4LP. This book may
not be lent, resold, hired out or otherwise disposed of by way of trade in any form of binding or cover other
than that in which it is published, without the prior consent of the Publishers.

10   9   8   7   6   5   4   3   2   1

Designed by Sue Lamble
Typeset by Graphicraft Limited, Hong Kong
Printed and bound in Great Britain by Biddles Ltd of Guildford and King's Lynn.

The Publishers' policy is to use paper manufactured from sustainable forests.

For Anne, Ben, and Jack

Contents

part I Preparing the organization for IT projects

part II Planning for success

part III Design and development

8 Project building blocks: people   183

part IV Project delivery

Preface

This text is an introduction to the wide range of topics which collectively form the basis of an information technology (IT) project. Central to the theme of the book is the significance of people, processes, and technology within the project and the relationships between them. For example, the experience, skills, and commitment of the individuals engaged on the project will be as important to its success as the effective selection and deployment of information technology.

Aim of the book

The aim of this book is to equip you with sufficient information to help ensure that your next IT project is a success. Real-life case studies will help identify the pitfalls and traps experienced from projects from which you can learn valuable lessons, whilst 'best-practice' techniques are identified throughout the lifecycle of the project to promote clarity and understanding. By the time you have reached the end of the book, you will know where the pitfalls lie in each stage of the project lifecycle, 'early-warning' symptoms of failure, and the corrective action that can be taken if necessary to ensure successful IT project delivery.

Of course, we live in the real world and no one book can guarantee to eradicate project failure. This book *will* guarantee that if you follow the advice within it, then your IT projects will have a greater chance of success. If they do fail, then you will know *why* they have failed and be all the wiser from it. Learning the lessons from failure is one of the first and most valuable steps in achieving success.

This book is not just another book concerning project management techniques; there are many good books available on the subject already. Poor project management is indeed a cause of many IT project failures, but it is not the only cause. Even with an experienced and accomplished project manager at the helm, there are numerous organizational, financial, political, and technical issues that can, and often do, affect the outcome of an IT project.

Readership

This book will appeal to a wide audience across the business and IT professions, anyone in fact who is involved in an IT project. People as opposed to technology are the key component of IT projects, and the overall success of the project is very much dependent upon the actions and decisions made by key individuals who have a vested interest in its outcome.

In large organizations, specific job titles will often dictate the role performed by an individual engaged on an IT project (such as project manager, technical architect, business analyst, business sponsor, business consultant). In smaller organizations, a more informal project structure will often necessitate a broader categorization of job titles. In such circumstances, it is likely that each project member will be expected to perform a number of different roles within the project, such as project manager/technical architect. The book therefore is aimed primarily at the following individuals.

■ *Business sponsors of IT projects*

As business sponsor you must commit funds for IT development projects. By approving funding you are empowering IT delivery agents to build and deploy systems that will satisfy stated business requirements. In return, you expect to be rewarded with measurable business benefits within the economic life of the project.

Whilst you are able to champion the project and steer it through the many hurdles and obstacles every project encounters, you may well suffer from a lack in awareness of basic IT methodologies and techniques.

This book will provide you with a clear understanding of an IT project, both from an IT perspective and a business perspective. It will enable you to understand your role in the project and how performing that role and the decisions taken as a result can ultimately affect the success of the project.

■ *Project managers*

As a project manager you must deliver operational or strategic projects into the business community to an agreed timescale and cost. However, your success is often dependent upon, and ultimately judged by, individuals within the organization who cannot always decide what they require and why.

■ *IT professionals within the project team*

As an IT project member, such as a business analyst, developer, architect, software tester, e-commerce specialist, or security consultant, you will play a key role in developing complex business systems that must satisfy the objectives of those business individuals who have commissioned it. An IT project can provide the opportunity to work with some of the latest products and technologies but, without the full support and co-operation of the business, it can become a stressful and unrewarding experience. Whilst achieving personal success within a project is often considered unimportant to the IT professional, it increases self-esteem and can often trigger an increase in salary and enhance career development. This book will help you understand the relationship between the business and IT stakeholders in the project and how the project team can work effectively to build upon that relationship.

More importantly, many of the topics within the book will be of prime importance to the IT professional, such as: key stages within the software development lifecycle and their relevance to the project lifecycle; the role of IS methodologies within the project; and key software development risks and how to avoid them.

In addition, there are two other key groups of individuals who will benefit from the book.

■ *Business consultants*

As an external business or IT consultant you may be required to identify and rectify problems your client may be experiencing on an IT project. The client will have high expectations of what you are able to achieve, and the onus will be on you to identify the most likely source of their problems and ensure that there is a clear owner for any actions required. This book will provide you with a firm understanding of the scope of an IT project and the most common causes of project failure.

More importantly, it will identify the roles and responsibilities of both the customer (the organization with the requirement) and the supplier (the organization tasked with satisfying that requirement).

■ *Business users*

As a user of the IT system you have an ongoing stake in its success. After all, the system was designed and built to cater for your business needs, not to further the careers of the IT professionals who designed and built it. Within the scope of your business activity, you may have already been let down by your IT supplier and felt helpless to do anything to correct the situation. This book will help you understand the role of the business within an IT project and how you can operate within that role to help ensure that future projects within your environment are successful.

The structure of the book

The four sections that provide the structure for the book reflect a logical cycle for achieving success. In order to plan for success, we must first identify and understand the reasons for failure. Having established our defence against failure, we can then start to build solid project foundations using the most appropriate tools and techniques. Throughout the whole project, quality standards must be identified and assured, up to and including business acceptance of the system. The software delivery cycle is then complete when one or more products are delivered into a user environment.

Part I Preparing the organization for IT projects

The initial chapter in this section highlights the worrying gap that exists between the perceived success of the IT industry – the need to build complex information systems to meet the growing demands of an information-dependent global society – and the disappointing reality of software delivery. Rather than delivering clear benefits through the effective use of IT, many IT projects are now abandoned as expensive disasters before implementation or fail to deliver any benefit once they have been implemented, at huge costs to the business.

Subsequent chapters highlight the key topics that provide the foundations for a successful IT project. Embarking upon an IT project is not a miraculous event that will suddenly and automatically transform an organization. The IT project is an enabler of change and must be aligned closely with the overall objectives of the organization. Managing change, capturing business requirements, and adopting a suitable project framework are fundamental activities that must be performed successfully if the project is to stand any chance of delivering real benefits into the organization.

Part II Planning for success

Planning is of paramount importance if the project is to overcome the many problems that are likely to be encountered throughout its duration. Activities such as program and project management, risk management, and configuration management therefore represent key topics within this section. The final chapter in this section should act as a strong reminder to those who are in danger of forgetting what the ultimate objective of an IT project is – to deliver measurable benefits into the organization.

Part III Design and development

A successful IT project is one built with the agreement, endorsement, and commitment of many people within the organization. As the project moves into the design and development phases, the role of the project stakeholders will become even more important as the project team will require their continued support and commitment to ensure that issues arising which affect the project are owned and resolved as soon as possible.

This section of the book identifies and discusses the techniques and methods necessary to establish acceptable quality standards and controls throughout the lifecycle of the project. Managing the systems development process is a key activity within the majority of IT projects; without software development, even the most sophisticated computer hardware is worthless. With this is mind, the failure of many software development processes to meet even the most basic quality standards is quite incredible.

Part IV Project implementation

The transition of the project from development of one or more products to the release of those products into a user environment signifies a critical phase within the project delivery lifecycle. The implementation phase of the project will be where the project team will be under the greatest pressure to deliver to plan – even when key issues still remain unresolved. The focus within this section is placed initially on the importance of testing within the project, followed by the need for the transition from testing to product release to take place in a controlled and safe manner.

The book concludes with the most important and long-term organizational need – to learn the lessons from IT project failure. A key difference between those people who enjoy repeatable project success and those for whom success is always a distant memory is in their response to failure. Those who learn nothing from it, either through arrogance or ignorance, continue to fail; those who succeed learn from failure and strive for better things.

Appendix 1

The Guide to Learning the Lessons from Project Failure. At each stage throughout the lifecycle of the project, clear and pragmatic advice is given on the potential problems that may be encountered during the project, early-warning symptoms of potential project failure conditions, and corrective action that should be taken to ensure that successful project delivery is not compromised.

Appendix 2

The Project Health Check. A checklist of key statements to test how successful your project is likely to be.

Glossary

All the key terms, expressions and abbreviations used within the book in one place for quick reference.

The case studies

The case studies scattered throughout the book will demonstrate just how easily IT projects can fail even if only a small number of critical success factors are not met. The case studies themselves have been chosen as they represent some of the most common faults identified in failing projects. The case studies analyse failed IT projects both in the public sector and the private sector although, due to legal restrictions, out of court settlements and ongoing litigation, it has been difficult to obtain information on IT failure within the private sector. Luckily there are still a few companies who regard the disclosure of information on projects that have not been a huge success as something positive from which we can all learn. There are not many, and in some cases the names of these organizations and the sources within them have been withheld for commercial and legal reasons. The practice of seeking legal redress for IT project failures and the reluctance to disclose any information which might be legally or commercially sensitive in itself highlights the problem many who seek to redress the balance of project failure face. It also helps explain why, after over 40 years of commercial computing, the rate of IT project failure has reduced little. The case studies will also demonstrate that failure is not limited to massive multi-million pound projects; a relatively small software development project can fail for exactly the same reasons as TAURUS, the London Stock Exchange trading system, did in 1988.

Whilst no one enjoys being associated with a failing project, understanding failure should be seen as an essential part of planning for success. Only from learning the lessons of failure can new methods of working be identified. Of course, this book is not the first publication to review IT failures but, whilst it is easy to discuss the many causes of project failure, it is much harder to identify what should be done to prevent such disasters from happening in the first place. This book, through the use of actual case study material combined with a comprehensive review of successful IT planning and development techniques, will provide you with the skills and confidence to help put that right.

David Yardley, May 2002

Forewords

It staggers me that after 20 years in the IT Industry IS Project failure continues at such an alarming rate, despite a plethora of advice, guidance, methodology, standards and training. Why?

The truth is . . . we have been too trusting in processes and project management approaches. In this book David Yardley draws our attention to additional factors that influence the success of IS projects that lie outside the scope of conventional project management. Measurement of project progress and success is all too often misdirected at the process of project delivery, rather than the subject of the project or program. In fact measuring the success of project management may be exactly the wrong thing to measure. None would argue against the measurement of 'business benefits' (commercial or political) – but what are they and how do you measure them? Good project management will help ensure a 'worthy' project is a success. Poor project management screws-up most things.

This book, for the first time in a single volume, brings together a number of key elements:

- alignment of IS/IT strategy with business strategy
- business prioritization and requirements management
- benefits management and realization
- behavioral psychology (individuals, teams, customers and suppliers) and change management
- project development processes, risk and quality management approaches (the methodology).

Yardley also states that a worthy project or program is one that is conceived within and aligned to the organization's business strategy, is viable, and can deliver measurable benefits in an useful timescale. In a nutshell – SMART. However, making change stick and deliver value proves too tricky for most. Change has "the capacity to embrace all"! In reality far less than "all affected" may actually embrace change, rendering the whole exercise sub-optimal. He also brings out nuances of team dynamics during the project's development phase. I am firmly of the opinion that project success lies in the synergy of the development team, spanning the producer/consumer divide, and in this respect Yardley has identified key success factors and contributors to project success.

Michael Gough
Chief Executive, National Computing Centre (NCC) Ltd., United Kingdom
September 2002

This book pulls together the various essential elements to ensure successful project delivery. The author is to be applauded for not just focusing on current hot topics but also for covering the less fashionable but equally crucial aspects of the job. I believe the key theme of this book, which is also the central focus of DSDM, is to ensure that the project is business-driven rather than IS/IT-led. How often do we see IS/IT strategy unaligned to the organization's business strategy? How many projects have a non-existent business case or fail to plan benefits' management and realization? How many projects are "run" without the necessary rigor to provide a framework for delivering benefits to the business and reducing risk?

So, if you are frustrated with your IS/IT projects, or about to begin a career in this area, you will benefit enormously from reading this book. In particular, the case studies in *Successful IT Project Delivery* help bring the book's essential points to life. You could do a lot worse than put into practice the author's recommendations and turn potential project failures into project successes. It's never too late!

Those of you familiar with DSDM will recognize and support many of the points raised here; those of you unfamiliar with DSDM who like this book's content should make their next port of call the DSDM website – www.dsdm.org – it's a lot more than just an application development framework!

Barry Fazackerley
DSDM Chairman
September 2002

Acknowledgments

This book brings to a close an enlightening and rewarding exercise that has lasted many years. Throughout this period, many companies and individuals found the time to discuss with me the problems experienced within IT projects. Their contributions were invaluable and to them I offer my sincere thanks. In particular, I must thank those individuals who were more than happy to discuss the problems that had affected their own IT projects; their names and identifying details, however, must remain anonymous.

My thanks to Michael Strang at Pearson Education for his unstinting support from conception to publication. Thanks also to the reviewers of my original synopsis and the completed manuscript, their words of advice and encouragement were gratefully accepted.

Special thanks to my wife Anne, who not only had to suffer my constant questions and thoughts whilst I was writing the book, but also kept the kids amused when I needed a bit of piece and quiet.

Finally, my sincere thanks to Michael Gough and Barry Fazackerley for kindly agreeing to write forewords for the book.

I am indebted to the following who kindly gave their permission for me to reproduce copyright material: Mary Henson, Global Operations Director, DSDM Consortium; Annelise Savill, Accounts Director and Pam Flynn, The Stationery Office; Anne-Marie Byrne and John Groom, Office of Government Commerce; David Harris, IBM; Dick Strange, Chief Executive Officer, Association for Project Management; Axel Catton and Angelika Schallerer, Audi AG. Thanks also to Gary Walsh.

Crown copyright material is reproduced with the permission of the Controller of Her Majesty's Stationery Office.

CA-Ideal® is a registered trademark of Computer Associates International, Inc.

Coca-Cola is a registered trademark of The Coca-Cola Company.

DSDM is a registered trademark of the DSDM Consortium.

FOCUS is a registered trademark of Information Builders, Inc.

Java and all Java-based marks are trademarks or registered trademarks of Sun Microsystems, Inc. in the United States and other countries. Pearson Education is independent of Sun Microsystems, Inc.

Pepsi is a registered trademark of PepsiCo, Inc.

Prince2 is a registered trademark of the Office of Government Commerce.

RUP is a trademark of The Rational Corporation.

UML is a trademark of Object Management Group Inc.

Windows, PowerPoint and Visual Basic are trademarks of the Microsoft Corporation in the United States and other countries.

Introduction

The IT project is now firmly acknowledged within organizations as an enabler of change. It is from the successful implementation of an IT project that an organization will realize material and financial benefits. Corporate success must, therefore, be dependent on the success of the IT projects undertaken within it.

The need to maintain competitive advantage is just one factor within the organization that has placed an even greater importance on the IT project; there are many others. Organizations can no longer afford to jeopardize their growth, and in some cases their very survival, by the failure of an IT project. Project failure, though, is not a technical issue; ownership for IT projects must exist within the business and their success will be dependent upon the effective engagement of individuals representing business *and* IT functions within the organization. Key business managers can no longer afford to pass the blame onto their IT counterparts for project failure; equally, IT managers can no longer ignore the needs of the business community in their strive for technological excellence.

Whilst we would all like our projects to proceed seamlessly from initiation to implementation, in reality, this rarely happens. Despite the enormous dependence placed on IT by organizations, it is still hard to believe that nearly two-thirds of all major IT projects fail in some way. A report, aptly named CHAOS,[1] based on research by the Standish Group, discovered that nearly one-third of IT projects were cancelled before they could be completed. Moreover, the research also indicated that over half the projects investigated cost almost twice as much as their planned budgets. Other reports suggest that over 70 per cent of all IT projects never deliver all their stated benefits. Without doubt, IT project failures certainly make good reading, not just in professional journals, but in the daily newspapers as well. On this evidence alone, marketing executives may well decide that the best way of attracting some welcome media attention is to announce that their project was delivered to time, budget, and quality, and it is on target to save the company millions.

Whether you are the director, sponsor or 'champion' of an IT project, a project manager, business manager, technical expert or business user, the unremarkable success rates experienced from IT projects suggest that you will have experienced project failure first-hand at some time within your organization. Those who can attest this will also know that seniority or status is no defence against the consequences of a failing project. Project failure has the capacity to affect everyone involved within the project, from the project team upwards into the wider organization, and ultimately, into the boardroom. Clearly, there is a need for everyone involved within an IT project to discharge their responsibility in a professional manner if the project is to be successful.

Of course, it is unlikely that the failure of a minor project will make the headlines throughout the global news networks. It will, however, have a significant impact on the individuals whose time, money and resources were invested in it.

It is a common belief amongst many project teams that project failure is only an issue for large, multinational organizations whose projects not only fail dramatically, but fail *publicly*. This is not the case. Even small IT projects, such as the implementation of an 'off-the-shelf' software package within a relatively small organization can fail to deliver any business benefits whatsoever, and worse, never recoup any of the finance invested in it.

As business and IT professionals, we all have a vested interest in the successful outcome of an IT project, yet the commercial sensitivity that often embraces a failed project ensures that individuals engaged on future projects are unlikely to learn the lessons arising from past project failure. The culture of non-disclosure is a constant reminder of the changing attitudes towards failure. It is a sad but inevitable consequence of the high-profile IT failures experienced within industry that IT projects are now under close scrutiny from a litigious society, seeking recompense wherever failure has occurred. It is hardly surprising, therefore, to discover that those engaged on IT projects are more concerned with hiding mistakes than sharing their knowledge and experiences with others in the hope it may help reduce further failure. The threat of commercial litigation makes this course of action appear highly unlikely and, in many ways, irresponsible. The 'compensation culture' is, of course, not unique to the IT profession, but thankfully, it has yet to witness the so-called 'ambulance-chasing lawyers' that now plague the medical profession.

Successful IT projects do, however, deliver measurable benefits into the organization and promote the career development of those individuals working on them. Unsuccessful projects, however, bring uncertainty into the organization; strategically, due to their failure to enable change, and operationally, due to their failure to deliver workable solutions that will satisfy critical business requirements. As individuals, regardless of our status within the organization, we do not want to be associated with having worked on a failed IT project; it is an unwelcome label that can, and often does, damage our professional credibility and self-esteem. It would seem sensible, therefore, for us to seek answers to what clearly must be the two most important IT project-related questions.

- Why do IT projects continue to fail?

- How can I ensure that future projects I am involved in are a success?

This book will help you identify and fulfill your role within an IT project by discussing the key issues and topics which lie behind these questions. Through the use of real-life case studies, the characteristics of project failure, from initiation to implementation, will be identified, allowing you to benefit from the experiences of others before you. Having established the critical success factors for IT projects, this book will then guide you through the steps you need to adopt in your own IT project to ensure that it has the best chance of success.

Reference

1 *CHAOS '98: A Summary Review*, Research Note, Standish Group International Inc., 1998

 Part I

Preparing the organization for IT projects

If the blind lead the blind, both shall fall into the ditch
St Matthew, ch.15, v.14

Why do IS projects fail?

IS project failure is everyone's business

David Yardley

Since the advent of commercial computing during the mid 20th century, advances in IT have spawned the meteoric growth of a society that has become, for all intents and purposes, completely dependent upon IT; the "information society." The need to acquire knowledge through information has never been greater than it is now. How well that process can be performed within an organization will be a key factor in determining its future success.

Advances in technology, however, are of little benefit unless they can be harnessed in such a way as to deliver benefits to those individuals seeking a return on their investment. The development of Information Systems (IS) seeks to leverage IT to enable the successful deployment of business processes and services. It is the role of the IT project, or to be more accurate the IS project, to make that happen. On reflection, therefore, for accuracy, the title of this book should be: "Successful *IS* Project Delivery." The terms, however, do seem to be interchangeable within most contexts and so, where meaning and understanding is not compromised, from this point forward I will refer to the term "IS project" rather than use the rather clumsy tag "IS/IT project." The term IT will be used, however, when the context relates purely to the technological components of an IS project.

Not every IS project, however, is undertaken to deliver highly complex business solutions; small and medium-sized IT systems are commonplace throughout the world and feature significantly in the plans of many existing and planned IS projects. The implementation of commercial off-the-shelf (COTS) software packages for instance, still remains one of the most common IS projects undertaken in practically every business sector.

Clearly, undertaking an IS project is an important event in the life of any organization, both in the short-term and in the long-term. It would not be foolish, therefore, to expect that within an organization, an IS project should attract the full support of everyone involved within it, from the boardroom to the factory. We might also confidently expect that an IS project employs individuals of only the highest calibre and dedication within the organization. Based on the clear need and importance of IS projects, we should all, therefore, expect IS projects to be planned and implemented to textbook perfection.

Although what exactly *is* the "perfect" way to plan and implement an IS project? The following list provides *one* interpretation of what the "perfect" IS project might actually be – it might be worth considering how many of these observations are true reflections of how IS projects are delivered within *your* organization.

- Strategic business planning indicates a clear need for a number of IS projects.
- A business program is established to co-ordinate all IS projects within the organization and establish standards and best practice across them.
- The project manager is selected on merit.
- The project manager is given a detailed and unambiguous requirements specification.
- The project manager is given time to produce a plan and the understanding that a budget will be provided and all the resources needed to complete it.
- The project manager is given all the resources requested and the ones that had been forgotten.
- The entire organization knows how important the project is and give their full support and co-operation.
- The project manager is not infallible and the organization understands this. If mistakes are made in planning, there is a painless and straightforward process of change control.
- The project sponsor understands how last-minute changes to the scope of the project can substantially increase the risk of failure and withholds additional functionality for the next release of the product.
- At the end of the project, the project manager is first to thank the project team, closely followed by the users. Both parties are happy as the system

meets all expected requirements and significant business benefits will be gained as a result. The project has implemented key components of the business strategy and the efforts of those involved are recognized through the activation of the organization's reward and remuneration process.

The reality gap

Whilst we would all like our projects to proceed from initiation to implementation by following a few simple steps, as they often do in the confines of management training centers, in reality, this rarely happens. Despite the enormous dependence organizations have on IT, it is still difficult to accept that nearly two-thirds of all major IS projects fail in some way. Research undertaken by the Standish Group concluded that out of 23,000 projects: 28 per cent failed completely; 46 per cent were challenged by cost and time overruns and only 26 per cent succeeded. According to the Standish Group, corporate America spends more than $275 billion each year on approximately 200,000 application software projects. Many of these will fail, not for the lack of funding or technology, but for the lack of skilled project management.[1] Without doubt, IS project failures certainly make good reading, not just in professional journals, but in the daily newspapers as well. On this evidence alone, marketing executives may well decide that the best way of attracting some welcome media attention is to announce that their project was delivered to time, budget, and quality, and it is on target to save the company millions.

The statistics reported by various consultancy organizations provide little comfort to the IT industry as a whole and to business and IT managers in particular. What is most disturbing, however, is why the statistics on IS project failure never seem to improve substantially over time. It is certainly not through the lack of information on the management of projects; a quick perusal through any city center bookshop will identify many respectable publications on the subject.

Equally, a review of the popular professional computing magazines will also highlight the vast number of accredited training and consultancy organizations that supply training courses on project management skills and techniques. So, given the vast amount of information and guidance available for those responsible for IS project delivery, why do IS projects continue to fail?

The answer to this question can best be found by first identifying some of the main reasons for project failure. A recent survey undertaken by the management consultancy and services company KPMG highlighted six critical "failure factors" relating to IS project failure:[2]

- poor project planning;

- a weak business case;

- lack of senior management involvement and support;

- lack of user involvement;

- technology new to organization;

- lack of business ownership.

Any one of these factors may jeopardize the success of the project in many different ways; the culmination of one or more of these factors may ultimately introduce enough risk into the project for it to become no longer viable. If this situation becomes a reality, the premature termination of the project is likely to be the only course of action left open to the organization.

Types of IS project failure

IS project failure refers to the failure of an information system, most notably in its conception, design, construction, deployment, implementation, and use. In this context, the scope of failure is not just limited to that of an IT component, but means failure in the wider context of the project organization as a whole. IS project failure is one type of business failure, and therefore must include the failure of business functions on which IS projects are dependent upon, such as business planning, finance, logistics, and business operations. IS project failure can therefore be characterized by one or more of the following events:

- the degradation of an existing business capability;

- the degradation of competitive advantage;

- an increase in operating costs;

- failure to meet critical business requirements;

- poor levels of user satisfaction;

- loss of control over requirements management;

- loss of control over planning.

Given the high incidence of IS project failure within the global business community, it should come as no surprise to even the most casual of observers that the subject is a popular and regular discussion topic within many of the current academic and industry journals. What *is* surprising, however, is the fact that the vast majority of these identify IS project failure purely in terms of exceeding budget, timescale and quality constraints; the classic symptoms of *project management* failure, but not necessarily symptomatic of *project* failure.

Project management failure is certainly common, if only because it is one of the most visible causes of failure. Deviations from the project budget and schedule can be easily measured against planned and agreed targets, and even the most basic of project reporting mechanisms will ensure that such exceptions are made visible to key project stakeholders. If recent surveys are to be believed, project management success remains an elusive goal for many organizations, as the following statistics bear witness to.

- In 1985 a survey of IT projects found that 66 per cent of projects overran their allocated time and 55 per cent exceeded their budget.[3]

- A KPMG survey undertaken during 1992 found that 56 per cent of companies in the UK believed that 'runaway IT projects' occurred frequently within their organization and 62 per cent of respondents had experienced such a project within the last five years.[3]

- The 1994 Standish Group survey found that the average IT project took about 220 per cent of its planned schedule.[1]

- In 1998 the Standish Group reported a slight decrease in the number of US IT projects that were completed over budget or outside the original deadline. Still the figure does not offer too much hope – 46 per cent of projects were described as "challenged."[4]

▰▰▷ The scope for IS project failure

It would not be unfair to suggest that in the light of such statistics, there should be a genuine concern over the role of project management within a project. But it would be unfair, and indeed incorrect, to assume that IS projects fail purely as a consequence of inadequate project management. Successful IS projects rely on the alignment and synergy of many disparate components, some being internal to the organization, such as business strategy, IT strategy and the behavior of stakeholders within the organization; and others being external to the organization, such as politics, industry regulation and the behavior of suppliers. What is becoming clear is that many of the factors that influence the success of the project lie *outside* the scope of project management (Figure 1.1).

Whilst all stakeholders in a project are important, it is ultimately the customer who will play a leading role throughout the entire lifecycle of the project. Figure 1.1 identifies the customer as an external stakeholder, which is representative of projects undertaken by a third party, such as a consultancy organization. There are, however, many projects, in which the customer is an internal project stakeholder, such as those run within one organizational department for the benefit of another.

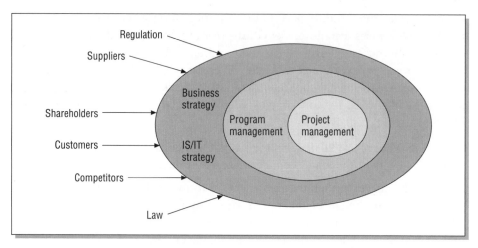

FIGURE 1.1 ▓ External factors influencing the success of an IS project

The role of project management in project failure

Whilst there is a clear relationship between the project and the process to manage that project, successful project management will not necessarily guarantee the success of the project. It is unfortunate then that there are numerous examples of projects undertaken by organizations that fail to deliver any benefit whatsoever, despite the use of popular and well-documented project management techniques.

The use of project management methodologies is now readily associated with the many complex activities and problems that are called a project. As a consequence, the success of the project management function within the project is now often directly associated with the success of the project as a whole. This is a common error within many IS projects, and many such projects wrongly employ measures typically associated with project management in order to determine the success of the project. It is the aim of this chapter to clearly define the boundaries of success within an IS project and to show that project management success and project success cannot be measured using the same criteria.

When discussing the role of project management in project failure, it is first necessary to accept that project management and the project are not necessarily directly related. The objectives of both project management and the project are different and therefore the control of time, costs, and quality, which are acknowledged objectives of project management, should not be confused with measuring project success.

In order to distinguish between the project and project management for the purposes of identifying potential causes for failure, it is necessary to establish clear definitions for each term. A project can be defined as being the achievement of a specific objective, involving a number of tasks and activities which consume resources. This objective is completed to a set specification and within a finite timescale.

In contrast, project management can be defined as the process of controlling the achievement of the project objectives. This function includes defining the requirement and scope of work, allocating the resources necessary to complete it, and monitoring progress against the plan, managing deviations when necessary.

Initially, these two definitions may appear to be synonymous; both, clearly, are heavily oriented towards the achievement of the project. There is, however, a clear and very important distinction that can be made between the two terms. A project is concerned with identifying and defining a task that will ultimately be of benefit to the company. That benefit may be financial, operational, technical, or even political in nature, and will tend to be long-term, based on the total life-span of the project. In contrast, project management is oriented towards planning and control. Essentially this task supports the project through on-time delivery, managing expenditure, and maintaining appropriate quality standards.

Defining project success

From the definition of a project, it should become apparent that project success is oriented towards the achievement of a commercial or political goal and the realization of financial benefits (Table 1.1). Experience has shown, however, that it is still possible to achieve project success even when the project management process has failed. Indeed, there are many examples of projects that were relatively successful despite not being completed on time, or within budget. The project to develop Concorde is probably one of the more well-known ones and is featured later in this chapter.

TABLE 1.1 Project objectives and how their success can be measured

Project objectives	Project success criteria
To effect change	Achievement of a commercial goal
To achieve a commercial goal	Realization of financial benefits
To implement business and IS strategy	Achievement of political objectives
To realize financial benefits	Delivers functionality and usability to the satisfaction of the users
To achieve a political goal	Completes to the satisfaction of the business stakeholders

It is clear that the dependency between these two concepts is much less than many organizations assume. As a consequence, for us to be able to measure project success, a distinction must be made between the success of the project and the success of the project management process.

Effective project management will help ensure a worthy project is a success. Even if the quality of the project management process is poor, a worthy project will ultimately overcome management weaknesses and deliver benefit into the business. If, however, the project fails to achieve its longer-term objectives, then it will ultimately fail, regardless of the expertise of the project manager.

Consider the situation where the project has failed whereas the project management activity has been perceived to been successful. In this scenario, the project may have failed because it did not deliver the expected return on investment to the sponsor, was not used as intended once implemented or failed to secure the organizational change necessary to succeed; while its implementation was completed to time, budget, and scope. Project management, in this case, could not have prevented the project from failing as this activity is merely a subset of the wider criteria that identify project success. Although the subset of criteria has been satisfied, the wider set has not been.

 CASE STUDY

Concorde

The project to build Concorde, the world's first supersonic commercial aircraft, was wholly sponsored by the British and French governments, and was initiated to develop and promote a joint European aerospace industry. In terms of project management, the Concorde project was a failure – the project vastly exceeded its budget and schedule.[5] Taking over seven years to develop at a cost of £1.5bn ($3bn), the Concorde project was dubbed the most expensive marketing experiment in history. In fact, the plane even gave rise to the phrase 'Concorde fallacy' – the belief that it is a waste of money to end a project after considerable sums of money have been invested in it.

Years after the Concorde project, many analysts have moved away from the opinion that the project was a complete failure. Quite the opposite in fact; contemporary opinion seems to view the Concorde project as a success, despite the obvious failure to remain within budget and schedule. The main reason why this opinion had credibility was simple: the project achieved its *primary* objective. Unusually, this objective was not a commercial one (due to the sheer cost of development and operation, Concorde was never expected to return a profit), it was political. The joint development and operation of Concorde by Air France and BOAC resulted in the convergence and alignment of two of Europe's leading aerospace companies, an objective that had been given a high priority by both governments.

TABLE 1.2 ▨ Project management objectives and how their success is measured

Project management objectives	Project management success criteria
Define the project	Completion to budget
Reduce the project to a set of manageable tasks	Satisfying the project schedule
Obtain appropriate resources	Adequate quality standards
Build a team (or teams) to perform the work	
Plan the work and allocate resources to tasks	
Monitor and control the work	
Report progress to project sponsor	
Closedown project	
Review project and learn lessons	

Defining project management success

It is only through the sheer arrogance or ignorance of senior executives that there are still organizations whose cultures define a successful project as one that only meets the success criteria for project management (Table 1.2). For instance, a project that was delivered within budget may well be identified as being successful, even if the expected benefits of the project may never be realized. Whilst the use of *de facto* project management methodologies will provide assistance in how to plan and control resources, budgets, and activities, they cannot *guarantee* project success, even if the project management objectives have been satisfied.

In this situation, the only criticism that can be levelled at project managers is that the potential risks for project failure should have been identified during the early stages of the project (in particular, the project feasibility stage) and the project sponsor informed as a result. The sponsor then has the option to either abandon the project or take action to reduce or remove the risk. This is a fundamental concept that is lacking within many organizations. Not only is there a lack of importance placed upon *project* success, there is *too much* importance placed on the success of project management.

Project management plays a role in project success, but that role is affected by many other factors outside the direct control of the project manager. This goes some way to explaining why IS projects can succeed or fail independently of the project management process.

The incentives for project managers to deliver an agreed specification of work within the constraints of cost, time and quality are commonplace; indeed, the performance-related bonuses for project managers are usually dependent upon the satisfactory achievement of precisely these three goals. As well as the obvious desire not to incur further costs of staff, especially overtime costs if the project is behind schedule, a project manager may be under enormous pressures to deliver quickly for many other reasons.

- Key staff on the project have been allocated to another project and must leave within a specified time. The project must complete before these staff leave.

- Senior management have told the project manager a promotion is likely if the project is delivered on time and within budget.

- Internal power and control structures may bypass business goals to achieve project goals.

- The project manager may know of complications that could arise soon after the project has gone live. This may be for a number of reasons, but it has not been unknown for a project manager to compromise software testing and software quality assurance tasks in the plan if there is a risk the implementation date will not be achieved as a result. However, if the project can be implemented as soon as possible he will be promoted whilst leaving his successor to deal with the problem – a variation of the 'Peter Principle'* of management.

The overlap between the project and project management

The project team, and more specifically the project manager, is only concerned with a small part of the overall project yet is often held responsible for the success of the entire project. From the diagram shown in Figure 1.2 you can see that the project team are only involved in stages 2–4 of the overall project, at which point they will leave and most likely move onto another project. Business involvement, however, must span the full lifecycle of the project, namely stages 1–6. The overall responsibility for the project, therefore, should not rest with the project manager, but with an individual from the business who has a wider view of the project – the business sponsor or champion is the obvious choice.

---

* The principle that within a hierarchy, an employee will be promoted to his highest level of incompetence. (*The Peter Principle*, 1969)[6]

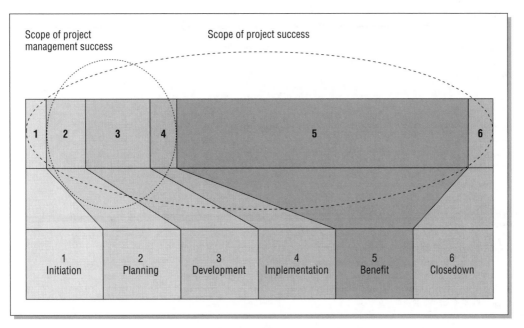

FIGURE 1.2 ▨ The scope of project management and project success

Project vs project management failure

Critical failure factors for IS projects are not limited to project management, but must also include those project activities that lie outside the scope of project management. Some of these factors will originate from within the business, such as strategy, organization, roles, and responsibilities; others, such as competitors, politics, and regulation will be external to the business.

Those failure factors that are internal to the organization can therefore be broadly categorized into two key areas; project failures and project management failures. A summary of these failure factors is shown in Table 1.3.

Key contributors to project management failure

Inexperienced project managers

Considering the importance and visibility of the project management function, it is incredible to discover how many project managers have no formal training in project management skills. Not so long ago, the state policy in California did not require IS project managers to possess experience in project management, or

TABLE 1.3 ▨ The scope of project and project management failure

Failure condition	Scope of failure
Weak ownership	Project failure
Immature or unproven technology	Project failure
Lack of user involvement	Project failure
A weak business case	Project failure
Poor communication	Project failure
Failure to examine existing business processes and goals before deploying technology	Project failure
Inexperienced project managers	Project management failure
Poor project planning	Project management failure
Poor requirements management	Project management failure
Dependency on project management tools	Project management failure
Never saying goodbye	Project management failure
Weak leadership	Project management failure
Inadequate testing	Project management failure

even in the field of IT. Yet, upon the shoulders of the state's project managers rested the success of literally billions of taxpayers' dollars.

I am sure I am not alone in having witnessed the incredibly poor selection of a project manager for an IS project. Unfortunately, the selection criteria for a project manager within many organizations is based on technical competence alone, and almost inevitably, such organizations are likely to promote a highly skilled programmer or analyst into the role of project manager without any thought of what such a role entails.

Inexperienced project managers lack strong communication, leadership, and management skills, so it is no surprise to discover that many IS projects fail due to the disproportionate focus placed on technology at the expense of the business, specifically the *users* of the system. Whilst the technology-led project places emphasis on IT delivery, the business-led project places emphasis on the achievement of business objectives and user satisfaction.

Poor project planning

The lack of adequate project planning is a common cause of many failed projects. Indeed a KPMG survey[2] identified inadequate risk management and a weak project plan as the main causes of poor project planning. Identifying tasks and resource usage is fundamental to project planning, yet it is often performed in an *ad-hoc* manner. For instance, one of the most common errors made during the planning process is to assume that project resources are available for the project 100 per cent of the time (i.e. every minute of every day is spent working on the project). In reality, the figure is much lower; 80 per cent usage is a more realistic maximum.

Poor requirements management

The requirements definition phase in any project is often the place where many basic and easily avoidable mistakes are made. To compound an already serious problem, errors that are made during the requirements definition phase are not always identified until much later in the project, by which time it is too late to correct them without affecting the project schedule and budget. Typical errors made during the requirements definition phase of a project are likely to include the following.

■ *Not capturing sufficient requirements*
I have seen requirements specifications that redefine the word "brief." In one particular instance the document was little more than a few paragraphs in length, drafted by a senior business manager, expressing more of an interest in, than a requirement for: ". . . the implementation of a billing system, using Oracle."

This is a good example of two common failures: first the obvious lack of detail in the requirements specification. "A billing system" can mean many things to many people; the foundations for system development activities must be based on clear and specific requirements. Second, in this example, it would appear that the solution has already been identified by the business. Maybe the users were invited to a supplier's sales conference and returned, eager to see the glitzy sales demonstration being turned into reality in their department. Users have a vital role to play in the project and their views must be respected at all times; but their role is not to identify the technical solution necessary to satisfy their requirements.

■ *Capturing a "shopping-list" of requirements*
The scope of a project is a key factor in determining both its length and its cost. It is also a good indicator of the level of impact the project will have on the business once it has been implemented. IS projects often require significant sums of financial investment to implement and can cause widespread disruption to the business as a result. Business tolerates such disruption in the knowledge that the

project will ultimately deliver benefits, but often demand the most sophisticated and "functionally-rich" IT systems in return for their financial support. Demanding high levels of functionality for a new system may be technically achievable, but if the time needed to develop such functionality extends way beyond current business plans it may ultimately put at risk some of the benefits originally stated. Doing too much is clearly as risky as doing too little.

Whilst the business stakeholders are regularly blamed for the excessive number of requirements specified at the start of a project, few books and articles on the subject ever acknowledge that IT stakeholders are often as much to blame for this as their business counterparts. It is not uncommon for IT directors or IT program managers to try and sneak in a few extra "system" requirements prior to development, in the hope that this will negate the need for them to formally request funding for new IT software and hardware in the future. Prime examples of this type of behavior would include the "need" to: upgrade key system and application packages and tools; purchase additional hardware; upgrade current hardware. "Business-critical" projects often provide the perfect excuse for IT directors to request funds from which they can satisfy their outstanding objectives – caused by their failure to plan and implement the IT strategy effectively. Not surprisingly, for many IT directors, Year 2000 "millennium bug" projects were a blessing in disguise.

■ *Changing requirements*

Even using a development methodology such as DSDM (Dynamic Systems Development Methodology), which accepts that requirements will change during the lifecycle of the project, it is essential to agree the scope of requirements at a high level. The failure to manage requirements effectively has been the downfall of numerous IS projects, from the smallest of implementations to global IS deployment programs. If the business stakeholders cannot agree requirements or constantly change the requirements specification, especially during the development and testing stages of a project, the probability of failure increases dramatically. Requirements that change significantly or frequently are also one of the main reasons why projects exceed their budget. Change requests made to the supplier from the customer will almost certainly result in the customer incurring substantial charges. If the frequency and scope of changes requested during the project cannot be controlled, the probability that the cost of the project will outweigh the expected benefits becomes ever more likely.

Dependency on project management tools

In some organizations, the only requirement for a project manager is the ability to use a project management tool. Skills such as communication, leadership, and negotiation are secondary to the need to become expert in the use of a project management tool. The preoccupation with software tools has been elevated to such a high level that they often appear to be the most important aspect of project management.

Clearly this is a potentially dangerous situation as it encourages the stakeholders of the project to find answers to their problems from a planning tool, at the exclusion of some of the more important human elements of the project. A project management tool is not a magical software-based solution to an organizational problem – it will manage tasks, schedules, and resources, but it will not manage the project.

If you are a poor project manager, then using a software tool will probably make you even worse. If you are a good project manager, then using such as tool will give you greater control of your project and will increase your ability to communicate key planning information to your team and the business stakeholders. If the use of analogy helps, think of the project manager as a car mechanic. A poor mechanic with a good toolkit is still a poor mechanic. An expert mechanic with a good toolkit is one hell of a mechanic!

Never saying goodbye

If a project does not have a clear start and end-date, this is a clear indication that there is little understanding of the overall project plan. If there is no exit point for the project, there is a risk that the project will be perpetuated for an indeterminate period of time. The most common cause for a project to be running years after its original deadline is a lack of clear objectives for it. Once in the main thrust of a project, especially one that has a multitude of deliverables, a project manager can often lose sight of the project's primary objectives; i.e. the real reason why the project was undertaken in the first place. There will always be extra functionality that can be "bolted on" to the existing system, but this should be out of scope for the project unless formal methods for change control have been established. The inability to stay focused on the project objectives is influenced heavily by the duration of the project; the lengthier the schedule, the greater the probability that it will drift off-course. If people are still working on the same project years after it should have completed, motivation and morale are often the first casualties. What started out as a good career move has now become a nightmare.

Weak leadership

Do not be mistaken into thinking that a project brimming with management is an effective one. Successful projects are a consequence of strong leadership rather than excessive management. To manage is one thing, to lead is an entirely different matter, and one which requires a combination of skill, experience, dedication beyond the call of duty, and charisma to motivate and empathize with the project team.

Inadequate testing

If planning and software development activities slip their milestone dates, which is not beyond the realms of credibility, they often do so at the expense of the schedule for testing. So whilst development activities may often take months to complete, it is quite likely that testing will be truncated to a few days in order to meet delivery milestones.

Testing is very much a business activity, yet it is not unheard of for users to abdicate their responsibility for performing this function, and leave it up to the software development team. This is a grave mistake as developers do not possess an expert level of business knowledge. A developer will place more focus on the performance of the systems rather than how well the solution meets the needs of the business.

 CASE STUDY

Company W

In this particular project, a relatively inexperienced applications developer was one of a number of IT staff nominated to be a project manager within the company's millennium compliance program. Clearly the company thought the most effective way of introducing IT staff to the subject of IT project management was to give them one of the most important projects ever undertaken within the company. The risks of project failure were already well-known within the company; if the company did not pass an audit conducted by an external regulatory body they could be forced to cease trading. Maybe that is why the company sent their "new" recruits on a popular and highly acclaimed project management course. However, as the course delegates soon discovered, a week's intensive training in project management techniques, even one conducted by a leading business school, is no substitute for experience. This clearly showed in the subsequent weeks and months of the project. Considering the pressures that these project managers were subjected to, it was hardly surprising that they felt exposed and vulnerable. At the time, the legal consequences of failing to ensure IT systems were millennium compliant was being widely discussed in IT magazines and journals.

Had a program of mentoring been introduced to help the new recruits feel less exposed, and at the same time learn their trade in relative safety, it might have mitigated some of the problems. This, unfortunately, did not happen, and it was only a matter of time before the fledgling project managers resigned from the company to enjoy more rewarding careers – careers which were more aligned with their own personal career aspirations, to become technical experts in their respective fields.

As for the project, it was restarted using external contract project managers, many of whom had over 30 years' project management experience each. The project was a success in terms of achieving their sole business objective – but at what cost?

Key contributors to project failure

Weak ownership

With any project must come a certain degree of accountability and responsibility from those who seek to gain advantage from it. The owner/sponsor of an IS project has a particularly important role, and at the very least must identify and justify the need for the project, assess and manage risks and raise finance for it. Despite this, the clarity and role of ownership within a project is often weak, and at worst, non-existent. Senior executives have a clear responsibility to track the progress of a project and to provide clear direction and leadership; they must lead by example. If they show no interest in the project apart from sacking the project manager if the project fails to meet their expectations, then their judgement and competence as directors must be questioned. Senior executives are in a perfect position to track the progress and cost of projects within the organization, but often fail to do so until it is too late. In a KPMG survey,[2] only 19 per cent of project failures were identified by a budget overrun being noticed at a senior level – the vast majority of them, 72 per cent, however, were recognized by the project team.

Immature or unproven technology

Whilst technology has advanced at a phenomenal rate over the last five years, the speed of change has had a negative effect on many IS projects. The "lure of the leading edge" is a common weakness within many organizations who dangerously assume that the "latest" is also the "best." The much-hyped client-server bandwagon during the 1980s was responsible for many impressive IS project failures within large organizations. Almost without any regard for the risks in deploying relatively immature technology, trusted, extremely powerful mainframe computers were replaced with much smaller UNIX servers – at the time, the very epitome of client-server technology. Within a matter of weeks (days in some cases), many organizations were finding it impossible to operate due to the failure of the new systems to cope with daily business workload. In the race to acquire new technology, business and IT managers had failed to ensure that the processing power of their UNIX server (especially its batch processing capability) was equal to that of the mainframe computer.

Lack of user involvement

IS projects are initiated to satisfy business objectives. Initially, these may be focused on strategic objectives, but ultimately, the project will need to satisfy objectives at an operational level – and that means understanding the roles, responsibilities and requirements of business users. A project that is technology-led as opposed to business-led cannot hope to satisfy business objectives; at most it will develop technology that satisfies IT objectives.

A major consequence of technology-led projects is the absence of high levels of user involvement throughout the project. Whilst the completion of a particularly complex piece of code may well excite the development team working on the project, it is the needs of the business that must be satisfied first, starting with and ending with those who must use it. The actual, or indeed perceived, resentment of a new system from users within the organization is one of the main reasons why IS projects routinely fail to realize their potential benefits. Whilst it is the role of IT professionals to build and deploy technology for business use, to perform this role without actively involving business users, the very people who must use this technology, is foolish and arrogant.

A weak business case

If a project is to be a success, it must have a strong business case with measurable (financial) benefits to justify the investment that must be made to implement it. If there is no obvious benefit to be gained from the project, why is it being undertaken in the first place? Equally, if the actual benefits gained from the project cannot be measured against the planned benefits identified in the business case, how can the success of the project be established? The business case must directly support the organization's business and IT strategies; there must be a clear explanation within the proposal of how the project directly supports the strategic objectives of the organization. In reality, many organizations do not have a clear, well-communicated business strategy, nor do they possess an IT executive on the main board. If the business strategy of the organization is weak or unclear, the chances are that any business case based on it will also be weak.

Poor communication

A successful organization is dependent upon the existence of effective communication channels between staff, management, and senior executives. An IS project is no different.

Communication is the life-blood of a project, and without it the ability to make effective decisions can be seriously compromised.

Failure to examine existing business processes and goals before deploying technology

The leverage of technology within an organization, in isolation from existing business practices, cannot guarantee IS project success. Deploying IT within an organization can only deliver benefits if it supports new or existing business processes and procedures, and then only if these operate efficiently and effectively within the organization. It is important, therefore, that all relevant business processes and procedures have been analysed before developing IT systems to automate them. If procedural problems already exist prior to the deployment of IT, such as process bottlenecks, then the introduction of IT systems within the organization is likely to add little value, and indeed make matters worse.

References

1 *CHAOS Chronicles II*, Standish Group International Inc., 2001

2 KPMG, *What Went Wrong? Unsuccessful Information Technology Projects*, 1997, www.kpmg.com

3 A. Dooley, "The real causes of project success and failure," Chairman, The Projects Group plc, *Project Manager Today*, February, 1998, 8–15

4 *CHAOS '98: A Summary Review*, Research Note, Standish Group International Inc., 1998

5 P.W.G. Morris and G.H. Hough, *Preconditions of Success and Failure in Major Projects*, Major Projects Association, Oxford, 1986

6 Dr L.J. Peter and R. Hull, *The Peter Principle: Why Things Always go Wrong*, William Morrow & Company, Inc., New York, 1969

2

Enabling change – the business of IT

Change is not made without inconvenience, even from worse to better.

Samuel Johnson, *Dictionary of the English Language* (1755)

Through the effective use of IT, organizations possess the capability to invoke change. If this were not the case, there would be no need to undertake an IS project in the first place. Change is fundamental to the long-term survival and prosperity of an organization, and its success will be dependent on how well the change supports the strategic decision-making processes within the organization.

Any business organization displays purposive and goal-seeking behavior; the former establishes one or more goals within the organization and the latter ensures that the organization strives to achieve them. Investment will be necessary if these goals are to be attained; supporting each investment will be a number of business drivers which will act as catalysts for change. Typical business drivers will most likely identify the need to increase profit margins, gain increased market share or reduce operational costs (Table 2.1).

TABLE 2.1 ▨ Common business drivers

■ Reduce threat from competition

■ Improve business performance

■ Improve service quality

■ Gain competitive advantage

■ Automation of business activities

■ Satisfy an externally imposed constraint, such as a legal or regulatory requirement

⧓ Strategic business planning

In order to plan and implement change within the organization, there must be some decision-making structure that can be used to establish goals within that organization. Without a business plan, formal or informal, for the development of the business, its products and its markets, there exists the likelihood that inappropriate short-term decisions will be made to the detriment of longer-term success.

Strategic business planning provides a framework in which corporate decisions can be made, such as *what business do we need to be in?* and subsequently refined and decomposed in order for operational decisions to be made, such as *how can we improve our order processing capability?* Strategic decisions may well affect the long-term direction and success of an organization and are likely to be both complex and risky in nature. The strategy of an organization, however, is not always determined by market forces, but also by the values and expectations of those who influence the strategy. In some respects, strategy can be thought of as a reflection of the attitudes and beliefs of those who have most influence within the organization – a theme that is often reflected in the *mission* of the organization. The decision by Lord Simpson, the chief executive of Marconi, to change the company's direction from being a defence contractor to a telecommunications company was ill-judged, given the fact that telecommunications companies were no longer seen by many analysts as a fashionable stock to hold.[1]

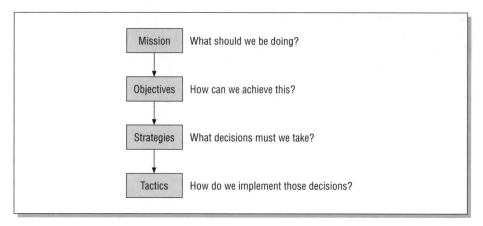

FIGURE 2.1 ■ The strategic business planning process

Whilst there are organizations whose business planning process is based, quite successfully, on "gut-feelings" and intuition, a more formal approach to business planning within organizations is often necessary. A typical business planning process takes the form shown in Figure 2.1.

Mission

During the 1980s, the mission statement became a popular way of communicating the core intentions of an organization. It was primarily aimed at employees, but has since become an important means of communicating key messages to customers. The mission statement should set out as clearly as possible the basic corporate strategy for the company in simple terms:

■ its target market;

■ how it will gain competitive advantage in that market;

■ how it will achieve superior profitability;

■ the key competences it will require to achieve its mission;

■ how its success will be measured.

A mission statement can be of a general and intriguing nature such as:

. . . to boldly go where no man has gone before . . . (the *USS Enterprise* – from the popular *Star Trek* TV series)

which is probably the most well-known mission statement of all, or specific and inspirational such as:

To be a high integrity software and systems company which provides excellent business solutions to our clients, a stimulating and rewarding environment for our staff, and an excellent return to our shareholders. (CACI Limited, a wholly owned subsidiary of CACI International Inc.)

or just plain and simple, such as:

To be the world's number one airline.

Objectives

The long-term objectives of an organization will have been alluded to in its mission statement, but now is the time to be more specific. Organizational objectives will identify key targets which are to be achieved in the medium to long term. Typical examples of objectives will specify markets, products, market share, turnover, and profitability.

Strategies

Strategies may exist at a number of levels within the business.

- *Corporate* strategy identifies the business of the organization and decisions taken at this level will have repercussions throughout the organization as a whole.
- The second level of strategy can best be thought of as a *competitive* or *business* strategy. It is at this level where decisions affecting specific parts or functions of the business are made, such as "how can our European manufacturing division compete with manufacturing companies in North America and Asia?"
- Supporting these two levels is the *operational* strategy, which is concerned with how the different organizational functions (marketing, finance, manufacturing, etc.) contribute to the other levels of strategy.

In comparison, an organization's IS/IT strategy identifies the strategic applications and IT solutions that must be adopted in order to satisfy the key objectives of its business strategy. Only through the combination of an effective IT and IS strategy can the organization hope to achieve competitive advantage and attain critical business goals and targets.

Tactics

Any strategy is worthless unless it can be implemented successfully. For instance, there is no point adopting a strategy that is focused on the deployment of a global IT infrastructure to support the organization's global business functions if the required technologies or skills are not available. IS/IT strategies must be realized through a coherent and viable program whose main objective is to deliver measurable benefits into the business within an agreed timeframe. An IS program can be considered to be a coarse, high-level approach to satisfying strategic business requirements; it is the many IS projects within that program that ultimately deliver benefit through the design and implementation of specific products.

Aligning the IT strategy with the business

It is with cruel irony, that, despite the benefits that can be achieved through the effective use of IT within an organization, the role of IT is often perceived by business managers to be:

- a necessary evil that is needed to automate large, mundane, and repetitive tasks;

- a huge waste of money;

- unable to deliver any business benefits;

- inflexible and an inhibitor of business change;

- ignorant of basic business methods and financial controls.

These damning indictments clearly suggest that the IT function within many organizations is largely alienated from the rest of the business. It should come as no surprise therefore, to discover that the some of the fundamental causes of IS project failures are:

- the absence of any clear link between the business strategy and the IT strategy;

- the failure of information systems planning to become part of the business planning process;

- the absence of business planning;

- the failure of business managers to own the proposed solutions and their implementations;

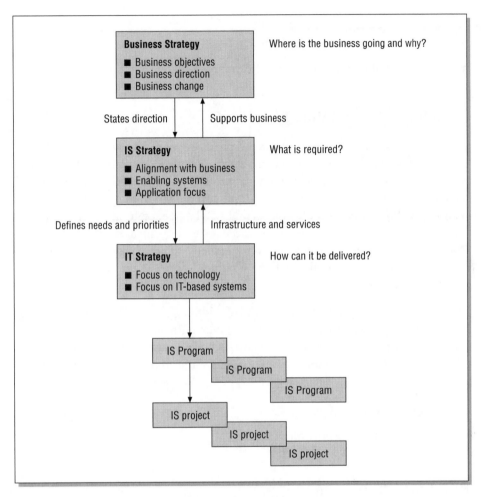

FIGURE 2.2 ▩ Implementing the IS strategy

- the lack of communication and participation between IT and business, reducing further, commitment and ownership;
- the failure to identify and track benefits.

It is evident, therefore, that to be effective, the organization's IT strategy must be aligned with its business strategy if it is to encourage corporate and business management to value information as a business resource (Figure 2.2). During the development of the strategy, it is vital that IT directors take every opportunity, possibly drawing on case studies or business events, to:

■ make key people aware of the value of information;

■ demonstrate how IT can add value to business operations;

■ provide a platform on which to reform and enhance business processes.

Implementing the strategy

The IS strategy sets the direction for the provision and management of IT solutions to satisfy business requirements. Once approved, detailed implementation planning will identify and justify one or more IS programs. Each program will have distinct business objectives that align with the IT strategy. Further detailed planning will identify a set of projects that will be needed to implement the program. Each project will have its own objectives and justification that support the objectives of the program. This hierarchy ensures that the objectives of each project can be shown to be making demonstrable progress towards the implementation of the strategy.

The selection of candidate projects will be a defining moment during the implementation of the IS strategy. If this is not given sufficient thought then the very foundations of the strategy will be weak. As no responsible builder would build a house on quicksand, no business manager should initiate a project unless they are in possession of:

■ the business case, followed by;

■ the project initiation document.

▶ Building the business case

Planning and presenting the business case to senior management is often the largest hurdle facing those wishing to initiate an IS project (or a portfolio of projects contained within a business program) as it is the mechanism used to obtain funding for the project. It is the development and approval of the business case that empowers IT, as delivery agents, to enable change through the development and deployment of business systems.

The sole purpose of the business case is to justify the business need for the project in order to secure capital funding. The guarantee of adequate funding will then allow a program or project to be established as a means of delivering the desired benefits. Whilst the business case can be used to secure funding and authorization for the entire duration of a project, it is more likely to be used to authorize funding to proceed to a given point in the project lifecycle for each project identified within the business case.

The business case is a business document and whilst IT stakeholders will need to make a significant contribution to it, in terms of structure and content, the responsibility for producing and owning this document must lie firmly with the major business stakeholder and primary risk-taker, the business sponsor.

 CASE STUDY

Company X

Shortly before the new millennium, a transit company established a business program to remediate a number of its critical business systems. The program was to manage and control a portfolio of business process projects and IT system remediation projects. Business projects were to include processes that dealt with communication and safety systems. IT projects were to concentrate on IT systems such as stock control, reservations, billing and financial control systems. Planning time was limited for the project initiation phase – all teams were given two weeks in which to plan, scope, and cost their findings. After that time, they were to present their plans to the program steering committee.

As a member of the project noted, "there was a direct conflict with two of the instructions identified during the project initiation meeting. Firstly, we were told to make sure that we used a 'least-cost option' approach, but were then told that any remediation activities must be undertaken in accordance with the IT strategy. It was clear to most of the project team that no one actually *knew* what the IT strategy was, and in any case, the two constraints given clearly created a conflict situation. In many cases, the least-cost option did not conform to the IT strategy so further clarification was sought."

Structure and content

A business case should not be considered as a "one-off" document produced solely to justify investment for the project; it should evolve during the formation of the project and act as a reference once underway. Typically, a business case is developed in three progressive stages:

1 strategic outline case (high-level scoping and planning – investigative);

2 outline business case (refined and indicative – feasibility);

3 full business case (validated and precise).

Each stage comprises a number of financial, economic, technical, and commercial components that are initially identified at a high level in the strategic outline

TABLE 2.2 ▆ Building the business case section by section

Criteria for project approval	Business case section
Why are you doing this now?	Background
What do you intend to achieve?	Benefits
What value will be realized?	
How will we provide evidence that the benefits are achievable?	
How will you know you have succeeded?	
What are you planning?	Project definition
What is the scope of work?	
What is the impact of that work?	
What are dependencies on the project?	
What are the deliverables?	
What could go wrong?	Risks
What do you need to accomplish the task?	Resources
What method of financial appraisal will be used?	Financial appraisal
How will you manage cashflow?	
How will you plan the task?	Project planning
How will you maintain control?	Project control

and subsequently refined and updated to form the outline business case. The final stage of business case development is the creation of a full business case which contains the same content, but validated and refined to a more accurate level.

At the start of the project it is unlikely that sufficient information will be known in order to complete the main sections of the business case (Table 2.2) – the investigative stages are there to find that out. At this stage, the business case, whilst lacking accurate information on the project, does provide a benefit which will be vital if the project is to succeed – it promotes commitment for the project through the need to engage key stakeholders and fundholders.

Strategic outline contents

The strategic case – strategic fit, business need and scope

- Alternatives for meeting project objectives (including doing nothing).
- The strategic context. How does the project support the organization's strategy, related projects, programs and policies?
- Need and drivers for change – what is wrong with the status quo?
- Key stakeholders and their interest in the project.
- Investment objectives, scope, and desired outcomes.
- Constraints.
- Risks.

The economic case – identifying appropriate options

- Alternatives for meeting project objectives (including doing nothing).
- Criteria to assess alternatives.
- Long-listing and short-listing of options.
- SWOT analysis.
- High-level benefit appraisal (financial and non-financial).
- High-level appraisal of costs (where information is available).
- High-level analysis of strategic risks.

The project management case – achievability

- Critical success factors.
- Project management arrangements.
- High-level project risk assessment and risk management strategy.
- High-level commitment from stakeholders.

The financial case – affordability

- High-level affordability analysis.
- Ability and willingness of budget holders to meet the resource implications of the project.
- Statement of (financial) support from stakeholders.

Refined outline contents

- Updated and includes review to ensure that objectives are Specific, Measurable, Achievable, Realistic, and Timebound (SMART).
- Full description of business outcomes and service requirements.

- Updated and includes detailed assessment of options (e.g. based on discounted cashflow analysis); formal assessment of costs; formal assessment of risks; sensitivity analysis on preferred option.

- Updated and includes more detailed assessment of critical success factors, more detailed project planning, including risk management, benefits management, change management, post-implementation monitoring, and review.

- Updated and includes detailed affordability analysis, commitment statement from senior management team and key stakeholders, and/or evidence of their involvement in planning the project.

▬▶ # Managing change

Developing and implementing an effective IS/IT strategy requires human, technical, and financial resources; the absence of one or more of these resources can limit the scope or approach of the IT strategy and its implementation. More importantly, the IS/IT strategy is only a blueprint; implementation of the strategy will require change. Despite the need for change, the management of change and its impact upon the organization is often found to be lacking within many organizations. The failure to address the subject of change in a rational and effective manner is likely to be a determining factor in the long-term success of an IS project.

New technologies, systems, business rules and processes are the most common deliverables from an IS project, and represent the most visible business impact resulting from change. The relative success of that change, however, is likely to be measured by individuals who have been affected as a result. What is now becoming clear to many organizations, is that individuals react to change in different ways. Typically, change divides human behavior into two broad categories.

- *Opportunistic*. This group believe in the need for change and want the change to succeed. Opportunistic people relish change.

- *Ritualistic/traditional*. This group views change as unnecessary – they are change-averse. They do not want to deviate from the status quo and will fight to resist any change that affects the values and welfare of themselves or their group.

Situations such as these, characterized by the absence of any noticeable "third-way" or feasible accommodation of opinion, can create conflict within the organization. In turn, this conflict may ultimately cause IS project failure. In this context, the costs of failure are not just financial; there may be a significant human cost (such as key business and IT staff leaving the organization).

To resolve the conflict between these two opposing behaviors, it is important to understand and manage the fundamental values that each group holds. Each group must first begin to accept the value of change to them on a personal basis. Only once this has occurred can their core needs and values be managed and aligned with the other group. Education programs and effective communication are all techniques which have been used to "manage down" the expectations and values of the opportunistic or *change-hungry group* of people, and to "manage up" the expectations and values of the ritualistic or *change-averse* group of people (Figure 2.3).

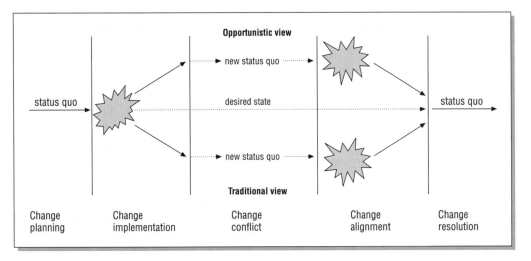

FIGURE 2.3 ▓ The dichotomy of change

The change cycle

The dichotomy of behavior shown in Figure 2.3 highlights the fact that change has the capacity to affect many people within the organization. Such is the potential impact of change within the organization, the effective management of change will be vital if it is to produce the outcome desired by those proposing the change in the first instance. The change cycle shown in Figure 2.4 is a popular approach to managing change within the organization and provides a fundamental component to many of the change programs used within successful organizations.

The management of change, however, is no guarantee that change will indeed trigger the outcome desired by the sponsors of change. During December 1984, key individuals within the Coca-Cola Corporation decided unanimously to change the formula of Coca-Cola®, just before its 100th anniversary.[2,3] They could not have predicted the massive public outcry from their customers which followed.

"New Coke", as it was branded, received heavy criticism from those who considered it to be inferior to "*Coke*", which to many was an icon of the American "dream". At the peak of the crisis, over 8,000 calls a day were being handled by the company and over 40,000 letters of protest were being processed. The company suffered a substantial drop in sales, giving Pepsi-Cola®, their fiercest rivals, a welcome boost in market share. The situation was unsustainable and the company was eventually forced to withdraw *New Coke* and revert to the original formula.

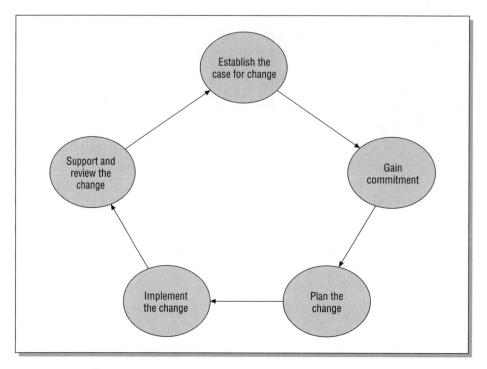

FIGURE 2.4 ■ The change cycle

Establish the case for change

In the initial stage within the change cycle, focus is placed upon the current state of the organization, the future desired state of the organization and the activities that could be performed to drive the process of transition forward.

Establishing the case for change is a major activity that must be undertaken before any change occurs. "Gut-feelings" for change based on anecdotal evidence alone are insufficient if change is to occur successfully within the organization. At a minimum, the case for change must identify the needs for change, the risks of performing that change and the impact of change within the organization:

- the proposed change in detail;
- the current state of the organization;
- the desired future state of the organization;
- alternative solutions which will achieve the same result;
- the inhibitors to change (internal or external);
- the direct or indirect impact of the change on the business function;

- the effects of change on people, processes and technology;
- the factors that can influence the effects of change;
- the consequences of failing to change.

Gain commitment

This stage is concerned with developing alliances, gaining commitment from the organization and creating a culture that will allow the change to occur.

- Do you have a set of clear, unambiguous messages which describe the change and its benefits?
- Are you still committed to the change process?
- Do you have a change sponsor who will champion the process?
- Do you know who the stakeholders are and where their interests lie?
- Do you know what you need from each stakeholder?
- Have you created a plan and discussed it with these stakeholders?
- Is there a communications strategy for the change?
- Is there a culture of openness and honesty within the organization?
- Are you confident people have the opportunity to provide feedback to the plan?
- Have you identified the financial, human, and technical resources you will need to implement the change?
- Have you a strong business case for the change?

Plan the change

This stage of the change cycle focuses on identifying the scope and impact of the change and the resources and activities needed to implement it. Successful project management is a key part of this stage.

- Are you still focused on the "to-be" situation as opposed to the "as-is" situation?
- Have you broken the main components of the plan into small manageable units of work?
- Have you identified the dependencies on other projects?
- Have you identified any critical risks which could affect the success of the project?
- Have you identified the organizational areas and functions which will need to contribute resources to the project?

- Have you communicated the plan to all stakeholders and obtained unanimous agreement?

- Are you building a project team?

- Are you following an appropriate project methodology?

- Is there a clear governance program in place to manage quality and methods?

- Are you confident you can measure the success of the project?

- Are there any training requirements which need action?

- Do you know how the change will be supported on completion of the project?

Implement the change

This stage of the cycle focuses on the actual process of change. The ability of the change sponsor or champion to drive through the change and prevent the process from stalling will be vital throughout this stage.

- Have you identified the cultural impact of the change within the business?

- Do you know how people will have to change their roles and activities for change to occur?

- Have precise details of new procedures been distributed?

- Are people aware of systems that will remain unchanged?

- Has a new organizational structure been developed and communicated to all staff?

- Does everyone know their new roles and responsibilities?

- Are the payroll, appraisal, and training programs aligned to meet the needs of the new structure?

Support and review

Change does not end when the project has been completed. Too many change programs fail as a result of not performing ongoing reviews of the change and developing a culture of continuous improvement within the organization.

- Are there any barriers that will prevent the change being sustained?

- Has the project delivered the expected results?

- If not, is there a plan in place to deal with any non-conformances?

- Is there a plan in place to ensure the ongoing support for the change initiative?

- Is there a plan in place to resume the status quo, i.e. "business as usual?"

Resistance to change

Whilst IT can be considered an enabler of change, that change can only be effected if the individuals within the organization who will be affected by the change posses the will to change. Providing the technological *means* for change is only one element in the change process and probably the simplest to overcome, as studies of change have constantly shown that human nature is fundamentally averse to change. Whilst it is acknowledged that people resist change whenever their individual or group values are threatened, it is much harder to identify exactly what those values might be. From the vast quantity of case-study material on organizational change collected over many years, it is now generally accepted that the vast majority of these values can be explained as being either: Political, Legal, Economic, Social or Technical – commonly referred to as PLEST (Table 2.3).

As there is no reason why we should assume that the individuals engaged on an IS project will have values and beliefs that are fundamentally different from those identified from previous studies into change, there now exists the potential for serious conflict at the very heart of the project. Elaborating upon the hypothesis identifies a clear dilemma for those seeking change from the successful alignment and implementation of the business and IT strategies. The project is a means of instigating change within the business, yet the very people whom the project will affect are naturally and fundamentally averse to change. As we have seen in the previous chapter, even an experienced and competent project manager cannot guarantee project success; if the project's *raison d'être* is challenged and resisted by the people who will be stakeholders within it, then disaster must surely be a likely outcome.

TABLE 2.3 PLEST factors that influence the level of resistance to change

PLEST factor	Example
Political	Loss of influence with superiors
Legal	Loss of rights
Economic	Loss of income
Social factors	Loss of comfort factors; loss of peer group
Technical	Loss of skills; forced acceptance of undesirable skills

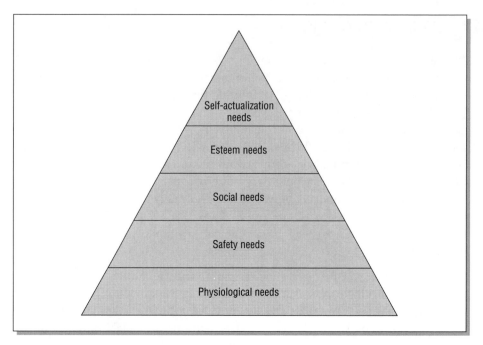

FIGURE 2.5 ■ Maslow's hierarchy of needs

Human motivation

The motivation of people and their ability to cope with change within the organization are critical to the success of an IS project. For a program of change to be successful therefore, it must connect with the very beliefs, values and needs of the people whom it affects.

The needs structure of individuals has been the subject of many studies into the psychology of human behavior. Abraham Maslow's theory,[4] suggesting a "hierarchy of needs" (Figure 2.5), is one of the more popular ones. Although not conclusive, it does provide a useful framework for the study of motivation and, therefore, the factors determining the success of change within an organization, and ultimately, the success of IS projects undertaken within it.

Maslow's theory, first formulated in 1943 and updated in the 1960s, established a simple hypothesis; most people are motivated by the desire to satisfy a wide range of needs, which can be categorized into five broad groups (Table 2.4).

The second and most crucial point of Maslow's theory is that people will tend to satisfy their needs in a hierarchical manner. Physiological needs must be

TABLE 2.4 ▨ The hierarchical nature of human needs

Need	Explanation
Self-actualization	The need for self-fulfilment (achieving personal goals, status or kudos)
Esteem	The need for self-respect, self-esteem and the esteem of others
Social	The need for close relations with others, the need for a partner
Safety	The need for a stable and secure environment, free from threats
Physiological	The basic needs to sustain life (food, sleep, oxygen, etc.)

satisfied first (the lowest group of needs), then others following their order in the needs hierarchy. For example, a person in desperate need of food and water will not be motivated by the thought of gaining self-respect and respect from others. Indeed, in extreme circumstances, people have been known to kill each other for food – the need for survival therefore surpasses any other need.

 CASE STUDY

The Piper Alpha disaster

Piper Alpha was the name of an oil platform in the North Sea which caught fire and burned down on July 6, 1988. It was the worst ever offshore petroleum incident during which 167 people died and a billion dollar oil platform was almost totally destroyed.[5-7]

The disaster began with a routine maintenance procedure to replace a backup propane pump. The valve in the pump was removed, leaving a hole in the pump where it had been. However, because the workers fixing the pump could not get all the equipment they needed by the end of their shift, they asked for and received permission to leave the work until the next day.

In what was to become a catastrophic sequence of events, the primary pump failed at 10 pm that night, and as the staff in the control room did not know the backup pump was under maintenance, they decided to switch it on. Gas under immense pressure escaped from the hole left by the valve and exploded with such force it blew down the firewall separating different parts of the plant; soon large quantities of oil were burning out of control. Tragically, the automatic deluge system, designed to flood the fire with water, did not activate – it had been turned off.

By 10:20 pm fire had spread across most of the levels within the platform – at its peak the flames reached over 300 feet (91.44 m) high and the heat could be felt from over a mile away. Being furthest from the blaze, the living accommodation area became the only 'safe' haven for the workers, but as the accommodation blocks were not smoke-proof, it was only a matter of time before conditions there worsened. It was now obvious to the workers that they would have to evacuate – their lives were now seriously threatened by the inferno that was raging out of control on the platform. Unable to reach the lifeboats as their route was blocked by smoke and flames, some workers realized the only way to escape would be by jumping into the sea. The decision was not based on reason, it would involve jumping 150 feet (45.72 m) onto a surface of water alight with oil. Those who did jump in then had to juggle between staying underwater in the freezing North Sea and staying on the surface to cook in the intense heat, in the hope that they would be rescued by boat. Sixty-seven men were saved in this way, most of the other 167 who stayed on the platform died from carbon monoxide and fumes poisoning.   .

Learning the lessons

The events of the Piper Alpha disaster now feature highly in many management theories, concluding that people will not change from the status quo unless they are faced with an immediate and fatal danger. In fact, many studies of change now conclude that the "Piper Alpha" approach is one of the best approaches to change management, i.e. given that human nature is so averse to change, the only way to effect change is to create a situation of immense pain. As a result, the risk to the individual must be immediate and fatal; the only option available to the individual is therefore to ignore the status quo and take a completely different course of action. The only oil platform workers that survived the Piper Alpha disaster were the ones who jumped into the sea (which was alight with oil), *actions that directly contravened the company safety policy*.

The "Piper Alpha" approach to change is not common; fundamentally, human nature is averse to change. Within business, such resistance to change is an obvious threat to the success of key projects. IS projects *enable* change, so if the rate of change is insufficient to achieve the desired outcome it becomes a critical issue for those individuals who are seeking benefits from the change.

The "Piper Alpha" approach to change management offers a basis on which change can be effected, even when a culture of resistance to it exists within the organization. To effect IS change (and therefore organizational change), an *artificial* crisis must be created which will cause the same level of pain and therefore bring about change in the same manner.

To illustrate this more effectively, let us consider an organization that is about to embark on a program of change. The board of directors have decided to introduce a number of strategic IS programs which will radically change the working practices and systems within the company. Let us also assume that the employees of this company are highly motivated individuals; their motivational needs are at the *top* of Maslow's hierarchy (self-actualization needs). Resistance to any organizational change, therefore, is likely to be high as it might threaten the core values and beliefs of the employees. However, based on Maslow's theory that needs are satisfied hierarchically, an artificial "crisis" can be created within the organization that will force individuals to change their behavior and move from their status quo position.

A situation which causes "immediate and fatal pain" is a fundamental principle of the "Piper Alpha" approach to change management. Within organizations, the principle can be upheld by displacing the higher-order needs of individuals with those that exist at a much lower level in the hierarchy. For example, someone who is initially against having to leave their current and well-respected team to join a new project team who are not regarded as "high-flyers" by their peers (the need for respect from others; a *high*-level need in the hierarchy) will soon view the situation differently if they are told they might lose their job if the project they are moving to does not succeed (need for job security; a *low*-level need in the hierarchy).

Status quo behavior can also be changed in a similar manner as a result of, or under the threat of:

- legal action (e.g. lawsuits as a result of a failed IS project);
- political action (e.g. government interference in how public sector IS projects are managed);
- executive decisions within the organization (e.g. the need to rationalize the business);
- a disaster which has affected the operational capability of the organization (staff, buildings, power, plant, and equipment).

The "Piper Alpha" approach to change management is fairly draconian, but it is effective and therefore not uncommon among organizations. There are, however, many other, more subtle ways of achieving a similar outcome, such as:

- the establishment of "assessment centers" to review the skills, values, beliefs, and experience of all staff as a pre-requisite to a major change program;
- the reorganization of the company structure to reflect the new change program – in many cases, staff must reapply for new positions within the new structure;

- the "ship is leaving the harbor" speech – the executives of the organization establish a series of presentations outlining the company's change in direction and their need for a program of change. The company is basically informing staff that their commitment and dedication to the new program is crucial to its success and that if they are not fully behind the program (onboard the "ship") there can be no role for them in the new structure;
- changing employee pay structures – reducing basic pay and implementing a commission or other 'deliverables-based' pay structure.

The Milgram experiments

The Piper Alpha study is a classic example of how people will not change from the status quo behavior unless a situation of immense pain is created in those from whom change is desired. Another classic change case relates to the experiments conducted by Stanley Milgram, which came to be known as the "Milgram experiments".[8] The experiments ultimately demonstrate just how difficult it is in practice to change human behavior, even *when the status quo is manifestly wrong*.

The first experiment was based on assessing the ability of a group of volunteers, the "teachers," to teach simple word-pairs to the other group, the "students." Teachers were told to administer an electric shock to the student every time they made a mistake, as a form of punishment.

Before the experiment, Milgram had asked a number of observers to predict how many of the subjects would actually inflict a form of torture on someone else, *purely because they were told to do so by a person in authority*. There was almost total agreement that all the subjects would refuse to obey the order.

At the start, the shocks were small, but they increased in intensity each time a mistake was made.* By the end of the experiment, Milgram discovered that two out of three teachers had administered electric shocks up to a level that was clearly marked "fatal," simply because an authority figure had told them to do so. In actual fact, none of the students received an electric shock, although the volunteer "teachers" were led to believe the students were actually receiving the shocks they themselves administered.

---

* A similar experiment appears with amusing effect in the film *Ghostbusters*.

In a variation of this experiment, Milgram decided to study the effects of a group in defying authority – in this case the experimenter. His experiment began by providing two assistants to help the subject, the teacher. Testing of the student would now be performed by a group rather than by an individual. The experiment began with one of the assistants administering the shocks. He then refused to continue, argued with the experimenter and withdrew to the corner of the room. The second assistant resumed the testing, but after a while, also refused to continue, leaving the "real" subject to continue administering the shocks himself. The experiment was then repeated 40 times, each time with a different subject. In 30 of these cases, the subject, having seen his colleagues defy the experimenter, also defied the experimenter. When the group pressure (or support) for defiance was lacking, only 14 subjects defied the authority figure.

The effects of authority and peer-group pressure are often overlooked within IS projects, yet they are often responsible for causing many of the problems that exist within team situations. This is especially true if the team contains a number of inexperienced or naïve members. For instance, if a relatively inexperienced project member is exposed to an authority figure away from the team, such as the business sponsor or a product supplier, it is not inconceivable to suggest that the person in authority may use his or her position to direct that individual to undertake a particular course of action which could introduce a number of important risks into the project, such as:

■ agree to include extra functionality in the final deliverable;

■ change the design of the system;

■ make changes which have not been approved;

■ bring forward the implementation date;

■ approve a technical solution which is complex and ambitious;

■ bypass formal control mechanisms;

■ pursue high-cost/high-risk strategies.

It is possible, however, that peer-group pressure can be used to modify unacceptable behavior within the team. It is often the case that an individual within the team feels they deserve higher status within it as they have more qualifications than others in the team, or a greater depth of technical knowledge. This situation can easily lead to conflict, creating a status quo within the team that is clearly unhealthy. Direct action from the project manager may exacerbate the situation, but peer-group pressure from the other members of the project team can ensure that the individual is aware that their behavior is unacceptable to the group, leading to a change in behavior.

⭐ CASE STUDY

Philips Electronics

During the 1980s, Philips Electronics[9] had a strong reputation for being one of the most successful manufacturers of domestic electronic equipment. Based in the Netherlands, its financial strength was unparalleled, matched only by the excellence of its engineering workforce, which at the time was undoubtedly the finest in Europe. The research and development of new products had been a significant factor in establishing Philips as a market leader, pioneering the development of products such as the audio cassette, video recorder, and compact disk.

Despite a strongly decentralized organizational structure which promoted competition and strengthened loyalty within each business unit, Philips experienced problems trying to get products to market in a timely fashion. Product excellence was not a problem, but with strong competition coming from Sony and Panasonic, who were operating with much lower manufacturing costs, Philips' margins were being squeezed and as a result, their market share – once unrivalled in the Netherlands – was now dropping substantially.

The problems that faced the Philips executives were classic in the manufacturing sector – the pace and quality of product development; the slow time to market and high cost of manufacture – and despite being tackled by two different CEOs during the 1980s, Philips were heading for their biggest operating loss in history. The issue that confounded the executives of the company the most was that, even after they had redefined the management responsibilities and articulated the problems facing the company to the lower levels of management, there was no improvement in the company's performance.

What the executives had not realized was that there was no employee support for the program of change within the organization. The lower levels of management within the organization, and their subordinates, had effectively refused to accept the need to realign their own goals with the new goals of the organization. In hindsight, the problem could have been predicted as the company's existing culture, i.e. its norms, beliefs and unwritten rules, clashed with the program of change taking place. Philips, historically, had been able to offer its employees a 'job for life' in return for loyalty to the company and to individual managers. The bond between a manager and his or her subordinates was a strong one, based on informal relationships rather than any formal system.

Responsibilities and boundaries of work were limited, and the success of subordinates was measured by meeting the demands of line management rather than meeting organizational challenges or aspiring to greater personal goals. Seniority directly affected an employee's career growth, workers had no incentive to work harder nor to exceed their manager's minimum expectations for performance.

By the time Jan Timmer took over as CEO, the company was in crisis, net operating income had dropped from 223 million guilders to 6 million guilders and the net operating loss was projected by analysts at 1.2 billion guilders. Jan Timmer faced a number of challenges to improve the company's position in as short a time as possible. First, he had to establish a program of change and, more importantly, initiate a process by which the employees could accept that change. In tackling these two areas, Timmer hoped to change the culture of the organization and improve its profitability by establishing relationships between an employee's commitment and the outcome of the change process.

Timmer, expecting the inevitable resistance to change from employees and managers, introduced a number of shock tactics. He invited the top 100 managers to attend an off-site meeting in the company's training center. At the meeting he explained the crisis affecting the company, and even handed out a hypothetical press release explaining that the company had gone bankrupt. It was the task of the people in the meeting to turn the company around – Operation Centurion had begun.

From the start, Timmer made his objectives clear: he offered his managers new contracts; the contracts, which were agreed by both parties, gave each manager targets for a reduction in headcount (a 20 per cent reduction in headcount was required overall), and operating costs. Commitment was established and performance was to be measured against achievement of these targets; career development and bonus payments were directly linked to meeting the stated objectives. In the days and weeks that followed the meeting, Timmer kept a high profile, reinforcing the urgency of the situation and the need for employees and managers to commit themselves to making the "new" organization work.

Commitment was established at the lower levels of management by negotiating new contracts with business unit managers across the regions. At the same time, workshop sessions were introduced for employees and managers to discuss the consequences and impact of the change program. Timmer himself attended many meetings to talk directly with employees and to encourage them to support his program. His style and approach were inclusive, and it soon became clear that the employees were listening and the company was changing.

By the end of 1991, the workforce had been reduced by 22 per cent. Those who had not achieved the targets set in their contracts were dismissed, including Timmer's successor in his previous business unit, the consumer electronic division. More importantly, Timmer had managed to change the culture of the organization; "loyalty deals" and the culture of patronage were no longer the values and norms of the company. If the management skills needed for prosperity did not exist within the company, Timmer recruited from outside the company; by mid-1994 only four members of the original senior management team remained, and only five of the 14 were Dutch.

The successful change program was also reflected in the financial strength of the company. Operating income rose from (4.3 per cent) of sales in 1990 to 6.2 per cent in 1994 and the share price rose from 20.30 guilders to 51.40 guilders.

Fundamentally, Timmer changed the company's fortunes by creating a crisis to change the status quo behavior of individuals within his company. As in the "Piper Alpha" approach to change, a successful outcome was only achieved by those who changed their behavior and ignored the status quo.

⏩ The psychological impact of change

The psychological impact of change is a key factor in determining IS project success. From my own experiences, the technical issues of a project are generally of less importance than those issues which directly affect our work and the environment in which we undertake that work.

I do not for a minute underestimate the complexity of contemporary IT systems, but that is insignificant, compared to the complexity that surrounds the behavior of our fellow human beings. We do not conform to any known standards; we are not always rational and our reasoning process is likely to be based on emotion rather than logic. From this we can draw the conclusion that the management of change from a human perspective is a critical step within the organization and, indeed, within the IS project.

One of the leading figures on the subject of human relations and organizational change was Professor Elton Mayo, whose association with the "Hawthorne studies" identified a number of vital considerations regarding human behavior within the workplace.

The Hawthorne studies

At the time of the studies, Elton Mayo (1880–1949) was Professor of Industrial Research at the Harvard Graduate School of Business Administration. He became involved in the studies after being approached by executives from the Western Electric Company (based in Hawthorne) for advice. The company was already proud of its welfare facilities for its employees, but had begun a number of studies to determine the effect of lighting on its workforce. In particular they were keen to discover whether changes to the lighting affected the productivity of the workers. What the executives found, before the arrival of Mayo, was that the workers who were the subject of the study improved their productivity, regardless of whether the lighting was improved or not.

A further study was carried out, this time with the help of Mayo and his colleagues, which would eventually become known as the Relay Assembly Test Room. Six female workers in the relay assembly section were segregated from their colleagues and subjected to variances in working conditions. The women were well aware of the changes before the study commenced and were comfortable with the study. The variables which were changed during the study were such things as the number and length of rest breaks and the time and duration of the lunch break.

The major observation from this study confirmed the results of the first study undertaken by the company executives; productivity increased regardless of changes to working conditions. At no point during the study was any attempt made to analyse the attitudes or the social relationships of the workers. Further studies changed the working week within the study group – the outcome was the same, productivity increased. The women's reactions to the study – their increase in productivity regardless of the changes made to their working environment – have come to be known as the "Hawthorne Effect." The Hawthorne Effect states that the behavior of individuals changes when they become the subject of a study – they are a special group and, as a result, display different behavior.

The Hawthorne experiments demonstrated the importance of human psychology in achieving change. If a group is perceived to be "special" they will behave differently to other groups and their productivity will increase as a result. Mayo's findings, however, are still hotly disputed by contemporary theorists.

Those who discredit the Hawthorne studies support the view that, apart from the fact that everyone likes to be noticed, the experiments were of little significance. Despite this, at least agreement has been reached on one key point; the studies represented the first major attempt to undertake social research. The debate will continue I am sure, but we have, however, learnt a number of key lessons as a result:

- Individual workers cannot be treated in isolation, but must be seen as members of a group;
- The need to belong to a group is more important than financial incentives or good physical working conditions;
- Informal (or unofficial) work groups exercise a strong influence over the behavior of workers;
- The social needs of workers must be satisfied if workers and managers are to build loyal and trusting relationships within the organization.

Valuable lessons for the project manager and business sponsor can be learnt from these studies. Every project is important to the organization; if it was not, it would not be undertaken, and as such, it is vital that the project members feel important. Organizational charts displaying the project structure and roles are a useful start in helping the project team understand how their group maps onto the wider picture. A much more effective approach would be to establish a series of "kick-off" type meetings, first with the project team as a whole, and later with each individual member of the project. The purpose of these meetings is simple; to communicate to the group and the individual a number of key messages:

- *Why* they are needed for the project;

- *What* they will be expected to perform;

- *How* the achievement of their personal goals will contribute towards the project's goals;

- *How* the success of the project contributes to the overall success of the organization.

Unfortunately, it is typical of many people engaged on IS projects to display energy, commitment, and high levels of motivation early on in the project, to be replaced by low morale, poor self-esteem, and resentment later on. Attending to the needs of the project members throughout the lifecycle of the project is crucial if the motivation of the team is to be sustained.

A possible remedy to this is the "away-day," a concept that is rapidly gaining importance within many IS projects. Being similar to an introductory "kick-off" meeting, but taking place at key stages throughout the project, the away-day is a relaxed, informal day away from the office. The objective of an away-day is to bring a group together to discuss plans, ideas, and to communicate openly and honestly with each other in a "safe," "no-comebacks" environment. The emphasis of the day is very much on people and people issues.

Herzberg's motivation–hygiene theory

One of the strongest theories so far to emerge from the studies performed by Maslow, is the study of human motivation undertaken by Frederick Herzberg in the 1950s.[10,11] Unlike the Hawthorne studies, which were concerned with the behavior of factory workers, Herzberg's research drew particular attention to the higher level needs in the motivation of professional (and subsequently other) groups of employees.

The research was undertaken using a sample of 200 accountants and engineers in Pennsylvania, USA and concentrated on satisfaction at work. Employees were asked to describe events within the workplace that had made them feel exceptionally pleased with their jobs and events that had produced exceptionally bad feelings. From the results collected, the research team came to the conclusion that certain factors were a key determiner of job satisfaction and that certain factors led to job dissatisfaction. The former, Herzberg called the "motivators;" the latter, "hygiene factors" (Table 2.5).

An interesting observation that can be made about these motivators is that they represent the "higher-order" needs of the individual and therefore relate to the higher levels within Maslow's hierarchy of needs. Indeed, during the studies

TABLE 2.5 ▨ Factors affecting job attitudes

Factors leading to extreme satisfaction	Factors leading to extreme dissatisfaction
Achievement	Company policy and administration
Recognition	Supervision
Work itself	Relationship with peers and supervisor
Responsibility	Working conditions
Promotion	Salary
Growth	Security

undertaken by Herzberg, these were seen as more important than other factors such as pay and status and were intimately related to the *content* of the work. Analysis of the hygiene factors, however, indicates that they are more closely related to the *context* or environment of work than to the job itself.

The relationship between the motivators and the hygiene factors is not merely a simple measure of the level of job satisfaction within an employee. Whilst the presence of motivators in the organization caused enduring states of motivation in employees, their absence did not lead to dissatisfaction. Hygiene factors, on the other hand, produced an acceptable working environment, but they did not increase satisfaction; their absence, however, did cause job dissatisfaction. Hygiene in other words, cannot ensure good health, but can act to prevent ill-health within the organization.

Both these approaches (motivation and hygiene) must be done simultaneously within the organization if the studies into job attitudes are to be of benefit. More specifically, it is the responsibility of those individuals overseeing the project to ensure that these factors are adopted throughout the project if they are to benefit those individuals engaged within it.

Fortunately, Herzberg's motivation–hygiene theory has been well-received by practising mangers and consultants in the field of human relations for its relatively simple distinction between the causes of satisfaction and dissatisfaction at work. Simply allocating work to individuals is no longer sufficient to keep highly motivated professionals satisfied. Job enrichment and job enlargement schemes are necessary, therefore, to ensure that jobs can be designed to contain the optimum number of motivators.

By understanding the motivation of individuals within the work environment, the organization can benefit from increased productivity, decreased absenteeism and improved working relationships. Equally, individuals within the project will enjoy a more satisfying role and improved morale for a number of key reasons:

■ They will have an individual identity and a group identity through which their needs will be satisfied;

■ Self-fulfilment will be experienced for an individual where consideration has been given to ensuring that their job is creative and gives job satisfaction;

■ They will have a status within the project providing their role is investigated to make their work more interesting.

 CASE STUDY

Cerner

During the early part of 2001, the CEO of Cerner, a US healthcare company based in Kansas City, sent his managers the following e-mail:[12–15]

> We are getting less than 40 hours of work from a large number of our K.C.-based EMPLOYEES. The parking lot is sparsely used at 8 a.m.; likewise at 5 p.m. As managers, you either do not know what your EMPLOYEES are doing, or you do not CARE. You have created expectations on the work effort which allowed this to happen inside Cerner, creating a very unhealthy environment. In either case, you have a problem and you will fix it or I will replace you.
>
> NEVER in my career have I allowed a team which worked for me to think they had a 40-hour job. I have allowed YOU to create a culture which is permitting this. NO LONGER.
>
> At the end of next week, I am planning to implement the following:
>
> 1   Closing of Associate Center to EMPLOYEES from 7:30 a.m. to 6:30 p.m.
>
> 2   Implementing a hiring freeze . . .
>
> 3   Implementing a time clock system, requiring EMPLOYEES to "punch in" and "punch out" to work. Any unapproved absences will be charged to the EMPLOYEES' vacation.
>
> 4   Hell will freeze over before this CEO implements ANOTHER EMPLOYEE benefit in this culture.
>
> 5   Implement a 5 per cent reduction in staff . . .
>
> I STRONGLY suggest that you call some 7 a.m., 6 p.m., and Saturday a.m. team meetings with the EMPLOYEES who work directly for you. . . . I suggest that you call your first meeting – tonight.

My measurement will be the parking lot: it should be substantially full at 7:30 a.m. and 6:30 p.m. The pizza man should show up at 7:30 p.m. to feed the starving teams working late. The lot should be half full on Saturday mornings. . . . I will hold you accountable. You have allowed things to get to this state. You have two weeks. Tick, tock.

In response, offended employees within the company hit back, posting the e-mail on the Internet (a *Yahoo* financial message board). Within days, the e-mail had found its way onto numerous business-related websites. The e-mail was to have a severe affect on the value of the company's stock, it dropped nearly 22 per cent. Ironically, the company had been included in *Fortune* magazine's list of the 100 best companies to work for in America during 2000.

Although the CEO followed up with an apology, which he e-mailed to his entire staff, he maintained that he was just trying to motivate his workers. "I did it with a lot of satire, never thinking it would be communicated to my associates or broadcast to the outside," he explained. "But I lit the match. That match has started a firestorm."

Change: critical success factors

- There must be a clear, well-defined goal or desired state which must be understood and supported by all participants.

- The values, beliefs, and ethics of the organization must be supported and accepted by all participants.

- The program of change must be openly supported by key stakeholders. There must be a change "champion" who must be the visible figure for change.

- People must be kept informed prior to, during, and following the change program. Information must be filtered down the organizational hierarchy to ensure that there is a clear, consistent message being communicated throughout the organization.

- Change is a complex issue requiring specialist skills. If these skills do not exist within the organization, they must be brought in from outside.

- Change will only happen if it has the full support of all the key stakeholders within the change program.

- The human effects of change are often the most difficult to resolve. Charisma, motivation, undying nerve, and courage in adversity are just some of the essential qualities the change manager must possess if change is to be successful.

References

1 *Lord Simpson: The man who broke Marconi*, September 7, 2001, http://news.bbc.co.uk/1/hi/in_depth/uk/2000/newsmakers/1527551.stm (accessed 2001)

2 M. Pendergrast, *For God, Country & Coca-Cola*, Orion Business, London, 2001

3 M. Ritson, "It's the real thing?," *Business Life*, November, 2001, p. 27

4 A. Maslow, *Motivation and Personality*, third edition, Harper and Row, New York, 1987

5 BBC Online Disaster Series: Piper Alpha www.bbc.co.uk/education/archive/disaster/piper.shtml

6 Hon. Lord Cullen, *The Public Inquiry into the Piper Alpha Disaster*, HMSO, London, 1990

7 D. Conway, V. Salazar and S. Byrd, *Piper Alpha: The Disaster and Beyond*, supporting course material, Rice University, US, www.owlnet.rice.edu

8 S. Milgram, *Obedience to Authority*, Tavistock, London, 1974

9 P. Strebel, "Why Do Employees Resist Change?," *Harvard Business Review*, May–June, 1996, 88–90

10 F. Herzberg, B. Mausner and B.B. Snydeman, *The Motivation to Work*, New York, 1959

11 F. Herzberg, *Work and the Nature of Man*, World Publishing, Cleveland 1966.

12 A. Wheat (2001), *'Oops'*, April; www.business2.com/articles/mag/0,1640.11286, FF.html (accessed 2001)

13 *Workforce Magazine*, "Electronic Invective Backfires," June, 2001

14 *Behavior Biz*, June 2001, (6) www.cultureworx.com/cultureworxnewsletter/ newsletterjune01.htm (accessed 2001)

15 P. Delves Broughton, 'Boss's angry e-mail sends shares plunging', The *Daily Telegraph*, April 6, 2001

Further reading

W. Currie, *Management Strategy for IT: An Internal Perspective*, Financial Times Management, London, 1995

The President and Fellows of Harvard College, *Harvard Business Review on the Business Value of IT*, Harvard Business School Press, Boston, 1999

J. Ward and P. Griffiths, *Strategic Planning for Information Systems*, John Wiley & Sons, Chichester, 1996

3

Managing the requirements

No one means all he says, and yet very few say all they mean, for words are slippery and thought is viscous.

Henry Brooks Adams

The capability for change becomes a reality when the business requirements necessary to effect that change are satisfied through the implementation of an IS project. The management of requirements is, therefore, fundamental to the construction of IT systems which deliver business functionality and support business processes. According to Fred Brooks,[1] "the hardest single part of building a software system is deciding what to build . . . no part of the work so cripples the resulting system if done wrong. No other part is more difficult to rectify later" – he is not wrong.

It is widely acknowledged that many IS projects fail because they have been designed to satisfy the wrong requirements. Moreover, it is apparent that many projects fail, not because they do not work, but because they do not work *in the right way*. Failure of system developers to understand the real needs of the business can be as damaging to an IS project as failure arising from the deployment of unsuitable or erroneous technology.

In a dynamic and volatile business environment, where the needs and priorities of business users are constantly changing, such failures should not come as a surprise. It is the aim of requirements management, therefore, to ensure that the capability delivered from an IS project matches the expectations of the users, within the constraints of feasibility, corporate strategy, regulatory standards and other limiting factors.

What is requirements management?

Requirements management is a broad and complex subject area that governs the process through which the needs of business users can be captured, documented, and expressed formally within the limits of what is financially and technically achievable. Fundamental to this approach is the need to minimize the variation and conflict of requirements, and to provide stability and conformity through change management, itself a necessity in the high-pressure climate of IS development.

Requirements management has three key objectives.

1 To gain agreement on the requirements from the all stakeholders within the project. Stakeholders will exist from many different groups, namely management, end-users, developers and third parties who will have diverging perceptions of what is needed.

2 To provide a basis for software design. Specifications of functional and non-requirements must provide a precise input to software developers who are not experts in the business application domain.

3 To produce a specification against which the system specified will be tested, and subsequently accepted or rejected. The specification will be used as input into the validation process, which will ensure that it complies with the requirements of the users, other stakeholders and the business objectives.

The requirements management process is widely acknowledged as being vital to the development of information systems, and despite being ignored by many IS professionals, requirements management forms an important part of the software Capability Maturity Model (see Chapter 9).

The failure to adequately manage requirements is not uncommon within many IS projects. A likely reason for this will be that requirements management is perceived to be a task largely undertaken by software development teams. Whilst successful requirements management is within the scope of software project management, it is vital that business stakeholders accept that they have a significant responsibility in providing the project team with a clear and prioritized set of requirements.

Numerous investigations into the causes of software project failure have repeatedly concluded that deficiencies in requirements management have been amongst the most important contributors to the problem. According to the authors of one such report[2] "in nearly every software project which fails to meet performance and cost goals, requirements inadequacies play a major and expensive role in project failure." The value of good requirements management, however, and the importance of performing it well increase significantly with the size and complexity of the system being developed. If performed well, the benefits of requirements management are clear:

- agreement amongst developers, users, and other project stakeholders on the scope of work and the acceptance criteria for the delivered system;

- a sound foundation from which resource and cost estimates can be derived;

- quality assurance through improved system usability, performance, and maintainability;

- the effective achievement of goals, as a result of less rework, fewer omissions and a greater understanding of requirements.

It should be clear, therefore, that a complete set of requirements must not only identify those that will help identify business functionality, but also the technical or system requirements that are needed to support that functionality. It is not, however, the objective of requirements management to identify practical solutions to any given set of requirements, but to establish a brief for systems developers or third-party suppliers.

The requirements management lifecycle

Regardless of the terminology used within software tools that support the requirements management process and systems development methodologies, there are a number of generic processes that translate unformatted business requirements into a formal requirements specification. These processes are known as the "requirements management lifecycle" (Figure 3.1).

The requirements lifecycle is generally considered to be a sequential and mechanical process – unstructured and diverse requirements are fed into it and a series of formal system requirements are produced from it. In reality, the lifecycle resembles a series of iterative steps that can be adopted to help identify, refine, and formally express user and system requirements. Iteration is an important part of the process to ensure that feedback and control is maintained throughout the process. For instance, requirements that turn out to be inconsistent or in conflict with existing requirements already captured can be reworked and refined by introducing them back into the elicitation or analysis phase.

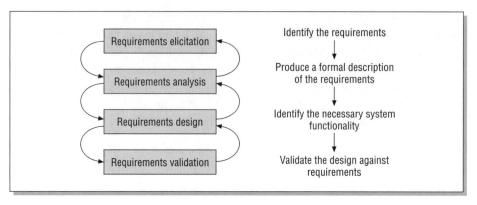

FIGURE 3.1 ■ The requirements management lifecycle

Whilst the elicitation process is generally accepted to be the initial phase in the requirements management lifecycle, analysis can actually assist the elicitation process before it begins. At the outset of the project, it is vital that the scope of the requirements elicitation phase is fully understood beforehand.

The identification of quantifiable business objectives will set the parameters for what information must be elicited from stakeholders, within the context of organizational strategy, assessment of risk, and other project constraints. These objectives, and the business information that is needed to achieve them, will be produced from the business planning process for each business function. The information–objective matrix, shown in Table 3.1, is a simple and straightforward means of representing this information for each business function. Its main benefit is that it allows a simple cross-check to be made for information needs that do not appear to contribute towards any business objective and business objectives that do not have the means by which they can be satisfied.

Analysis of the business using structured techniques contained within methodologies such as SSADM (Structured Systems Analysis and Design Methodology) or DSDM will help identify the groups and individuals who either 'own' requirements or who use or manage data, and so will be a vital contributor to the elicitation process.

Requirements elicitation

The initial stage of the requirements management process is typically the most difficult; yet it is the most critical as it provides the foundations from which all subsequent phases develop. Traditional requirements elicitation makes two key assumptions: that a mechanistic approach using techniques (such as interviewing,

TABLE 3.1 ▨ An information–objective matrix for a sales and marketing business function

					Information needed				
				Time order delivered					
			Time order received						
		Service level							
	Sales by customer								
Sales by product									
Objective									
Produce statements within 24 hours									X
Process payments within one working day							X		
Statement error rate < 1 in 1000									
Turnaround 95% of orders in 24 hours							X	X	X
Increase sales by 5% per year						X	X		

structured questionnaires, and prototyping) must be adopted; and that this in itself will be sufficient to elicit the requirements from business stakeholders. A more contemporary view of requirements elicitation is based on a more 'human' approach where requirements are identified through discussion and negotiation.

The need to capture requirements effectively from specific users has led to the development of a number of techniques such as JAD (Joint Application Development) and prototyping, which promote shared responsibility for design and development activities. In practice, successful requirements elicitation will involve discussion and negotiation between users, managers and developers and possibly external bodies, and agencies. Through the course of negotiation and later, within the requirements analysis phase, the demands of all the stakeholders in the system should be formulated and agreed. Whilst effective requirements elicitation establishes a consensus of requirements through discussion and co-operation, poor elicitation does not stimulate people to communicate openly. This inevitably imposes an interpretation of the business that is likely to be unacceptable to many people within the organization.

Key deliverables

During the requirements elicitation stage, large amounts of information will be captured by the requirements management team. These must now be documented, structured, and put into some sort of context so as to be relevant to the wider project team. Whilst there are many different ways of expressing both business and system requirements within the software development methodologies available (such as data and process modeling techniques), there are a number of general techniques that provide a useful starting point for expressing the context within which the requirements will exist.

▨ *Business context diagram*

Business context diagrams (see Figure 3.2) help explore the interactions between the major business entities that will use, or interface with, the proposed system. As a consequence, they can be used to validate that all the key participants in the project have been identified as well as the significant information flows

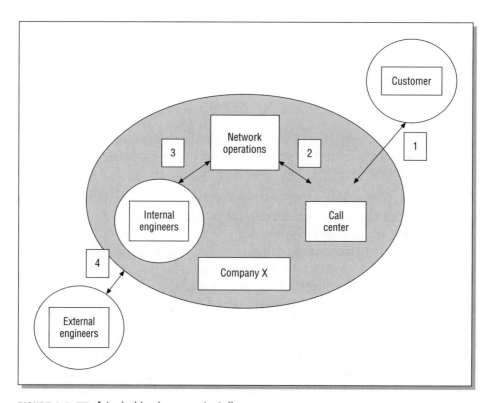

FIGURE 3.2 ▨ A typical business context diagram

TABLE 3.2 ▨ A typical business event list

Interaction 1 (Customer/call center)

Event number	Business event	Related requirement
E1.1	Customer contacts the call center to report a fault.	1
E1.2	The customer contacts the call center to enquire about the progress on an existing fault call.	5
E1.3	The call center contacts the customer with an update on an existing fault call.	4,6
E1.4	The customer provides the call center additional information relating to an existing fault call.	3,10
E1.5	The call center contacts the customer to check service has been restored. If the fault has been resolved, the call center can close the fault call.	11,15

between each business area. They do not, however, describe the sequence of these interactions, nor any processes operating within each business area. Up to this point, only the business requirements are known, and so business context diagrams do not show the IT systems involved in the solution, nor whether any interfaces between business areas are manual or automated.

■ Business event list

For each interaction within the business context diagram, the main business events are listed and cross-referred to the specific items with the requirements specification that support that event. As the diagram shown in Figure 3.2 represents the interactions within a product support function, the list of typical business events that might exist between the customer and the call center (interaction 1) is likely to resemble the list of business events shown in Table 3.2.

Requirements analysis

Requirements analysis provides a basis for developing a formal design from a given set of requirements. It is within this phase that the information obtained from requirements elicitation must be processed and verified for accuracy and consistency. The elicitation of requirements from business users and stakeholders is, without doubt, a complex process, and the likelihood that errors will have been introduced into the process will be high.

Requirements are generally gathered in many different ways and from diverse sources, so formal analysis of the requirements is a necessary activity if the customer and supplier are to be able to commit to proceeding with further development. Traditional structured analysis techniques, found in many systems development methodologies such as business modeling and in more contemporary techniques such as prototyping, are vital during this phase as they promote understanding and participation between users and developers.

Key activities

During the requirements analysis phase, a number of key activities will be performed and often repeated until all issues concerning requirements are resolved. These activities are typically as follows.

Assessing potential problems

Requirements captured through elicitation from users must be assessed for their feasibility and for problems such as ambiguity, incompleteness, and inconsistency. If requirements are to be formally expressed as a precursor to systems development, they must conform to some basic rules:

- Requirements must be atomic. Each requirement must be a statement of a singular requirement. Inherently compound or hierarchical requirements must be normalized into multiple and dependent requirements.

- Requirements must be quantifiable. If there is a requirement for a new business process for example, when will it start? When will it stop? What will it need as input and what will it produce as output? Key Performance Indicators (KPIs) can be used to quantify specific performance requirements, such as transaction rate and response time for business processes and functions.

- Requirements must be consistent. The function and attributes of a requirement must remain consistent throughout the life of the system that it helps define.

- Requirements must be understood. The language and vocabulary used to express requirements must be common to both the customer and the supplier.

- Requirements must be complete. The definition of complete is that if a system satisfies every requirement, it will be acceptable to the customer.

TABLE 3.3 ▨ MoSCoW rules for prioritizing requirements

Priority	Description
Must have	Requirements which enable the objectives of the system to be met.
Should have	Requirements which, if omitted, will severely limit the operation and performance of the system.
Can have	Requirements which can be omitted, but if incorporated will provide additional functionality.
Won't have	Requirements which do not support the objectives and are therefore out of scope.

Prioritizing requirements

On average, the requirements elicitation phase will generate a huge number of requirements; now is the time to prioritize them. Too many IS projects fail as the scope of the project is so immense; nothing of any worth is delivered for years, by which time the business drivers have changed and many of the requirements have become redundant. Rapid application development techniques aim to mitigate this risk by ensuring that business capability is developed on a priority basis. As it is likely that 80 per cent of the requirements in a business system are satisfied by just 20 per cent of the system functionality, it seems sensible, therefore, to focus on building the most important requirements first.

A key factor in prioritizing requirements will be the need to assess each requirement against its ability to deliver functionality which will directly support the stated business objectives. Whilst there are numerous ways of identifying criteria against which requirements can be prioritized, the MOSCOW (or more accurately, MoSCoW) technique is one of the more common approaches used within IS projects and is outlined in Table 3.3.

Evaluation of feasibility and risks

Once requirements are documented and represented in a manner that can be understood by all project stakeholders, an assessment can be made of their feasibility. This assessment must include:

- technical feasibility (i.e. can the requirements be met with the current technology?);
- operational feasibility (i.e. can the system be deployed into the business environment without affecting current operations?);
- economic feasibility (i.e. can the requirements be satisfied within a cost that is acceptable to the customer?).

Categorizing requirements

■ *Functional requirements*

Functional requirements are *what* the users need. A functional requirement will therefore specify a function that a system or system component (software) must be capable of performing. Functional requirements can be stated from a static or dynamic perspective. The former will describe the functions performed by each entity and the way each entity reacts with others within the system; the latter will identify the behavior of the system under a number of specific circumstances or "states."

■ *Non-functional requirements*

Non-functional requirements are often overlooked during requirements management as they cannot be easily modeled using standard modeling techniques. Non-functional requirements (or *quality* requirements) identify *how well* the functional requirements must be developed. They include attributes such as conformity, efficiency, reliability, maintainability, flexibility, portability, auditability, security, usability, and reusability. Using techniques such as software quality assurance, the requirements management process can model non-functional requirements and the level to which related quality criteria must be delivered (for example, conformity has the related criteria of completeness, correctness and traceability).

■ *Design and implementation constraints*

The identification of constraints that affect the design should be treated as another set of requirements for the project. Constraints define *when* and *how* the system must be developed. In practice, constraints on design and implementation play a significant role in ultimately determining how the requirements, and ultimately, the proposed business system will be implemented.

Typical constraints on IS projects are likely to include one or more of the following:

■ operating in conjunction with existing hardware and software;

■ cost;

■ conformance to specific programming languages;

■ conformance to IT strategy and organizational policy;

■ architectural platforms;

■ recruitment of skilled resources.

The outcome of requirements analysis is the formulation of functional requirements, non-functional requirements, and design and implementation constraints. These requirements and constraints must be represented and presented in a manner that will fulfil the needs of all the stakeholders in the project, especially between systems developers and users.

Key deliverables

- The definition and documentation of the functions, performance, internal and external interfaces and quality attributes of the system under development.

- Estimation of the business benefits that can be achieved based on an evaluation of the proposed system.

- The identification and documentation of user requirements concerning business process, organization, user roles and responsibilities.

Requirements design

If requirements analysis can be considered to be the "what," requirements design is the "how." The analysis of requirements must be free from implementation constraints – essentially, it concerns objectives rather than methods. Requirements design, however, must identify the implementation that will meet the stated requirements – it must define and subsequently refine the end-to-end high-level architecture for the proposed system. The system context diagram (Figure 3.3) and the system data flow list (Table 3.4) are popular methods of identifying the scope of the proposed solution in terms of the impacted systems and the interfaces between them. The former focuses on the interfaces between the systems, whilst the latter identifies the high-level data flows within them. The system data flow list is a particularly useful device as it correlates the

TABLE 3.4 ▨ A typical system data flow list

Data flow number	High-level data flow description	Functional req. cross-reference	Business event cross-reference
	Interface 1: User – System A		
1.1	User creates a new fault ticket in System A	17, 21, 42	E1.01
1.2	User updates a fault ticket in System A	–	–
1.3	User assigns a fault ticket to one or more agencies for resolution	15	E5.01, E6.01, E7.01, E8.01
1.4	User performs query to retrieve details on a fault ticket	14, 17	E1.02, E1.03, E5.02, E6.02, E7.02, E8.02

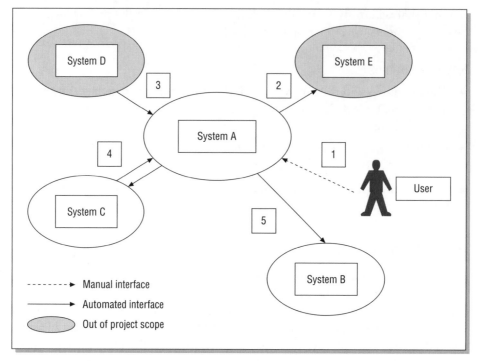

FIGURE 3.3 ■ A typical system context diagram

high-level data flow with the functional requirements and business events obtained during earlier stages in the requirements management lifecycle.

Key deliverables

- Program function/module/object design.
- Database design.
- Hardware and software interface design.
- Network design.
- File design.

Requirements validation

The process of verifying and validating requirements elicited from the business is just as important as the process that generates them. A failure to satisfactorily complete the final phase of the requirements lifecycle greatly increases the risk that development may commence with requirements that are incomplete, inaccurate or both.

Validation is best achieved if the systems designers walkthrough the intended design with the business users, explaining how the design will satisfy their requirements. Data flow diagrams, entity relationship models and other systems analysis and design techniques will form a key role in this process.

Techniques such as prototyping, whilst useful during requirements analysis to aid understanding and user participation, can also be used to validate and prove the feasibility of requirements. Prototypes or "straw-man" type models, when used to validate the proposed design against the documented requirements often highlight flaws that may not appear until much later in the development life-cycle. It is important to remember that the cost of rework increases significantly throughout the lifecycle of the software development process and, should the eventual cost of development outweigh the benefit to be realized from its deployment within the business, the project will have undoubtedly failed.

Evaluating requirements

Estimating the cost of requirements

Based on the estimated cost of requirements, it is expected that the benefits that will be realized by the implementation of an IS project will outweigh the costs of building and developing the IT infrastructure and architecture. The cost of implementing requirements, therefore, is an important measure in determining the feasibility and benefit potential of the project as a whole. The benefit calculations made for the London Stock Exchange's TAURUS project were measured in millions of pounds over the years following implementation. This might have been impressive had the calculations taken into account the enormous costs of designing and developing such a complex and functionally rich system.

Identifying the cost of business requirements (as opposed to the cost of IT infra-structure and architecture requirements) is a vital part of the evaluation process, yet one of the most difficult to perform. Some organizations try and establish basic costs based on business function or transaction, others by the technical effort needed to develop software to implement the business process. Fortunately, there are a number of useful techniques that can be used to estimate software development costs, and these can be found in Chapter 9.

The cost of non-functional requirements, such as availability, must also be investigated thoroughly. It is not uncommon for business users to specify that a system must be available most of the time. Clearly, there is a need to quantify exactly what is required here; does "most" mean 80 per cent of the time, or maybe even 100 per cent? Service Level Agreements (SLAs) are often captured as a key non-functional requirement because their objective is to guarantee the availability of the system within agreed parameters.

However, accepting a business requirement, regardless of whether it is a functional or a non-functional one, without investigating and assessing the costs involved in satisfying it is a common mistake made within many IS projects. For instance, an SLA that requires a system to be available 99.9 per cent of the year allows for the system to be unavailable for 8.76 hours in that time. An SLA requiring 99.99999 per cent availability allows for only four seconds of downtime a year. Both are achievable, but the cost of satisfying each option varies enormously.

If the value placed on benefits is insufficient, yet the project has an otherwise sound business case, attempts must be made to determine where the costs lie within the project. Only then can efforts be made to reduce them, while at the same time raising the value of the business benefits. One answer to this problem is to reduce costs by reducing the scope and therefore the requirements, of the project.

Assessing the impact of requirements

Whilst it is necessary for business stakeholders to take responsibility for providing requirements to the IS project team, it is equally important for them to consider the consequences of what they are actually requesting. Requirements such as "we need a 24 × 7 system," indicating that the system must be permanently available all day, every day, are very common, and often suggest that the business has merely produced a "wish-list" of requirements rather than the minimum set of requirements necessary to support the business objectives.

The costs of supplying an IT system that incorporates such a huge level of redundancy to ensure a continuous operation would be enormous. In many cases, the cost of such a system would be so great they would completely destroy the benefit case for the project. However, if the business can tolerate a 23 × 7 system or a 24 × 6 system, the requirement has a significantly lower impact on the cost/benefit case and may in fact, be achievable – negotiation is a key skill in requirements management.

A SLA that states system availability or "uptime" of 99.9 per cent may, at first glance seem fairly robust. The problem, however, is the failure to control the timing of the accepted loss of service (the remaining fraction of one per cent). This outage may be acceptable if the periods when the system is unavailable happens to coincide with traditionally "slack" periods of business when a small loss of service might go unnoticed or have a very limited impact on business operations. The impact may be considerably more significant if the seemingly insignificant outage coincides with a critical period in business operations, such as end-of-year accounting or stock-taking.

Barriers to effective requirements management

Whilst there are IS projects that result in failure due to errors made during systems development, testing, and implementation, many IS failures can be traced back to basic errors which were made during the analysis and design phases of a project. A report into the UK Government's troubled NATS (National Air Traffic Service) project stated, "system implementation was commenced with an inadequately comprehensive set of requirements specifications."[3]

The capturing of requirements in any project forms the foundation on which the rest of the project can be built – just like a house in many ways. If a house is built on a firm foundation, it can survive many years during which time changes can be made to the original design with minimal risk. However, if the house is built on weak foundations it is more likely to suffer from serious problems in later years.

The successful capture and agreement of requirements has, in the past, often been undertaken amidst a culture of misunderstanding, hostility, and conflict. The relationship between IT and the wider business community has often been strained due to the lack of a confidence that the other party has their best interests at heart. Clearly, relationships based on mistrust, misunderstanding, and contempt add little value to the project and may ultimately jeopardize its success.

Relationships based on power are not uncommon within many organizations and can be a major threat to a project when there is no accountability to ensure it can be controlled. For many years, IT professionals, having a monopoly on information and technology within the organization, have held that power. This situation has done little to improve the relationship between developers and users, as this power enabled IT stakeholders to blame their business counterparts for their failures. The failure of the business to define their requirements sufficiently well allowed IT professionals to abdicate any responsibility for a system which, when implemented, did not perform as expected.

Luckily, we have all moved on from this position, and there has been a significant shift in the power-based relationships of the past. As strategic thinking becomes much more focused on meeting business objectives rather than IT objectives, expert power, the power exerted through the use of information, has now been replaced by "business power." Business professionals no longer view IT as a controlling technology, but as an *enabling* technology, providing them with the services to allow them to achieve their objectives and goals.

As a consequence, business stakeholders now demand a much more profes-sional and responsive level of service from their IT suppliers. If the internal IT function cannot provide such a service, businesses are more than willing to employ external IT systems integrators, who they perceive as being more flex-ible, business-focused, and ultimately more accountable for their actions.

The field of business requirements engineering is now seen as a key skill that must be satisfied by IT professionals, either internally or externally. If, therefore, IT analysts have a problem with business customers who find it difficult to articulate their requirements, it is no longer purely a business problem. Owner-ship of the problem and ultimately the resolution of the problem must be accepted jointly by both the business stakeholders *and* the IT stakeholders.

Principal causes of requirements management failure

Organizational culture

The elicitation of requirements from business stakeholders can often be strongly resisted by an organization whose culture views change as a threat to the status quo. What is clear from many change management case studies is that the culture of the organization (i.e. views, beliefs, norms, and unwritten rules) can be a formidable barrier, making the requirements management process difficult, if not impossible, to complete effectively.

The experience of a US consultancy company who were planning requirements management for two clients is a perfect example of how the culture of an organ-ization can affect this process. One of the clients was a merchant bank, which had a predominantly entrepreneurial and highly-enpowered culture, driven by the need to compete with other merchant banks. The other client, a police organ-ization, had a rigorously strict and hierarchical culture, almost to the extent of being "paramilitary," where procedures were followed without exception. Any attempt to get the merchant bankers to take ownership of the problem and ensure user participation in documenting their requirements proved extremely difficult and ultimately failed. By comparison, the rigorous and formal systems analysis framework was totally accepted by the police organization as it was, to a large extent, seen as "business as usual."

Poor communication between users and developers

It is notoriously difficult to analyse and model the requirements within an organization, even with the use of sophisticated software tools. Organizations do not always encourage inter-departmental working and communication, which can result in a very limited and biased view of requirements being provided by business stakeholders. The irony of the situation is that the use (or more appropriately, *misuse)* of software tools to aid requirements capture can actually obstruct best-practice techniques, such as face-to-face communication, effective interviewing and numerous other "soft-skills." Software tools provide a method of working, which may not always be suitable for the specific business operation or organization. Simply put, whilst software tools define requirements in terms of entities, classes, normalized relationships and so on, these definitions and concepts are not understood by the majority of business users. To overcome this, two techniques are often used within successful IS projects:

- informal and open discussion involving the whole organization to obtain a consistent vision;
- the use of prototypes, models and simulations to encourage user participation and understanding.

Functional requirements do not reflect the real needs of business

There is an important difference between information *needs* and information *wants.* The former is the minimum required to achieve the critical success factors for the business system. The latter is merely an unwelcome distraction that often wastes significant amounts of time and money and delivers no benefit to the organization. Requirements must be prioritized against the objectives of the project and, if necessary, against the strategic objectives as identified in the corporate strategy.

Too many assumptions are made

Even with the co-operation and participation of highly-knowledgeable users, the requirements specified may include, possibly through force of habit, numerous operational assumptions. This poses a serious risk for the analyst who is not an expert in the application domain. A common assumption is that the new system will behave in a similar way to the old system and that existing work practices will be the same. As a consequence, users assume IT professionals know more about their roles and responsibilities than they actually do.

Assumption that requirements are frozen

To plan an IS project with the assumption that the requirements will not change is to invite failure. Of course, there has to be at least a high-level understanding and approval of requirements, but the expectation must be set that these *may* change.

For an IS project manager in this situation, the solution can be found by the use of impact analysis, change management, and risk management procedures. If and when requirements change, each change must be evaluated against the business objectives to assess the likely impact on the project. If the impact is high, a full risk management exercise must be undertaken to identify and mitigate any risk.

Many of the project case studies in this book represent classic examples of how constantly changing requirements can sound the death-knell for an IS project. Inherent in any project should be the knowledge that, whilst changes can be made early on in the project without causing a significant impact to cost and timescale, changes made later on in the project (i.e. during the systems development phase) can be very expensive and have an adverse affect on subsequent phases in the project. The failure to establish a baseline of requirements and subsequently to track and control deviations from that baseline is probably the largest single contributor to project failure.

Failure to agree requirements

Many IS failures are the result of human failings rather than technical failings; this is probably no better demonstrated than in the area of requirements management. A few years ago, the Hilton and Marriott hotel chains joined forces with Budget, a car rental company, and American Airlines to develop an incentives system that would allow their customers to earn the equivalent of "frequent-flyer" points for purchases.[4,5] The system would also allow customers to exchange their points for any of the participating companies' services. The benefits were clear and measurable; customer loyalty would be matched by an increase in revenues within each participating company.

A complex software system was commissioned which would allocate and track points earned for all customers. However, during the requirements management phase of the project, the software developers needed clarification on how the system would be expected to behave based on different scenarios (e.g. from input A, should the system choose function X, Y or Z?). The stakeholders could not agree on the answer. Forced to acknowledge deep divisions and incompatibilities among their business interests, the system was cancelled and legal proceedings were started. This is a classic case of stakeholders assuming they would each get what they wanted out of a project.

Lack of an agreed requirements specification

Business stakeholders and policy-makers who put excessive schedule pressure on project managers run the risk of achieving development milestones at the expense of spending sufficient time with the business users to find out precisely what they require. Collecting, verifying, and evaluating requirements is not a trivial exercise, and it is up to the project manager and business sponsors to ensure that this phase is performed fully and not just as a precursor to the implementation of a software tool.

What appears to be a simple business system to users when viewed superficially can actually turn out to be a complex set of interdependent business processes and functions when investigated in more detail. In situations where the potential time needed to perform requirements analysis is high, the requirements team must consider the best approach to follow. A purely sequential approach to requirements capture may ultimately fail as time available for the activity may expire before all the requirements have been captured.

In too many failed IS projects, enormous risks were taken, either through sheer arrogance or incompetence (or more likely due to a mixture of the two), by commencing development of the system before a full requirements specification had been documented and approved. Without a clear and concise specification of what is required, costs cannot be accurately assessed, estimated timescales will be incorrect, leaving the chances of successful project delivery very slim indeed.

Not so long ago saw the rollout of a huge military project in the U.S. It was, in fact, the Titanic of military projects with one noticeable exception – the Titanic was ahead of schedule when it sank. With a development budget that was already hundreds of millions of dollars over budget and years behind schedule, the system was passed over to the users. Despite a number of long-standing problems, such as indefinite quality, expectation of the system was high as was the confidence that it would sail past user acceptance testing.

Not long after the system was proudly presented in front of the users, they rejected it. Their dissatisfaction was simple – the system lacked features they had said were essential to their jobs. To add insult to injury, the system had also inherited a number of additional processes which not only increased the tedium of using it, but also placed an unnecessary burden on their workload. The project eventually died a visible and painful death amid litigation and congressional inquiries.

Although, like many other failed IT projects, this project was riddled with problems, it ultimately failed because the system did not satisfy the needs of the business. Do not be confused by the use of the word "business" in this context; if the main deliverable of an IS project is the implementation of a new business system, the business requirements must be provided by the business *users* – not the business managers and executives. In the failed project mentioned earlier, the developers of the system received most of their requirements from high-level supervisors and a number of "users" who did not regularly use the system. By contrast, successful projects are those where the level of user contribution is high throughout the whole project, especially during the early and formative phases.

Confusing expectations with requirements

The word "expectations" has probably been misused and misunderstood more than any other word in the lexicon of computing (with the possible exception of the word "benefits"). To many IT professionals involved in the requirements management phases of a project, expectations are those elements of the requirements that were not specified by the users (such as "it must be available every weekday and for five hours every other Sunday"). To others, expectations are the difference between what the users want and what they actually *need*. Expectations, however, are just another set of related requirements that can be analysed and modeled. They are often omitted because standard analysis techniques used to express requirements, such as data flow diagrams and use case diagrams, do not capture all the requirements for a business system, namely non-functional requirements and constraints.

Belief that buying a software tool will solve the problem

A software tool is a software package that helps solve a specific problem. Indeed, with the application tool market now fully mature, one can only wonder whether there is any major problem left that cannot be solved (or at least partially solved) by using a sofware tool.

Such is the ease with which a tool can be purchased and implemented nowadays, the IT community, in particular, has become far too reliant on such tools to solve what is often a business problem. Such reliance often sets expectations of what the tool can achieve to dangerously high levels and the tool eventually becomes a "silver bullet." From then onwards, IT managers feel obliged, or even compelled, to use the tool, perceiving it to be a solution to all their problems – as long as the business is prepared to change the way it operates in order for it to be compatible with the tool.

The reliance on software tools by development teams eager to overcome new technical challenges can often compromise an otherwise healthy project. As a consequence, many IS projects can fail due to the incorrect and inappropriate use of software tools. This is especially true of organizations that have a relatively small IT department.

In such circumstances, the scope for in-house IT development may be small, as will be the possibility of outsourcing important IT development activities to a third party. The solution becomes nothing more than a *fait accompli*. A software development tool is purchased, in the hope that it can be used or customized to support the business. The selection criteria for the tool, however, is likely to have come from the software development team (who may want to gain experience in a new and exciting product) rather than from a combination of business and IT professionals.

The dangers of using software packages

Whilst IS professionals are sometimes accused of knowing what the solution is to a business problem well before any functional requirements have been identified, based on their knowledge and familiarity with a specific software package, business users must also accept responsibility and accountability for their actions. As budget holders, business stakeholders under pressure to deliver a new system can often be influenced by the latest software fads and gizmos. I could name quite a few business managers who purchased software packages without a clear understanding of what functionality was needed by the business. In many cases, the choice of software package was in direct contravention of the company's IT strategy, and as the package was installed by a third-party vendor, the IT department refused to support it.

The relative ease of purchasing and implementing such tools combined with the lack of budgetary controls means that many organizations are not only buying too many unnecessary software packages, they are also buying too many of the *same* software packages. Buying the right software package is a huge risk, but with the application of some common-sense principles and effective requirements management, these risks can be minimized. The main question which must be answered well before the purchase of any software package is of course, "do we have an understanding of our requirements?"

Evaluating a software package

All business applications, packages, and software suites consist of:

- features;
- advantages;
- benefits.

Features are those parts of the system that are typically never used. For instance, how many of the "features" of Microsoft® *PowerPoint*® or *Excel* are actually used on a regular basis? Probably about 20 per cent. Wacky and insignificant features add nothing to the cost/benefit equation, but delay development time and accrue cost. The moral here is to identify the features and leave them out.

Advantages are those parts of the tool that make life easier for us – maybe they provide a few helpful routines or automation in particular areas. They are a "nice-to-have" and often cost more than the benefit they deliver. They are better than features, but not by much.

In the business case for any IS project, benefits that are tangible, measurable, and repeatable must be identified. Strategically, it is by the realization of benefits that competitive advantage can be gained and maintained within the organization. In the strive to deliver benefits, IS and business managers must be ruthless in their assessment of projects and the software tools they use. Benefits come from the early delivery of business requirements, so aim to go live sooner rather than waiting an inordinate time for the extensive functionality to be implemented. Benefits should be measured against initial investment costs, so focus core functionality on the most important business requirements.

Selecting the right software package

If the outcome of the requirements management phase has identified functionality which *may* be provided by a software package, it is important to understand the scope of work that *can* be achieved by using a software package and equally, what *cannot* be achieved from it. Do not rush out and buy any software before you have fully understood what it is meant to achieve. The following advice cannot be overstated to anyone even *thinking* about purchasing a software package:

- Don't window shop and opt for the best-looking.
- Do evaluate software packages against your critical functional priorities.
- Don't evaluate too many – you will not have the time.
- Don't class all your requirements as *must-haves* – you will end up performing unnecessary customization.
- Give suppliers a hard time in making sure the package meets your requirements – any salesperson worth their salt will state that the package has the *capability* to meet a requirement, but does that mean customization is required or is it from "out-of-the-box" functionality?
- Agree your package selection criteria and use it to assess each package uniformly – otherwise accurate comparison will not be possible.
- Choose your own reference sites – a supplier will only provide the favorable sites.
- Do not judge the software purely on the in-house demo. Make sure the supplier tailors the demo to meet your needs.
- Do assess the supplier as well as the package. How strong are their finances? Do they understand your business and the sector within which you operate? How good is their technical support – and where is it based?
- Be fair. Do not expect a 100 per cent fit – but do ensure that the critical requirements can be met.
- Do negotiate on price, including ongoing support and training costs.
- Do take legal advice before signing the contract.

Requirements management: critical success factors

- Make sure all stakeholders are involved throughout the requirements management process.

- Always prioritize requirements against the need to satisfy the stated business objectives.

- Do not undertake any key development activities until a requirements specification has been produced and agreed with all the stakeholders.

- Use whatever tools and techniques are necessary to ensure the requirements are understood by both customer and supplier.

- Validate all requirements and assess their impact on the project before approving them.

References

1   F. Brooks, "No silver bullet: essence and accidents of software engineering," *Computer*, **20** (4), April 1978, 10–19

2   M.W. Alford and J.T. Lawson, *Software Requirements Engineering Methodology (Development)*, RADC-TR-79-168, US Airforce Rome Air Development Center, Griffiss AFB, NY, June 1979 (DDC-AD-A073132)

3   House of Commons – Environment, Transport and Regional Affairs – First Report (Select Committee on Environment, Transport and Regional Affairs Memoranda), *Financial and Management Evaluation of the Swanwick Air Traffic Control Centre Project*, August 12, 1999

4   L.J. May (1998) "Major Causes of Software Project Failure," *Crosstalk*, July, 1998, http://stsc.hill.af.mil/crosstalk/1998/jul/causes.asp (accessed 2001)

5   The Standish Group, *CHAOS*, www.pm2go.com (accessed 2001)

Further reading

D.J. Flynn, *Information Systems Requirements – Determination and Analysis*, Second edition, Department of Computation, University of Manchester Institute of Science and Technology, McGraw-Hill Publishing Company, Maidenhead, 1998

R.H. Thayer and M. Dorfman, *Software Requirements Engineering*, Second edition, IEEE Computer Society Press, Los Alamitos, 1997

4

The IS methodology –
a framework for project delivery

This is the way, walk ye in it

Isaiah ch.30, v.21

What is clear from the KPMG survey[1] mentioned in Chapter 1 is that IS projects are most likely to fail from the very outset rather than from being mismanaged following an otherwise healthy start. The need for planning is paramount, and it is likely that a number of plans will need to be developed to manage the project, from initiation to completion. What those plans are and their effect on the project will be largely determined by the rules and principles adopted by the organization to enable them to complete IS projects – the IS methodology.

IS methodologies cover two main areas: project management and systems development. Project management methodologies help in establishing control over resources, tasks, budgets, and risks within the project. Systems development methodologies provide an approach to support the construction of business systems.

Project management methodologies have been in existence for many years and there is no shortage of material on them. PRINCE (PRojects IN Controlled Environments) and more recently, PRINCE2, for instance, are in the public domain and are essentially free to anyone who wishes to use them.

Equally, systems development methodologies have been documented in numerous publications and are widely used within the IT industry. Indeed, they are fundamental to the principles behind many IT-related disciplines and are also a popular topic within commercial training institutions all over the world. The effective combination of project management and systems development methodologies should, therefore, provide a definitive set of procedures controlling the management and delivery of IT systems within the organization.

The role of IS methodologies

IS methodologies have an important role to play if organizations are to successfully deliver IS projects. Structured systems analysis and development methodologies, such as SSADM, have evolved over many years and still remain two of the most popular development methodologies used by IS delivery teams worldwide. Project managers, by contrast, can readily adopt mature project management methodologies such as PRINCE2 in conjunction with the wide variety of software tools available, in order to manage the project effectively.

IS methodologies undoubtedly play a key role in the success of IS projects, and it is within this area that many of the fundamental issues influencing IS project failure lie. Whilst a detailed analysis and assessment of IS methodologies is beyond the scope of this book, it is expected that you will be able to gain a sufficient understanding of the factors affecting IS project failure, and so be able to determine that either:

■ there is nothing wrong with IS methodologies, but some other factor, external to the IS project is responsible for the widespread project failure experienced today;

or

■ there must be some critical issues relating to IS project failure that are not addressed within existing IS methodologies.

The limitations of IS methodologies

At the very heart of the organization and, more importantly, within the project are people – and that is the area in which many of the problems affecting the success of an IS project are likely to be found. Technology can be managed and changed easily – we can follow a set of rules and procedures and end up, more often than not, with the desired outcome. The same cannot be said of people. Managing people is a key factor that determines success within business, and an

IS project is no different – but it is one area in which many IS methodologies are clearly weak.

Within the average project management methodology, the success criteria for the project management process are often very different to the success criteria identified by the business. Implementing a system within time, cost, and quality constraints is not always perceived as a success criterion by those individuals who must use the system. The ability to satisfy the actual (as opposed to the perceived) needs of the business, combined with the usability of the system is often the defining factor for those outside the project management team.

Equally, many existing project management methodologies make many assumptions about the project team itself. There is a fairly large assumption, for instance, that the project manager and the project team have sufficient skills and experience to perform their responsibilities competently. Equally, existing methods assume that the project team (recruited from within business and IT departments) will work well together and form a cohesive unit within the organization. We have all had bad experiences of working with people who have different attitudes to work from our own, and when this affects the motivation and effectiveness of the project team, the chances of project failure increase dramatically.

Considering the huge numbers of projects that overrun their time and budgetary constraints, it is clear that even by following a project management methodology such as PRINCE, success cannot be guaranteed. The London Ambulance Service Computer-Aided Dispatch project which failed in 1992, is a prime example.

As a public sector organization, the London Ambulance Service was obliged to use the UK Government's recommended project management methodology, PRINCE. However, what is clear from the investigation into the causes of the disaster (discussed in Chapter 5), is that the organization put considerable faith in a methodology which, whilst being a *de facto* standard, was completely new to the organization and the people who were to use it. This represents a classic case of the so-called, "silver bullet"[2] syndrome. The term "silver bullet" describes a course of action which, by its very implementation, will produce the desired outcome. Unfortunately, as the London Ambulance Service discovered, the reliance upon a single factor at the expense of many other critical success factors can seriously affect the outcome of an IS project.

IS projects utilize technology to achieve a specific aim, but they cannot exist without the participation and co-operation of people from within the organization. The roles and responsibilities of managers, sponsors, suppliers, budget-holders, and users can all affect, and be affected by, the development of an IS project. Immediately, this raises the question of the extent to which ethical issues should influence project planning and implementation.

Ethics is an established subject within other professions such as law and medicine, but is a relatively new discipline within the IT industry and is noticeably absent from many software development methodologies. It can be argued that all IS projects have an ethical dimension, and therefore it is necessary to adopt a suitable ethical code throughout the software development process. Methodologies such as SSADM, for instance, which are used extensively all over the world, emphasize the formal and technical aspects of IS development, overlooking the human, social, and organizational aspects, which are equally important if business success is to be achieved. Whilst success may be achieved both technically, through the introduction of new systems, and financially, through the realization of tangible benefits, this may, however, be disguising ethical failure within the project.

Despite the weaknesses which may be inherent within established IS methodologies, following an established methodology is clearly better than following nothing at all, and will undoubtedly help plan and manage at least some of the key stages within the project.

Imagine, for a moment, the long-term consequences, if the implementation of a new system forces dramatic change to the working lives of the people who must use it. The deployment of technology is not always undertaken with people in mind, which is why after a 'successful' implementation, levels of user satisfaction may remain low.

User roles that were once challenging and performed with high levels of autonomy may now have become routine, unskilled, and unchallenging, increasing hostility and resistance towards IT within the organization. The ethical argument within the IT industry is still in its infancy and will no doubt raise serious issues which will affect the nature of IS projects in the future. Whether the success of an IS project can be measured using ethical criteria should be of importance to anyone involved in IS projects, but unfortunately, the subject is well beyond the scope of this book.

A comparison of popular IS methodologies

IS methodologies are a fundamental part of the IT industry; they represent many of the basic principles and procedures that organizations can adopt when choosing to develop and deploy computer-based systems. Many of these methodologies have been in the IT domain for many years and are now considered "mature." Equally, some continue to evolve, whilst others are being introduced to reflect new ways of thinking. Some of these methodologies thankfully remain the topic of theoretical discussion within the hallowed walls of academia, others have received mixed levels of exposure and acceptance within commercial environments.

Even a brief awareness of some of the more popular IS methodologies will be of benefit to all those engaged on IS projects. The remaining section of this chapter, therefore, will introduce and compare some of the more popular methodologies that are currently used within IS projects.

The information provided in this section, however, is only intended to provide an overview of each methodology. It is not a practical guide to their use within a project environment – there are numerous publications available that discuss these topics in much more detail and it is to these you need to turn.

Systems development methodologies

SSADM

SSADM (Structured Systems Analysis and Design) is a methodology covering the analysis and design stages of systems development. SSADM was originally supplied by Learmonth & Burchett Management Systems after being commissioned by the CCTA (Central Computing and Telecommunications Agency). Following its launch in 1981 it was used extensively to standardize the many IT projects being developed across UK government departments. Since 1981 SSADM has been refined and version 4.2 has been available since 1995. SSADM is now an open standard and freely available for use within the IT industry, with many companies offering training and automated tools to support its use.

Major features

SSADM revolves around the use of three key techniques; logical data modeling, data flow modeling, and entity/event modeling.

- Logical data modeling. This process identifies, models, and documents the data requirements for an IS project. The logical data model, which is produced from this process, identifies key business entities and the relationships between these entities – what other methodologies refer to as an entity–relationship model. A typical example of a business relationship that can be modeled using this technique is the relationship that exists between a customer and a customer order.

- Data flow modeling. This process identifies and documents the flow of data within the business area which has the IS requirement. The data flow model consists of data flow diagrams which are decomposed into: processes (activities that transform data from one form to another); data stores (where information is held); external entities (objects that send data into the system or receive data from it); and data flows (routes by which data can flow).

■ Entity/event modeling. This process identifies the business events that affect each entity and the sequence in which these events occur. An entity/event model consists of an entity life history for each entity identified within the business.

SSADM is based on a *scientific* paradigm; the analysis, modeling, and functional decomposition of information. Consequently, it does not focus on the human elements of an IS project, such as team structure, team roles, and management structures. The only element of an IS project covered by SSADM is *data*.

SSADM adopts a structured, rigorous approach to the development of data structures and processes, which limits the chances of the initial requirements being misunderstood. Equally, this also reduces the chances of the systems design straying from the functional requirements through the use of inadequate analysis and design techniques. However, SSADM assumes that the requirements, in the form of an agreed requirements specification, will not change during the development of the project.

Being a highly-structured methodology is both a benefit and a limitation. Having a clear set of deliverables at each stage of the analysis and design process ensures that the appropriate documentation is produced. It also makes the whole methodology simple and easy to use. Each stage within SSADM must be taken in strict sequence, and only when every stage is complete can the process be terminated. This can be of great benefit to inexperienced IT staff on the project, who require a process which is highly prescriptive in nature.

SSADM's weakness is that its sequential nature closely follows the "waterfall" approach to IS development; a series of cascading tasks which must be completed in turn to achieve the desired outcome (Figure 4.1). Rigorously following each step of SSADM can be time-consuming and, as a consequence, can lengthen the duration of the process from project initiation to project implementation. In the dynamic world of business, a three-year IS project using SSADM may well guarantee to meet the original requirements specification, but equally may well deliver a system that no longer meets the current business requirements.

SSADM has been in use for many years, and it is unlikely that its use will decline significantly in the future. Its longevity is mainly due to its one key benefit: from the simplest of IS development projects to the most complex, SSADM provides IT staff with a "tick-list" of tasks they must perform and documentation they must produce.

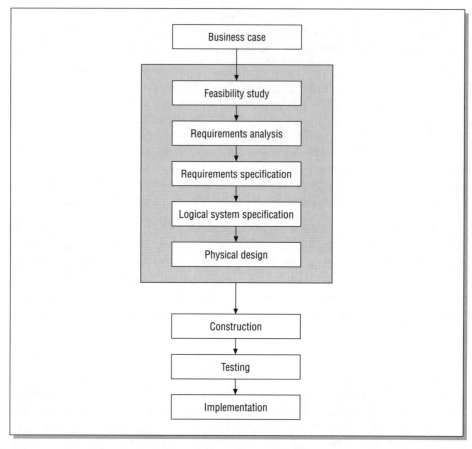

FIGURE 4.1 ▪ The scope of SSADM within the software development lifecycle

Key benefits

- Suitable for lengthy and complex projects where formal analysis and design techniques are required.
- Follows the majority of stages in the systems development lifecycle.
- Simple and easy to learn.
- Can be used for just about any type of IS development project.
- Extensive software tool support available.

Key limitations

- Assumes requirements are fixed at the start of the project.
- User involvement is limited.

- Construction and testing stages are not covered.
- The audience is limited to IT staff.
- Focuses on activities not products.

DSDM

DSDM* (Dynamic Systems Development Methodology) is gradually becoming the standard methodology for RAD (Rapid Application Development), and is currently gaining more formal support under the auspices of the DSDM Consortium. The DSDM Consortium itself is a non-profit making, vendor-independent organization that was started informally during 1994 by a number of like-minded individuals looking to establish standard principles for RAD that would foster cross-industry collaboration.

The DSDM framework enables users and developers to work alongside each other, designing, building, and testing IT systems in a collaborative manner (Figure 4.2). As DSDM actively encourages user involvement throughout the lifecycle of the methodology, the IT systems generated as a result map extremely closely onto business needs.

DSDM is based on a *pragmatic* paradigm. It does not promise to deliver all requirements in one attempt; nor does it allow the duration of the project to increase to ensure that all requirements are met. Time is very much a limiting factor in determining what functionality will be required. If there is no time to deliver additional functionality, it is not delivered. DSDM is a big supporter of the 80/20 rule – the majority of requirements can be delivered in a relatively short amount of time.

The key principles of DSDM

DSDM is built around nine key principles which have been refined and rationalized as a result of the practical application of DSDM.

Active user participation is imperative

DSDM is unashamedly focused on the user. In SSADM, the user acts as a supplier of business information and reviewer of results to the IS project; in DSDM the user is an active participant in the development process.

DSDM teams must be empowered to make decisions

DSDM teams consist of both developers and users. As such, they must be empowered to make decisions, as requirements may be refined or even changed.

---

* DSDM is a registered trademark of the DSDM Consortium.

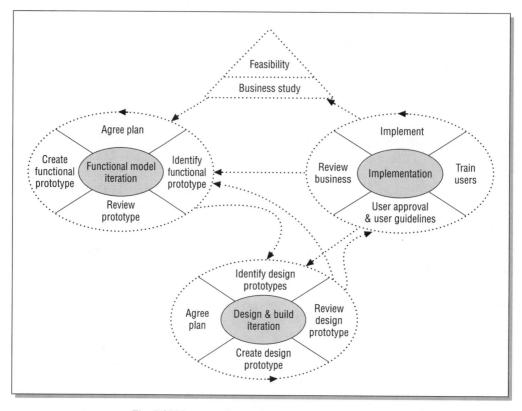

FIGURE 4.2 ■ The DSDM approach to software development (source: DSDM Consortium)

They must be able to agree acceptable levels of functionality without frequent recourse to senior management.

The focus is on frequent delivery of products
It is the objective of the DSDM team to agree on what products can be delivered in an agreed period of time (a concept often referred to as "time-boxing"). This enables the team to decide the best approach to delivering the products required in the time available.

Fitness for purpose is the essential product acceptance criterion for products
The focus of DSDM is on delivering business functionality at the required time. This is a major deviation from traditional systems development methodologies which aim to satisfy the contents of the requirements specification, whilst losing sight of the fact that these requirements are often inaccurate and do not support the business case for the project.

Iterative and incremental development is essential in order to converge on an accurate business solution
DSDM allows systems to evolve incrementally, allowing IT developers to make use of feedback given by users. Incremental development also allows partial solutions to be delivered to satisfy immediate business needs.

All changes made during development are reversible
Backtracking is a key feature of DSDM and is necessary if requirements can change. However, in some circumstances it is easier to reconstruct rather than to backtrack.

Requirements are baselined at a high level
High-level requirements are "frozen" and agreed to allow an investigation into what the implications of such requirements might be. Further baselines can be established later as development progresses.

Testing is integrated throughout the lifecycle
Testing is not treated as a separate activity. As the system is developed incrementally, it is tested and reviewed by users and developers. This ensures that the deliverables satisfy business needs and technical specifications.

A collaborative approach between all stakeholders is essential
Co-operation between all stakeholders in the project is vital in order to prevent the project becoming stifled by bureaucracy and restrictive practices.

Key benefits

- Particularly useful for identifying and agreeing all requirements in the early stages of a project.
- Can be used for large projects in conjunction with more traditional methodologies such as SSADM. DSDM will ensure that all requirements are captured and prioritized; SSADM will provide the formal analysis and design processes required to build the system.
- Aims to deliver the highest priority requirements first.
- Seeks to deliver small amounts of functionality on a regular basis.
- Assumes requirements can change.
- Better to be roughly right than precisely wrong.

Key limitation

- Not suitable for real-time or safety-critical systems or any systems development where the functional requirements must be fixed before development can begin.

OPEN

OPEN (Object-oriented Process, Environment and Notation), is widely acknowledged as a "third-generation" methodology that has been developed to focus on OO (Object-Oriented) and Internet-based software development.[3,4] OPEN was initially created from the merger of earlier methods, namely MOSES and SOMA, and has since evolved to embrace more recent techniques such as UML* (Unified Modeling Language).

OPEN is not a "true" methodology, it is often described more accurately as being a "methodological framework," mainly because it must be instantiated and customized for particular problems, projects and organizations. Even so, it is based around processes and, as a consequence, can be used with any modeling language, although it has strong associations with the *de facto* standard OO modeling language, UML.

Major features

Similar to traditional methodologies such as SSADM and contemporary OO methodologies such as RUP (Rational Unified Processes), OPEN follows the software development lifecycle, but also incorporates business concepts, such as decision-making activities, project management concepts, such as team and organizational roles, and sociological roles, such as usability. More specifically, in supporting OO analysis and development techniques, OPEN allows reuse, abstraction, inheritance, information-hiding, and polymorphism. Whilst methodologies that support traditional "waterfall" software development have been widely used for many years, it is only since 1996 or so that methodologies have been available to support OO development.

The processes within OPEN support three different levels of abstraction: the business-focused "product-lifecycle;" the software engineering process; and the modeling process (Table 4.1). Between them, they support key OO concepts, namely:

- iterative development (refining high-level requirements and products);
- incremental development (delivering products and sub-products through phased development and delivery);
- parallel development (working on multiple parts of the system concurrently).

---

* UML is a trademark of Object Management Group Inc.

TABLE 4.1 ▬ The OPEN process

OPEN phase	Key events
Project initiation	Feasibility study Establishing the business case Business case approval
Requirements engineering	Elicit user requirements Analyse and validate requirements Identify re-use potential for components
Project planning	Project lifecycle design Capacity planning Quality planning
Analysis and business modeling	Object design Construct business object model Design user interface
Build	Construct object model Coding Construction
Evaluate	User acceptance testing Regression testing
Deployment	Product delivery Post-implementation review

Key benefits

- Supports the complete software development lifecycle.

- Language-independent.

- Has close links with quality frameworks, such as the Software Engineering Institute's Capability Maturity Model (discussed in Chapter 9).

- In the public domain.

Key limitations

- Specific activities need to be developed with the appropriate techniques to create a development process that will meet the requirements.

- Still relatively immature.

RUP

The Rational Unified Process (RUP) is, like OPEN and DSDM, an off-the-shelf system development process that can be configured to be used within both small and larger software development projects.[5,6] Through the extensive use of tools, models, guidelines, and templates, RUP allows the following best practices to be adopted within the project:

■ develop software iteratively;

■ manage requirements;

■ use component-based architectures;

■ visually model software;

■ verify software quality;

■ control changes to software.

RUP adopts an iterative approach to software development, similar in style to DSDM and OPEN and, likewise, aims to rapidly deliver an initial version of a system. A number of key features within RUP successfully support the iterative software development model by ensuring that:

■ requirements are not assumed to be fixed at the start of the project, but can be refined as the project evolves;

■ RUP expects and accommodates changes;

■ high-risk areas are addressed very early in the software development process;

■ the emphasis is placed on software delivery; RUP lends itself to automation of many of the tedious activities associated with software development.

The RUP software development lifecycle

The software development process supported by RUP can be approached from two differing but integrated perspectives: a management perspective and a technical perspective. The former places the focus on dealing with the financial, strategic, commercial, and human aspects of the development process, whilst the latter places the emphasis on the quality, software design, and engineering aspects.

The RUP software development lifecycle can be broken down into four phases, representing the management view of the process. Moving through the four phases will progress the project from initiation (inception) to implementation (transition), as shown in Table 4.2.

TABLE 4.2 ▨ Phases within the RUP lifecycle

RUP phase	Key events
Inception	Establishing the business case for the systems and the scope of work to be undertaken. Project plan (showing iterations) and risk assessment produced.
Elaboration	Analysis and design of problem domain. Elimination of high-risk problems. Major functionality identified and architecture designed. Evaluation criteria for at least the first construction iteration. Development of 'throw-away' prototypes.
Construction	Building the product – all components and features are built and tested. Increased product stability through the iteration of components created during elaboration phase. Documentation produced. Evaluation undertaken on suitability for release and deployment to users (transition phase may be postponed if necessary).
Transition	"Beta-testing" to validate new system against expectations. Parallel operation with existing system that is being replaced. Conversion of operational systems. Users trained. Releases of product throughout organization, e.g. "beta" releases, standard releases, bug-fix releases.

The progression of work through these phases represents in RUP terms a development *cycle*. At the end of each cycle, RUP produces a version of the product, referred to as the software *generation*.

A software generation is an appropriate term for what other methodologies, such as SSADM, may call a "deliverable," as the product may evolve into another generation by repeating (reiterating) the same four phases. Such evolution could occur, for example, through suggested enhancement, technological advancement or reaction to external forces, such as competition or regulation.

From a technical perspective, software development is achieved incrementally through a succession of iterations; each iteration being concluded by the release of an executable product which can be utilized by the user community. Each release of a software product is accompanied by supporting documentation, plans, and designs. The activities performed within any one iteration (such as planning, analysis, design, construction, and testing) will, in various proportions, reflect the current phase where the iteration exists.

When the management and technical perspectives of the process are combined, as shown in Figure 4.3, each phase of the process, and in particular, the *end* of each phase, is synchronized with the completion of an iteration – i.e. each phase comprises one or more iterations.

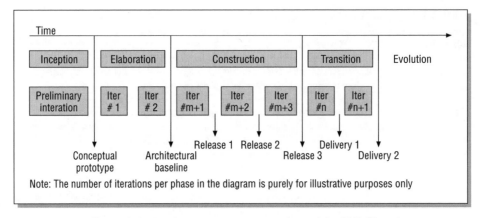

FIGURE 4.3 ■ The technical and management perspectives of the RUP lifecycle

Modeling within RUP

RUP uses four primary modeling elements as shown in Table 4.3.

RUP core workflows

There are nine core process workflows within RUP; six core "engineering" work-flows and three core "supporting" workflows (Table 4.4). An initial inspection of the six "core" engineering workflows may indicate a similarity with sequential phases in "traditional" development methodologies such as SSADM. Whilst this is true, it is important to remember that the phases of an iterative process are different, and that these workflows are revisited again and again throughout the lifecycle. The actual complete workflow of a project interleaves these nine core workflows, and repeats them with varying emphasis and intensity at each iteration.

TABLE 4.3 ■ Modeling elements within RUP

Modeling element	Description	Example
Workers	The "who." Defines the roles and responsibilities of an individual or group.	Jim is a designer and will be producing the object design.
Activities	The "how." An activity is a unit of work that an individual in that role may be asked to perform.	Review design or perform test.
Artifacts	The "what." An artifact is a piece of information that is produced, modified, or used by a process.	A model, such as the Use Case Model; source code; executables.
Workflows	The "when". A sequence of activities that produces verifiable output and shows interactions between workers.	Business modeling, project management, analysis and design. In UML terms a workflow can be expressed as a sequence diagram.

TABLE 4.4 ▨ RUP core workflows

Core engineering workflows
Business modeling
Requirements management
Analysis and design
Implementation
Test
Deployment
Core supporting workflows
Configuration and change management
Project management
Environment

Key benefits

- Supports the complete software development lifecycle.
- Highly configurable to suit many development requirements.
- Has close links with quality frameworks, such as the Software Engineering Institute's Capability Maturity Model (discussed in Chapter 9).
- In the public domain.
- Provides a guide for how to use UML, an industry-standard language for communicating architectures and designs.
- Supported by tools and can be highly automated.

Key limitations

- RUP provides a comprehensive set of elements which can be used to successfully deliver a product. Inexperienced or immature project teams may find it difficult to determine which elements of RUP are required for the project, especially if it is relatively small.
- Project participants can become too involved in a specific element of RUP at the expense of understanding the key process elements that are required to deliver a quality product.

Project management methodologies

PRINCE

PRINCE* (PRojects In Controlled Environments) is a method of managing projects, developed by the CCTA in the UK (now part of the Office of Government Commerce). The methodology was originally developed to manage UK government IT projects, but was put into the public domain in 1989. Since then, the methodology has been updated and adapted to become a generic project management tool, applicable to a wide variety of projects. The latest development of PRINCE, known as PRINCE2, was developed by a team of project management specialists with contributions from a review panel, which comprised 150 organizations familiar with PRINCE. PRINCE2 was completed and published in March 1996.

PRINCE is a structured set of guidelines and procedures which have been designed to enable the successful management of projects. Throughout the PRINCE methodology, the focus is on the business case which describes the rationale and business justification for the project. All the processes identified within PRINCE are driven by the business case, from initial project startup to project closedown.

In its simplest form, PRINCE has a number of components, positioned around a central process model (Figure 4.4).

The process model itself consists of eight distinct management processes which reflect the lifecycle of the project: initiating the project, tracking the progress of the project, and completing the project (Figure 4.5).

Key features

- There is a defined organizational structure for the project team.

- Planning approach is driven by the need to identify products throughout the whole process.

- Emphasis is placed on dividing the project into small, manageable stages.

- It is flexible and scalable; the level at which PRINCE is applied is very much dependent upon the nature and size of the project.

---

* PRINCE is a registered trademark of OGC.

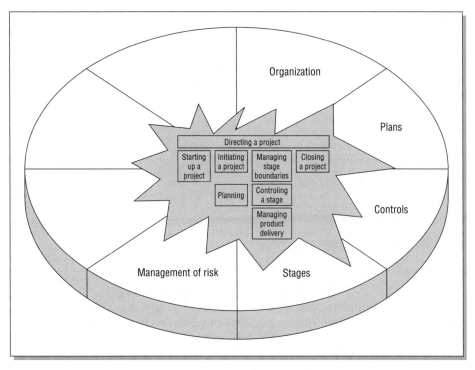

FIGURE 4.4 ▦ PRINCE processes and components (source: Office of Government Commerce)

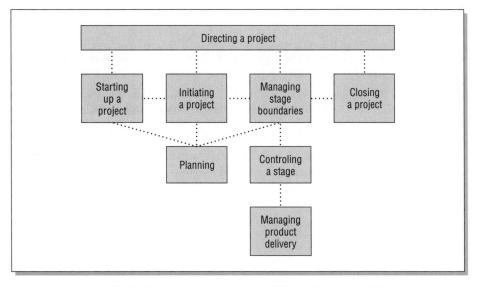

FIGURE 4.5 ▦ The PRINCE process model (source: Office of Government Commerce)

PRINCE components

Project initiation
This is concerned with ensuring that the project is established on a firm management foundation. PRINCE identifies the need for a PID (Project Initiation Document) containing:

- project brief;
- project scope;
- quality strategy;
- project plans;
- management organization structure;
- configuration management plans.

Project organization
PRINCE formally enforces the involvement and commitment of the senior management, users, suppliers, and IT staff throughout the project. The organizational structure within PRINCE allows a flexible hierarchy to be created covering:

- project ownership;
- project management;
- stage management;
- project support and assurance;
- team leadership.

PRINCE also defines the roles and responsibilities of these positions and job descriptions for each one. In addition the structure of PRINCE allows the creation and management of the PSO (Project Support Office) as an optional hierarchy. Roles and tasks for the PSO are also defined within PRINCE.

Controls
Control is established by use of management control meetings. Each meeting has a defined agenda to reach a specified objective. Control meetings include:

- project initiation;
- end stage assessment;
- project exceptions;
- checkpoint meetings;
- project closure.

Configuration management and change control
Guidelines and roles are provided for those organizations wishing to introduce this process. The importance of change control is recognised, and it can be performed as a stand-alone activity or as an integral part of configuration management.

Product breakdown principles
This is probably the most powerful feature of PRINCE. These principles enforce a rigorous approach to planning and control by concentrating on products rather than activities. The approach ensures that all products are identified and defined before the planning process can begin.

The scope of PRINCE
Whilst PRINCE operates within a business environment, the scope of the methodology does not address all related business functions and techniques. Figure 4.6 shows the scope of PRINCE within the organization.

PRINCE is a mature project management methodology, but it does not aim to provide extensive coverage of all aspects of project management; these are covered by existing methods and techniques. PRINCE does, however, contain many interfaces to other methodologies and so these are excluded from core PRINCE components. Examples of these include:

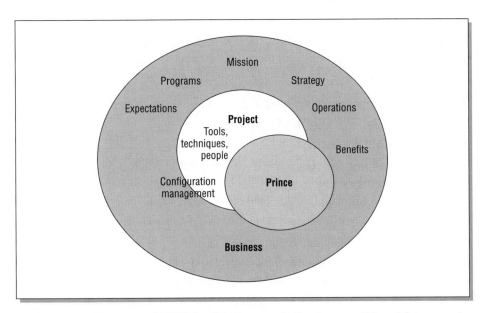

FIGURE 4.6 ▨ The scope of PRINCE within the organization (source: Office of Government Commerce)

- people management techniques, such as motivation, delegation, and team leadership;

- planning techniques, such as Gantt charts and critical path analysis;

- risk management techniques;

- the creation and management of quality management and quality assurance systems;

- the creation and management of the business case;

- financial project evaluation techniques;

- budgetary control;

- benefits management.

Key benefits

- Identifies management, specialist and quality products and helps ensure that they are produced on time and to budget.

- Separates the management and specialist aspects of organization, planning, and control.

- Allows control to operate within all levels.

- Ensures that project progress is visible to senior management.

- Ensures communication between all stakeholders in the project.

- Ensures that work progresses in the correct sequence.

- Involves senior management in the project at the right time and in the right place.

- Allows the project to be stopped and, if required, re-started in a controlled manner, at any time during the project.

- Allows flexible decision points.

- Provides planning interfaces to external program, configuration and risk management processes.

- Offers software tool support.

Key limitations

- PRINCE is a mature and comprehensive methodology which, if it is to be understood fully, requires extensive training and mentoring.

- Due to the many planning, management, and control stages within PRINCE, many organizations use an abbreviated method – often key processes are omitted.

- There are no IT specific parts to the methodology, such as software risk management and software quality assurance.

- There are no processes which directly manage the realization of benefits.

- The various structures within PRINCE only act as guidelines and do not provide a prescriptive set of tasks to perform.

- PRINCE2 and its predecessor PRINCE have often been accused of being unnecessarily complex and lengthy which makes them difficult to deploy within an organization. As a result of this, a number of publications now exist tackling the broad subject area of "how to make PRINCE work."

MITP

MITP* (Managing Implementation of the Total Project) is a project framework that was developed and used within IBM and its customers during the 1990s.[7] MITP was eventually superseded by WSDDM (World-wide Solution Design and Delivery Method) and, ultimately, by WWPMM (World-wide Project Management Methodology), which remains in use within IBM. As many of the key features of MITP were adopted in subsequent IBM project management methodologies, an overview of MITP should still provide a useful source of information.

MITP provides a view of the lifecycle of the project by identifying four key stages within it:

- before the project can start;

- establishing the project;

- managing project performance;

- ending the project.

These four stages are then decomposed into nine practices which ultimately form the MITP model (Figure 4.7).

MITP organization

Prerequisites
These define the criteria which must be established in order for the project to begin. The standard MITP list covers:

---

* Copyright IBM. From D. Harris, (1992) 'MITP IBM's method of managing projects', *Project*, Volume 5, issue 4 and appears courtesy of the Association for Project Management, formerly Association of Project Managers.

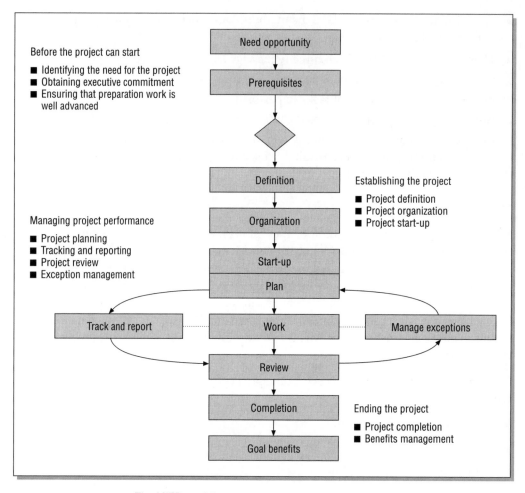

FIGURE 4.7 ▓ The MITP model

- identifying the business need;

- defining the target solution;

- assessing the feasibility;

- understanding the risks;

- establishing and agreeing the business case;

- identifying the key people.

Project definition
Once the prerequisite work has completed for the project, and approval granted, the definition of the project can begin. This activity concentrates on providing a

simple overview of the project and ensuring that all the key stakeholders understand what the project is and how it will be managed. The project definition workshop is the place where this is initiated, by first gaining the commitment of key stakeholders.

Organization

An organizational structure for the project is created within MITP which is intended to cross existing line boundaries – maybe even company boundaries. Key players within the organizational structure will be identified: the business sponsor will have a particularly important role within the structure as they have the most to gain but, conversely, the most to lose.

Within the broad structure there is a need to establish an effective method of managing work. This is achieved with the establishment of a number of sub-projects (typically between 3 and 12) as the main units of work. This enables the project manager to introduce the most appropriate method of management for each sub-project.

Startup

Once the definition and organization practices of the project have been completed, the project can commence. During startup, project and management plans will be created which will be needed during the performance stage of the project.

Managing project performance

This stage will ensure that the project is kept on track by use of a standard control loop: planning, tracking, reporting against the plan, reviewing, and taking action if necessary.

Ending the project

This is the stage where lessons learned from the project can be identified and stored for use by future projects. More importantly, it is the objective of the completion of the project to ensure a smooth transition of systems and procedures into the normal working environment – "or business as usual." This part of the project can have a significant part to play in the success of the project, and so can often start early.

Following on from the formal completion of the project is the key area concerning the management and delivery of benefits. In one particular use of MITP, the business sponsor managed the benefits management sub-project for some time after the end of the project and succeeded in delivering the project benefits well ahead of the plan. In this particular case, identification of this sub-project took place very early in the plan, in the Project Definition stage.

MITP management techniques

As well as MITP providing a framework to help plan and manage the project, it also provides a number of management techniques which can be used throughout the lifecycle of the project. There are two sets of techniques within MITP: key techniques and support techniques. The former covers the basic tasks which can be performed to manage any project, the latter can provide new techniques or show how the key techniques can be modified in certain situations, such as the use of sub-contract staff.

The eight key techniques within MITP are as follows.

Scope management and objectives
Used to identify and agree the overall goals, objectives, and scope of the project. These techniques will be used extensively during the Project Definition stage and throughout the management of the project.

Work breakdown structure and deliverables
Used to identify all the deliverables (internal and external) to be developed by the project and the management of these throughout its progress.

Organization
Used to establish the key management roles throughout the project: sponsor, project manager, sub-project managers, project office manager. For each role, job descriptions, responsibilities, and objectives should be established.

Planning and estimating
The development of the work breakdown structure into a set of objectives – probably by sub-project – and the combination of these estimates into the plans and schedules at an overall project and sub-project level.

Progress management
Used to measure actual progress against planned progress at a project and sub-project level. This technique will ensure that progress and status activities are carried out during the project, such as the scheduling of regular progress reviews and the management of issues.

Risk management
Used to identify any eventualities which jeopardize the success of the project and the actions which must be performed to mitigate them.

Quality management
Used to ensure that the deliverables produced by the project conform to the required level of quality.

Financial management
Used to develop the business case to justify investment in the project. An extension of the business case can then be used to budget for the project, both being managed throughout its lifecycle.

Key benefits

- Imposes consistency across a number of projects.

- Flexible approach to implementation.

- Can be used for a wide range of projects.

- Business oriented.

- Provides techniques for some of the difficult tasks in the project, such as estimating, risk management and financial planning.

- Ensures that benefits are managed as part of the project.

Key limitation

- No longer used.

IS methodologies: critical success factors

- Ensure that the strengths and weaknesses of any methodology are known and understood before adopting it.

- Using a popular or *de facto* IS methodology will not guarantee project success – but it can help.

- Make sure the project team have been adequately trained in the use of the methodology before using it.

- A methodology is only a framework. The processes that support the framework should be refined with experience.

References

1   KPMG, *What Went Wrong? Unsuccessful Information Technology Projects*, 1997, www.kpmg.com

2   F. Brooks, "No silver bullet: essence and accidents of software engineering," *Computer*, **20** (4), April, 1978, 10–19

3   B. Henderson-Sellers and B. Unhelkar, *OPEN Modeling with UML*, Addison-Wesley, Harlow, 2000

4   B. Henderson-Sellers (1996) *"The OPEN methodology,"* submission to *Object* magazine, **6** (9), 56–9

5   P. Kruchten, *"A Rational Development Process,"* Crosstalk, **9** (7), July, 1996, 11–16

6   *Rational Unified Process: Best Practices for Software Development Teams*, Rational Software Whitepaper, 2002

7   D. Harris (1992) 'MITP IBM's method of managing projects', *Project*, Association of Project Managers, **5** (4)

▪▪▪ Further reading

D. Avison and G. Fitzgerald, *Information Systems Development: Methodologies, Techniques and Tools*, McGraw-Hill, Maidenhead, 1995

C. Bentley, *PRINCE2 A Practical Handbook*, Butterworth-Heinemann, Oxford, 1997

CCTA (The Stationery Office), Managing Successful Projects with PRINCE2, 1996

P.B. Checkland, *Systems Thinking, Systems Practice*, Wiley, Chichesher, 1981

N. Jayaratna, *Understanding and Evaluating Methodologies*, McGraw-Hill, Maidenhead 1994

S. Rogerson (1996) *"An ethical review of information systems development and the SSADM approach,"* Ethicomp 96 conference proceedings, **1**, 384–93

J. Stapleton, *DSDM: Dynamic Systems Development Method*, Addison-Wesley, Harlow, 1997

 Part II

Planning for success

If you fail to plan, plan to fail

Popular business adage

5

Planning the project

If one does not know to which port one is sailing, no wind is favourable

Seneca ('the Younger') *c.4 BC–AD 65, Epistulae Morales* no.71

Whilst the strategic alignment of business and IT objectives is fundamental to the concept of business change, it is of limited value unless there is a well-defined and agreed mechanism within the organization for these strategies to be implemented.

The IS project is an instrument of change that can be utilized by the organization to deliver long-term benefits. Fundamental to this capability must be the need to plan the project to ensure that strategic objectives are translated into manageable units of work, yet many plunge into the task without asking even the most basic questions, such as: why are we doing this? what are our assumptions and expectations about the project and our roles within it? how are we going to work together?

What is a project?

Let us first define exactly what we mean by the term "project." Almost any piece of work undertaken within an organization can be considered to be a project if it has:

- a finite and defined lifespan;
- a clear, well-defined set of deliverables or products;

- a set of resources;

- a reason for its existence;

- an organizational structure, identifying specific roles and responsibilities which must be established to manage the project.

Consider the PRINCE definition of a project:

A management environment that is created for the purpose of delivering one or more business products according to a specified business case.[1]

Another definition might be:

A temporary structure set up to manage the delivery of one or more deliverables within a specified period of time to an agreed level of quality.

Projects, as we have seen from Chapter 2, are usually undertaken as a consequence of the business planning process, and, with the exception of the "sub-project," provide the lowest level of granularity of managed effort within the organization. IS projects in particular can be undertaken at all levels within the organization and may represent a stand-alone activity, such as the implementation of a specific software package, or a program of related projects, or they may form part of an overall corporate strategy.

Activities such as ongoing support and maintenance of existing systems, however, are generally not regarded as projects as they have an indefinite lifespan. Support activities and other "non-projects" may well adopt a new set of objectives after a period of time and continue to operate in an ongoing manner. Projects, on the other hand, are temporary in nature, and as such, have a definite beginning and a definite end. Despite the fact that many projects may take years to complete (either due to their complexity or simply as a result of inadequate planning), a project must always have an end point. That point is either when the project's objectives have been reached, or when it becomes clear that the objectives cannot be met and the project is terminated. Of course, the temporary nature of projects does not mean that the products or services created on completion of the project will necessarily be temporary.

It is the objective of a project to deliver a unique product or service – in the sense that it has not been done before within the organization. IS projects may indeed develop solutions which are common to many organizations, such as order entry and billing systems, but that individual product is unique as it will have a different owner, different programmers, and different business users to other identical products deployed elsewhere. The unique nature of a project dictates that there is a need to incrementally plan the distinct activities that must be performed in order to articulate what is to be achieved. At the start of the project, these activities will be broadly defined, but they must be refined and detailed during the lifecycle of the project as the project team increase their understanding of the problem.

Types of IS projects

Simple projects

Whilst no project can be said to be "simple" and risk-free, there are some projects where, by the time the initial investigation into the project has been completed, much of the information normally obtained from later stages in the project will be known. Simple projects are most likely to arise from the combination of relatively small business objectives and the experience of the organization and the project team in tackling similar projects. A simple project is therefore characterized by a high level of confidence and a low level of risk because:

- there is a detailed plan for the whole project;
- all the resources needed to complete the project are available;
- there is little impact on existing business operations;
- there is a single and obvious solution.

Simple projects do not normally require the lengthy feasibility and investigation stages that are necessary for more complex projects, but they must, however, still undertake regular project reviews and controls to ensure that the project remains focused on meeting business objectives and, above all, remains viable.

Fuzzy projects

Whilst we would all prefer to undertake projects which lie comfortably within our bounds of knowledge and experience, in some cases we must work in unknown territory. "Fuzzy" projects are those where the precise details of what to implement and how to undertake the work are not known. Fuzzy projects are, therefore, characterized by the need to perform and re-iterate investigation and feasibility stages until a sufficient understanding of the situation can be gained.

Must-do projects

These are projects where there is an overriding commitment placed upon the business to satisfy a specific requirement, such as one laid down by a legal or regulatory body. Such is the nature of the requirement, the business is unlikely to be able to continue to operate until it has been met. These types of projects are not commonplace, but many Year 2000 compliance projects had as their main business drivers the need to prove their capability to operate safely before and after the date change by satisfying legal requirements issued by regulatory bodies.

For instance, Year 2000 projects undertaken within the airline industry were driven by safety and legal directives issued by national regulatory bodies for the airline industry, such as the Civil Aviation Authority (CAA) in the UK and the Federal Aviation Administration (FAA) in the US.

Emergency projects

Reality dictates that there will be times when projects must be authorized and initiated as soon as possible – they are just too important to delay. Not undertaking such a project would cause disproportionate damage to the organization, either financially, legally, or commercially. Emergency projects carry enormous risks, but luckily they should be a rare occurrence within a well-structured and managed organization.

Likely risks for these projects will ultimately focus on the disruption to existing budgets and programs, and so great care must be taken in classifying any project in this category. It hardly needs saying, but for clarification, an emergency project should not be used as an excuse by management who have fallen behind in meeting their objectives.

Hallmarks of a healthy project

It is not the aim of this chapter to provide a comprehensive assessment of project management tools and techniques currently available for use on IS projects. A brief search through any good bookshop will identify a multitude of perfectly adequate books on the subject that will complement the topics contained within this book and, in particular, this section.

Without doubt, many projects are doomed to failure, even before they have produced any deliverables. The title of this chapter provides the reason why. In the absence of adequate planning, the risk of IS project failure is greatly increased, yet by adopting a disciplined approach to project planning, many risks introduced as a result of poor planning can be mitigated. What follows is a list of attributes associated with planning and performing a successful project; the hallmarks of a healthy project.

User involvement

The concept of "management" within the project (such as project management, change management, and risk management) is a regular theme expressed within many project plans and customer presentations; and for good reason – it indicates control and direction flowing downwards from the most senior levels within the project hierarchy. Whilst this is a necessary requirement for a successful project, if allowed to manifest itself throughout the project, it reinforces the idea that project success is solely determined by the authority and direct involvement of senior management.

It is important to remember that the only reason why the project exists in the first place is because the business requires an IT solution to a specific problem. The business – lest we forget – comprises users who, by definition, must use a business system in order to met one or more business objectives and measures. End-users are, therefore, a vital element within an IS project, and they must be identified as soon as possible within the lifecycle of the project so that their requirements and concerns can be captured.

Whilst senior management may welcome the implementation of a new business system that broadly delivers what was desired in terms of processing capability, their feelings may not be supported by the users of that system. Frustration at slow response times, exposure to complex user interfaces, and the enforcement of vastly different business process do little to endear non-technical business users to the system and can ultimately result in the rejection of that system by the business community.

Any IS project whose outcome affects the roles and responsibilities of individuals has ethical consequences, and the issue of implementing *ethical* IT systems is now becoming greater all the time. Historically, very little attention has been given to business users during the lifecycle of the project prior to the user acceptance stage and, as a consequence, systems have been implemented which force users to adopt inefficient, unnatural, or unhealthy methods of working.

Whilst it is easy to state the importance of user involvement throughout the project, it is much harder to ensure that any user involvement is positive, constructive and of a high quality. In a climate where solutions are often focused on the capability of technology to meet business requirements, the need for effective communication between individuals within the project must not be underestimated.

Failure to discuss issues and concerns, report progress, and identify changes to working methods and procedures are probably some of the most common complaints from users. This is especially important for projects that are dispersed across geographic boundaries, where the need for effective, scheduled communication is paramount. Global projects, in particular, are highly dependent upon effective methods of communication, if planning, control, and information-sharing activities are to succeed throughout the duration of the project.

Many management texts often suggest that it is the quality of the user community that ultimately determines the effectiveness of user involvement within a project. This is true, but reality dictates that in many cases the project manager and, indeed, the business sponsor have little control over the selection of users. Mindful of the dependency on the business to second willing and capable users onto the project, the project manager must, as a minimum, ensure that the users:

■ are aware of the scope of the project;

■ are aware of the objectives of the project;

■ are aware of the timescales of the project;

■ have an ongoing and mutually beneficial relationship with the rest of the project team;

■ together with the project team, understand and agree the system functional requirements.

Executive support

A project must have as its sponsor an executive within the organization. In the top-down hierarchy of organizational strategy, this executive may have already initiated a number of key projects; if the project has developed from a "bottom-up" requirement, an executive must be found. In each case, the executive must have a vested interest in the success of the project and their success must be dependent upon the success of the project.

As the project sponsor, the executive must have a stake in the success of the project. This might seem obvious, but too many times executive sponsors fail to keep in touch with the progress of the project, only to discover, when it is too late, that the project has run into serious difficulties.

Endorsement and support for the project can be gained through the presentation and approval of a well-defined project plan. This will ensure that the sponsor is fully aware of the activities and the resources necessary to satisfy the business objectives (which should be a subset of the sponsor's overall objectives). Once the formal project initiation activities have been dispensed with it is vital that the project manager and executive sponsor communicate with each other throughout the remaining stages of the project. There will be many hurdles ahead – some technical, others of a financial or political nature – in which case the sponsor must be prepared to take whatever action is necessary to protect the project manager and the team. If the career progression of the sponsor is dependent upon the success of the project, seemingly insurmountable barriers can often be removed without adversely affecting the project timescales.

Executive support for a project may seem an obvious necessity for those managers who require funding from strategic rather than operational budgets, but the scope of their involvement must extend well beyond that of providing financial support. Executives and senior managers within an organization have the power and authority to make key decisions which can affect the outcome of an IS project. Successful projects rely on timely decisions being made by those who are part of the management decision cycle. If senior management expect IS project success, they must ensure that they maintain their support for it throughout the duration of the project. More importantly, they must realize that a failure on their part to make accurate decisions in time to promote action or effect change within the project can only increase the risk of project failure.

A capable and experienced project manager

Project management is a key role within the project and, if performed effectively, brings together and establishes commitment both from the supplier of the service, in the form of the IT community, and the customer, in the form of the business. The project manager must, therefore, be more than just a good manager; they must be a leader of people, a motivator, and a good listener. Strength of character is often lacking in many project managers, especially when the project runs into difficulties and, as we have already discussed in the earlier chapters of the book, many of the problems experienced within an IS project are not related to traditional project management activities.

A capable and experienced manager will recognize the warning signs early on and rise to the challenge. If the fundamental objectives of the project, as identified by the business sponsor, are wildly optimistic and unachievable, the project manager must be bold enough to question them. Too many project managers capitulate much too readily when put under pressure from their sponsor, only to bitterly regret their decision later on.

It goes without saying that the project manager must be committed to the project and to the team. The project manager must be part of the team – but is their leader and must act like one. My own experiences within IS projects have brought me into contact with project managers who, when faced with the potential wrath of the business sponsor, have chosen the easy option, and disavowed the project team to protect their own interests. Not surprisingly, these managers never gain the respect of their subordinates.

Clear business objectives and requirements

IS projects are undertaken to satisfy one or more clearly-defined business object-ives. They are not undertaken to keep the project manager in work, nor to fur-nish the IT department with all the latest technical products and gadgets. Before the project can begin, therefore, there must be a complete understanding of what it is meant to achieve and why – in business terms.

The standard approach to business planning dictates that most projects are initially seeded from a vision or mission – a "what-if" scenario with a beneficial outcome. This vision must then be translated into a number of clear, precise business objectives. These business objectives, in conjunction with a complete financial evaluation of the costs of the project, the business requirements, and the financial benefits it will realize, must form the business case for the project. At a minimum, the business case must identify the return on investment for the project.

Whilst contingency must be made for requirements to change, it is essential that the initial requirements of the project are agreed and approved before any development work on the project is undertaken. All requirements gathered must be prioritized by the business; starting with the "must-haves" and ending with the "nice-to-haves."

In a perfect world, development effort is only required once firm requirements have been provided by the business. In reality, this rarely happens, but no one should be under the illusion that increasing the scope of the project is without risk. "Scope creep" has been the silent killer of many promising IS projects, purely as a consequence of failing to identify, and stick to, clear business object-ives and requirements.

By stating how the project will achieve its business objectives, it will also be necessary to identify the metrics which will be used to determine its success. Conditions of success must be identified, therefore, and refer back to the initial objectives and requirements for the project. A typical condition of success might be that project failure should be declared if more than 20 per cent of require-ments are not delivered or if one or more key business objectives are not met.

Small milestones

If popular research into what constitutes a successful project is to be believed, the optimum time for a project is between three and six months. Fundamental to this approach are the needs to prioritize requirements and to adopt an incremental approach towards project delivery.

The "big-bang" approach to the project, delivering huge amounts of function-ality in one go, many years after requirements have been captured is not necessarily the best way to plan an IS project. A much better approach is to break down the project activities into a number of smaller chunks of work, which can be managed and controlled more effectively.

There can be little doubt that, whilst the majority of software development projects are increasing in complexity, the timescales for project delivery are decreasing. In a climate where "first-to-market" is often the final arbiter between success and failure, organizations cannot wait years to realize the benefits of new technology. If the system proposed can be developed using a rapid application development methodology, such as DSDM, techniques such as time-boxing can be used to identify a number of small development milestones which are to be completed in a set time limit.

Competent and committed staff

Whilst we would all like to think that the individuals working on a project constantly display exemplary behavior, in reality, people are only human. If you expect to get the most from your staff you must first appreciate what motivates each member of the team. A project has a structure and a clearly defined objective, so it is vital that each member of the project team understands what the project is trying to achieve and why.

Equally, it stands to reason that those people within the team must have the necessary skills and competences to undertake their allocated tasks within the project. The project is not a charity nor is it a training camp, so whilst risking your popularity with others within the organization, it is crucial that you hold out for the best people you can get. If you need the best, do everything you can to make sure you get the best.

Remembering that we are, indeed, only human it would be naïve to think that competent and committed individuals on the project will remain that way throughout the project. Training, personal development schemes, bonuses, promotion, and salary reviews all have a place in the overall management of the project – and it is the wise project manager who is not afraid to use them.

Proper planning

At the heart of every successful project is a clear and detailed project plan which has been communicated to the business and approved by all the project stakeholders. Successful project planning is more than just developing a critical-path model or a Gantt chart based on a few key dates and dependencies; it must start with a documented and well-articulated business problem.

This document must identify the business problem and the resulting benefit to the organization if the problem is resolved. An initial requirements analysis exercise must then be performed in order to assess the feasibility of the project. Once a feasible solution has been identified, the use of an appropriate project management methodology can then be used to manage the tasks and resources necessary to deliver that solution. However, before any real effort is allocated to the project, it is essential that milestones are clearly identified within the plan and that a process is in place to track them effectively. Each milestone should represent, at least, the completion of one or more deliverables. The quality standards to which each deliverable must conform must also be agreed during the initial project planning stages.

Successful project planning acknowledges the fact that not everything turns out exactly as planned and incorporates appropriate contingency plans to manage the situation. Table 5.1, therefore, provides a few of the more popular methods for applying contingencies to a project plan.

Risk analysis also plays a key part in contingency planning, and it is the successful project manager who completes a risk analysis exercise before committing funds and resources to a potentially risky project. If project risks have been identified upfront, a successful project plan will be one based upon realistic assumptions and expectations of achievement, rather than promoting an optimistic and "best-case" schedule.

TABLE 5.1 ▨ Possible methods of applying contingency to a project

Method	Example	Note
Add dummy tasks.	Refine the activity "Write test scripts" (estimated to take 10 man days) into a number of smaller tasks and add a dummy task called "Review test scripts" with a duration of one day (10% contingency).	Probably the best technique, as this method does not distort task resources and deadlines.
Ensure that all resources are less than 100% available.	Identify resource availability as 4.5 days per project week.	Do not plan for resources to work full-time on the project – it will never happen in practice.
Add a standard rate of contingency to all tasks.	If the design phase of a project takes 100 man days, plan for 110 man days (10% contingency).	Not recommended as individuals will fill the time available to complete the task (and use up all the contingency).
Add contingency to the end of each project phase of appropriate duration.	Add 10 days for a "contingency" task at the end of the 'integration test' phase to resolve unknown problems.	Not recommended. The visibility of the contingency activity will tempt individuals on the project to use it.

Ownership

The best project plan in the world is worthless unless there is ownership of the activities identified within it. Ownership within the project is established by initially identifying the roles and responsibilities for each member of the project team and linking them to the project objectives. Each member of the team, whether from a business department or an IT department, must understand how and why they are needed for the project – and the consequences of failure.

Identifying and allocating resources to activities within the project plan is, however, of little benefit if the resources are unavailable when required. Project stakeholders, in particular, must be prepared to release individuals from their normal business duties to undertake key project activities, such as user acceptance testing, when required.

Clearly, it is not acceptable for project stakeholders to abdicate responsibility and ownership independently of authority. Ownership and commitment must be demonstrated throughout the whole project if it is to stand any chance of success.

With ownership must come accountability. Where individuals within the organization have the power to make decisions, yet are not accountable for their actions, they represent a significant risk to the success of the project. Accountability must be established through organizational structure, and if the current organizational structure does not reflect the accountability and authority for the project, it must be the responsibility of the project sponsor to effect the necessary changes.

Managing project constraints

The desire to satisfy the constraints of time, cost, and quality should not overshadow the need to satisfy the objectives of the project. It is likely, therefore, that the project management process may need to be flexible in its approach, depending on the overriding constraints governing the project.

For example, a project to develop an air traffic control system cannot compromise on quality, as human lives are at stake. Timescales must, therefore, be of secondary importance. On the other hand, an organization may decide that they can accept a system that is not perfect, but available for deployment, rather than wait for all their requirements to be met and miss a business opportunity.

Project success will depend on how well the project manager and the business stakeholders understand this flexibility. When planning the project the following questions will need to be answered by the business:

- How important is the project to the business?
- How important is it for the project to achieve its timescales?

■ How important is quality?

■ How important is cost?

The project to rescue the Apollo 13 mission,[2] for instance, was heavily constrained by scope; the parameters within which the project had to operate were very small. Year 2000 compliance projects on the other hand were least flexible on time, as systems had to be compliant by December 31, 1999, if not sooner. Figure 5.1 provides an indication of the constraint flexibility that might exist

Apollo 13 rescue

	Least flexible	Moderately flexible	Most flexible
Scope	X		
Timescale		X	
Budget			X

IS development projects

	Least flexible	Moderately flexible	Most flexible
Scope			X
Timescale		X	
Budget	X		

Year 2000 compliance project

	Least flexible	Moderately flexible	Most flexible
Scope		X	
Timescale	X		
Budget			X

FIGURE 5.1 ■ Constraint flexibility within projects

within three different types of project: the Apollo 13 rescue mission; a Year 2000 compliance project; and a typical IS development project.

The project plan

One of the initial deliverables in any project is the project plan. The creation and distribution of the project plan satisfies a number of key planning objectives, the first and most important one being the declaration of a statement of intent. The project plan is one of the main forms of communication within a project as it states the intended activity to be undertaken within the project and the expected future outcome.

Remember, the project plan is, indeed, only a plan, and no plan can be 100 per cent accurate, even assuming it is refined as the project progresses. Don't fall into the trap of spending so long trying to produce a perfect plan that you wish you had spent the time more wisely in the later stages of the project. Remember, the project plan must identify what *should* happen and what must be done if this is not achieved.

Failing to understand the level of detail required in a project plan is likely to be the main reason behind the generation of worthless project plans by inexperienced project managers. Difficulty often arises when project managers do not have sufficient detail for the plan in the early stages of the project. The solution to this problem is to identify high-level milestones within the plan such as:

- milestone 1   requirements specification produced
- milestone 2   high-level application design documentation produced
- milestone 3   high-level database design documentation produced
- milestone 4   system testing completed
- milestone 5   user acceptance testing completed
- milestone 6   implementation plan produced.

Obviously, experience of similar projects and the implementation of different business solutions will enable the project manager to identify planned activity with more accuracy. This is a good example of how future projects can benefit from the experiences gained from previous projects within the organization. If you do not already do so, ensure that all your previous project documentation is made available to anyone working on a project within your organization – even if the project was not a success (*especially* if the project was not a success!).

Gaining benefit from the plan

A project plan is often considered to be merely a checklist of activities that must be completed with, perhaps, an indication of their cost. There are, however, many other uses for the project plan which can provide additional benefits to the project. By extending the use of the project plan, the plan can add value far in excess of cost.

As meeting key milestones within the project plan is likely to be paramount for any IS project manager, this may be satisfied at the expense of failing to appreciate the public relations aspects within the project. Typically, communication and understanding between business and IT managers is poor; but a good project plan is one of the most effective ways to establish and maintain a relationship within the business whilst promoting commitment and ownership at the same time.

Of course, such advice should always be applied with care in the light of experience. One key lesson that was learnt from London Ambulance Service's failed Computer Aided Dispatch system project (which will be reviewed later in this chapter), is that a public relations exercise is no substitute for a genuine and participative dialogue with key parties.

Feasibility – the plan as a simulation of the project

In reality, a project manager may often only be informed of an imminent business crisis at the last minute. What happens next is unfortunately too common: panic sets in and the project manager rushes to the aid of the business, disregarding any notion of planning in the process.

The need for a plan is, therefore, quickly overtaken by the need to get a development team engaged and key systems built. Successful project managers know different, but even they have a tendency to produce a minimum plan as soon as possible; immediacy beats detail. However, the more detail that is put into a plan, the more likely it is that the plan will be effective. Consequently, as more detail is added to the plan, the more it changes in nature – it becomes less of a plan and more a simulation of what is about to happen.

All projects start off from a vision. A need for change now exists within the organization, which is quickly translated into the need for an IS project. Project kick-off meetings attempt to establish basic foundations, vague timescales, "finger-in-the-air" costs, and a fleeting attempt to propose a technical solution. Crucially though, up to this point, the project is based on enthusiastic discussion only and, as most bad ideas often sound like good ones to start with, it is extremely difficult for project managers to defend themselves against an accomplished and powerful business sponsor.

The first duty of the project manager must be to ensure that the project is indeed feasible. Apart from actually completing the project, the next best approach is to *simulate* the project; using the project plan. A detailed project plan will offer the best protection for the project manager and project owner in an uncertain situation; but what level of detail is required? This will obviously depend upon the time horizon of the project. If the project is expected to last a number of years, there is no point planning what you will be doing next Wednesday afternoon. In particular, if the project is to comprise a number of phases, you only need to plan the next phase in detail.

The last action of each phase should be, therefore, to plan the next phase. However, if the business you are working within operates within specific operational windows, possibly with penalties for systems that are not introduced in time, then there is a clear need to plan down to the last hour.

The plan as an approval document

Once the project owner or sponsor has been convinced that the simulation of the project is fairly realistic, the detailed plan then becomes the document which the sponsor uses to indicate their approval of the project (or not in some cases). At this point the project sponsor knows as much as anybody about the schedule and costs for the project. The plan has now become a visible definition of the project to which the business sponsor can add their signature. Ownership has been established, as has management approval – the plan has now become an internal contract.

The plan as an internal contract

The list of tasks within the project plan provides the project manager with an acceptable way of achieving an outcome. Commitment is established through the identification of resources against each activity in the plan.

Up until this point, project planning is usually an enthusiastic and idealistic affair; everyone is smiling and, if nothing else, the experience is much more interesting than the daily grind of the office. Everyone is pulling in the same direction and the level of camaraderie is high – that is, until the project starts and trouble begins. Some of the most common culprits are business managers who are often determined to increase the scope and functionality of the project once it has been approved.

As the plan identifies the scope of the project, the business managers and sponsor must realize that any changes to the plan will now incur a cost to the project. Use the plan as an internal contract. The printed plan with a few words added to indicate a contractual responsibility against each of the signatures will suffice.

Keep this document in a safe place and don't hesitate to produce it if trouble ensues.

The plan as the budget document

The two key elements in the project approval process which will come under most scrutiny are simply:

- how are we going to solve the problem?
- how much will it cost?

If the activities in the plan are anywhere near comprehensive and the rates for man-days-of-effort accurate, the plan will deliver a cost which can be reliably budgeted for. Budgeting without a plan is worthless, but budgeting as a result of a good plan is a step towards eventual project success. If the budget application is accompanied by the project plan, those individuals saddled with the pleasure of approving it will understand exactly what they are approving and what will be delivered for their money.

The plan as the customer contract

A large proportion of projects are now undertaken as a result of the successful acceptance of a contract from an external customer. If your current responsibilities include account management, bid management, or program management for a professional services organization, you will no doubt already be aware of the need to convince the customer that you and your organization are capable of performing the work in the specified time, subject to the conditions of the contract. The response to a typical project bid will therefore contain an approved, high-level project plan in the appendix.

In the average project plan, it is likely that a number of activities will need to be performed by the customer (such as the preparation of candidate data for testing). Immediately there is a dependency upon an external resource and the risk of control being lost. If the plan forms part of the customer contract, and has been approved, this will avert any finger-pointing and recriminations when problems arise. Nevertheless, it is important to ensure that the customer is present during the project review meetings which cover their designated activities.

The plan as a cold shower

If performed correctly, planning a project will always be of benefit to a project manager. In the worst-case scenario, it will prove that the project itself is not feasible. When budgets need to be planned months in advance, it is very tempting to allocate funds on the back of a few short paragraphs of justification; the assumption being, of course, that the project is, in fact, feasible. This budgetary procedure, when performed in isolation from a project plan, does not force the business stakeholders, sponsors, or IT managers to consider the details of the investment.

As the time approaches when the costs must be justified fully, the project manager will be asked to produce a delivery plan. However, by now, there may be insufficient time or resources available to complete the project in time. For instance, if new hardware and software must be provisioned, have critical lead times for delivery been passed?

The plan, however, has achieved its objective – to breathe the sobering air of reality onto something which was, up to that point, a good idea. The business sponsor and management team should be able to make a good case for the value of a discarded project plan being greater than that of an adopted one. To spend a small amount of money to prevent a large amount of waste is no bad thing. Budgets do not provoke thought – plans do. If it can't be planned, it shouldn't be done.

 CASE STUDY

The London Ambulance Service Computer-Aided Dispatch system

This case study illustrates the dangers of implementing high-technology solutions without having an adequate level of technical confidence, management organization, and due regard for people within the organization. The spectacular, but tragic, crash of the LAS (London Ambulance Service) system should send a clear message to sponsors and managers of strategic change that projects implemented without the full support and commitment of users are likely to fail.[3,4]

The LAS was founded in 1930 and is the largest ambulance service in the world. Covering an area of just over 600 square miles, it serves a resident population of over seven million people. During a working day, the LAS will receive between 2,000 and 2,500 telephone calls, of which between 1,300 and 1,600 are emergency '999' calls. It provides a transport infrastructure for 80 hospitals and community units, making over 500,000 accident and emergency visits and 1.3 million non-emergency visits a year.

Rationale for a new system

The nationally recognized standards for performance of ambulance services issued by ORCON (Operational Research Consultancy) state that from the receipt of an emergency call to an instruction being relayed to an ambulance station must be no more than three minutes. After dispatch, an ambulance must arrive at the designated location within 14 minutes. The LAS could not meet these standards with its existing manual system of dispatch. A summary of how the manual system operated might suggest some pertinent reasons why.

1 When a 999 or call is received from the control center, a control assistant writes down the call details on a pre-printed form. The location of the emergency is identified from a map book (a gazeteer), together with its geographical co-ordinates. The form is then placed on a conveyor belt with other similar forms which transports them to a central collection point within the control center.

2 The form is collected and reviewed by another member of staff who decides which resource allocator should deal with it based on the three divisions within the London area: North East, North West and South. At this point potential duplicate calls are also identified.

3 The resource allocator, from the current status and location of each ambulance within their sector (using information supplied by the radio operator and the activity form for each vehicle), must then decide which resource to mobilize (paramedic, ambulance, helicopter, etc.). Dispatching information is then recorded on the incident form and passed to the dispatcher.

4 The dispatcher then telephones the relevant ambulance station (if that is where the resource is) or passes mobilization instructions to a radio operator if the ambulance is in transit.

Given the operational pressures and a situation where the volume of incoming calls cannot be controlled, the LAS were already well aware of the deficiencies in the existing system, including:

▪ the amount of time taken to identify the precise location of incidents as a result of often incomplete or inaccurate details being provided by the caller;

▪ the sheer amount of paper-based processing that is required;

▪ the need for human judgement to identify duplicate calls and special incidents (which need a Rapid Response Unit (RRU) or a helicopter);

▪ the almost impossible task of maintaining details of vehicle status and location information using a mixture of operator intuition and information provided on the activity forms.

The aims and objectives of the new system

The basic aim of the project was to create an almost totally automatic system. The new role of the Central Ambulance Control operators would be to receive incoming calls and enter their details into the system. Only in the most complex of cases would human intervention be required to allocate the best resource.

The computer-aided dispatch system would therefore provide the following command and control functions automatically:

▪ automatic tracking of vehicles;

▪ automatic resource identification and allocation;

▪ automatic identification of duplicate calls;

▪ resource management, primarily the positioning of vehicles to minimize response times;

▪ computerized mapping with public call box identification.

Establishment of the project

Finding a supplier to develop the system did not prove difficult. From an initial interest shown by 35 companies, 17 proposals were received by a selection team comprising a career ambulance manager (who for some years previously had been responsible for LAS systems), and a contract analyst. The Chief Executive of the LAS had already stated that the systems manager role would eventually be filled by a properly qualified systems manager – making the current holder redundant.

The criteria used to assess each bid were prioritized as:

- ability to perform the tasks required;
- ability to handle throughput and response times;
- ease of use by staff;
- resilience;
- flexibility;
- ability to meet timetable;
- cost;
- additional features.

The tender, advertised on February 7, 1991, stated that full implementation was to take place by January 8, 1992. This date was non-negotiable. A number of suppliers questioned this date and also stated that they thought it was unachievable and suggested a phased approach to delivery. It is unclear whether these comments ever reached senior LAS management.

Despite receiving sound proposals from a number of established suppliers, the selection team opted for a bid based on a consortium of Apricot, a well-established hardware supplier, and a relatively unknown and small software supplier, System Options (SO). Their bid was significantly lower than any other bid; the next lowest bid being $1.05 million (£700,000) more expensive. As the policy of the LAS was to accept the lowest bid, the selection team had little option but to accept it. Despite cost being practically last in the criteria stated for acceptance, it was clearly much higher than the LAS were prepared to admit.

Prior to the bid being passed to the LAS board for ratifying the selection team passed it first to another ambulance service for approval. Whilst the technical evaluation of the project should have been adequately covered, there was no one within this team who had specific project or contract management experience.

The board ultimately approved the bid, but there was no evidence of any discussion as to the supplier selection process, the suitability of the supplier, and the extremely low cost of the bid compared with any other.

As the project became established, the project team was changed to include the following roles:

- director of support services;
- LAS contract analyst;

- control room services manager;

- director of operations;

- training manager;

- public affairs manager;

- Communication and Technical Services Ltd. representative (communications);

- administrative support;

- supplier representatives.

Whilst many departments within the LAS appear to be represented, there is no representation from the users (ambulance crews). Given the scale of the development performed by the supplier, it is also surprising there is no contract manager role within the team.

Project management

Whilst no specific reference was made in the contract, it was the intention for SO, as lead contractor, to take on the role of project management. As the project developed, this role became ambiguous; SO were struggling to manage their own input to the project which forced the LAS to accept responsibility for project management. The suppliers are clear that, in reality, it was the LAS, through the director of support services and the contract analyst who were providing project management. Whilst the director performed to the best of his abilities, it is clear that a professional project manager would have identified the huge risks in terms of the proposed solution, supplier selection, and timescales much sooner.

The LAS intended to use PRINCE project management methodology. However, no one in the LAS was experienced in its use and so, to overcome this, a short PRINCE course was provided to the project team. Given the scale of the task, this action seemed woefully inadequate and should have been identified as a risk to the project.

At a project group meeting on June 17, 1991, a number of issues of potential concern were raised and minuted. These issues were to have a significant effect on the success of the project.

- The LAS had no full-time participants assigned to the project.

- The lack of formal clarification of how the PRINCE methodology was to be applied.

- The lack of a formal program for project group and other meetings.

- Concern over the aggressive timescales for the project; six months was well short of the industry average for this type of project – 18 months.

- The draft plan distributed by the supplier left no time for review and revision.

Although these issues were discussed early on in the project, there is no evidence that any of them were followed up or escalated to senior management.

Ironically, whilst there was little understanding of how to apply PRINCE techniques to the project, the adoption of a PIR (Project Issue Register) did actually occur. What is astonishing though is that control and management of the issues affecting the project was given to SO, the lead software supplier. However, on the recommendation of a new LAS systems manager (who was not assigned to the project) the PIR system was eventually put under the control of the LAS project team. Despite the use of the PIR system, the 1513 PIRs that were raised represented only a partial record of project issues.

Systems development

The Systems Requirements Specification (SRS) was developed during 1990 and outlined a design that was based on five key components:

- Computer-Aided dispatch system (CAD);

- computer map display system;

- Automatic Vehicle Location System (AVLS);

- Mobile Data Terminals (MDT);

- Radio Interface System (RIFS).

Two of the components (MDT and RIFS) were already installed as a result of a previously aborted attempt to automate LAS operations. The functionality of the proposed design was extremely high and complex; not only did it greatly surpass the previously failed attempt to automate resource allocation, it was also more advanced than any other comparable system in the UK.

The SRS itself was extremely prescriptive in nature, reflecting the culture of the organization and providing little scope for additional ideas to be incorporated from prospective suppliers. There was no evidence of any formal sign-off for the SRS.

The computer hardware which was to support the CAD system was based on Apricot workstations, containing a 486 processor and running at 25 Mhz (which was considered very powerful at the time). The user interface to the CAD system was based on Windows® 3.0, providing a pleasant graphical user interface whilst allowing the multi-tasking of applications. The actual screens to be used with the CAD system were written in Visual Basic® which is a software development tool used for rapid application prototyping, rather than the generation of fast and efficient systems. As the project team was to discover, the unproven combination of Windows 3.0 and Visual Basic was a risk waiting to happen.

Organizational culture and operational change

Industrial relations between the management and staff of the LAS were not good. Undoubtedly, by 1990, at the end of a very damaging national industrial dispute over pay, the LAS stood in need of major change. The attitudes of the management and ambulance crews were so different they were almost confrontational. Ambulance crews felt that management were obsessed with meeting project deadlines at the expense of the occupational factors which they prided themselves on, such as speed of response and patient care. As a result they did not feel encouraged to challenge and discuss the rigid and inflexible deadlines being imposed for fear of being "sidelined" or being thought of as "negative."

The overall design of the CAD project was to automate as far as possible, the existing manual processes for the allocation of emergency resources. The design of the new system was to be based on the following operational process:

1 Call is received by the Control Assistant (CA) and entered into the CAD system.

2 Location of call identified using the mapping system and public call-box identification system.

3 The CAD system, using information obtained from the call, informs the CA on the severity of the call (1–10) and which skills and resources should be used (e.g. helicopter/RRU, etc.).

4 Using information on the status and location of each vehicle, a rule-based algorithm determines the closest appropriate vehicle.

5 The CAs allocate the indicated resources and the CAD system sends a mobilization signal and incident details.

6 The ambulance crew inform the system of their status as they manage the incident by pressing different buttons on their MDTs. This information, combined with the information from the AVLS, is used to update the CAD system so that it knows the precise location and status of all resources at any moment in time.

System testing and commissioning

Once a system has been developed, there are at least two key forms of testing which should be performed:

■ functional testing, to ensure that the system does what it is expected to do;

■ load testing, to test the ability of the system to perform under maximum load.

Considering the critical nature of the system, in the sense that failures could have life or death consequences, the testing performed within the project was of doubtful quality and completeness due to the eventual piecemeal delivery of equipment and implementation. There is no evidence of full testing ever taking place on the system before implementation in October 1992.

Whilst testing was always going to be a complex affair due to the real-time nature of faults, this should not have formed an excuse to ignore such a vital phase of systems development. Given the fact that, at the time, there were numerous automated testing tools available which could have helped identify and test such a complex system, it is curious that there was no evidence to suggest this option had been identified.

In particular, integration testing between the dispatch sub-system and the communications sub-system (MDT and AVLS) was never fully tested. A memo in the original LAS Enquiry from the Assistant Director of Operations to the Accident and Emergency team, sent prior to the original implementation date of January 8, 1992 states: "*Following the initial operating period of the CAD system*, a full review of the network capability will be carried out" (my emphasis). The implication is that testing would form part of the implementation exercise.

Implementation

Despite the planned implementation of the system in a single phase (a phased approach suggested by some of the suppliers being rejected), the inability of the suppliers to meet the agreed deadline forced a new, phased approach to be adopted.

- *Phase 1* Call taking routines are implemented, but the existing manual system is used for allocation (using activation boxes) and dispatch. The mapping functionality was also to be used, to help CAs identify the location of incidents more quickly.

- *Phase 2* As phase 1, but with the introduction of vehicle tracking through the use of the AVLS and MDTs. Voice dispatch is now eliminated.

- *Phase 3* Full implementation. Call takers allocate resources automatically provided that resources can arrive within 11 minutes of activation. Otherwise, allocators would identify and allocate resources manually. This phase was designed to run without paper backup and would operate over the whole of London rather than across three divisions. Staff in the control center are now grouped together by role in different parts of the room.

Phase 1 was broadly successful, but the printers used were not part of the original specification and were responsible for a number of system failures, such as screens locking and occasional server failures. This tended to undermine user confidence in the integrity of the system. It was, in hindsight, an inevitable consequence of the need to highlight a small, but significant, success in project delivery against a published implementation date.

Between January and October 1992, phases 1 and 2 were implemented in a piecemeal fashion across the different London Ambulance divisions. The following list highlights some of the main errors that occurred during this period.

- Frequent inaccurate or incomplete reporting of vehicle status by ambulance crews, caused by inadequate training, communication failures and alleged misuse of tracking equipment.

- Failure of AVLS system to identify every 53rd vehicle.

- Inaccurate ambulance location fixes; problems with MDT, both caused by faulty equipment, transmission black-spots and software errors.

- Overload of communication channels.

- Inability of system to cope with crews taking a different ambulance to the one allocated.

- Software bug in the resource proposal software causing it to fail to identify the nearest available resource.

During these months, the system was never stable as changes and enhancements were made continually. Despite the obvious lack of any formal change control and in the absence of a full systems test, a decision was made to go for a full implementation on October 26, 1992. At the time of the implementation, there were still two PIRs which identified severe service degradation and that the system would not function properly until they had been resolved. Incredibly, there were also 44 outstanding PIRs that would result in a poor level of service to the patient.

Full system implementation

The CAD system went fully live at 7 am on Monday 26 October 1992, nine months after the planned implementation date. The first problems became apparent when the workload on the system increased during the morning shift. It soon became clear that, due to the problems with the communications, vehicle status, and location sub-systems, the system rapidly knew the location and status of fewer and fewer vehicles. In addition, the system was "losing" calls, resulting in duplicate calls being made by anxious members of the public. As call volumes increased, the system rapidly became unusable and callers were experiencing a waiting time of 30 minutes "on-hold" in the call queue. As voice radio communication was restricted in the implementation, the timely feedback of incident information was prevented. Coupled with the physical changes which had occurred in the control room, the ability for the control room staff to intervene was severely reduced.

As the level of exception messages increased throughout the day, partly as a result of unresolved errors generating new exceptions, the congestion within the system became so great it became necessary to abort the full implementation and revert to a semi-manual system of operation.

This worked well until the early hours of November 4, 1992 when the system slowed significantly and then locked up altogether. All attempts to restart it failed, and on the advice of senior management, Central Ambulance Control reverted to the fully manual, paper-based system, using radio and telephone mobilization.

Reasons for the LAS project failure

Schedule pressure

At the time of the project, the LAS was still suffering from a history of poor industrial relations, low staff morale, and a lack of trust in management. The aggressive implementation of a system that would force widespread organizational change on its users without proper user involvement and consultation was clearly a major risk, given the critical nature of the Ambulance Service. LAS management were under immense pressure to improve operational performance and satisfy ORCON standards which undoubtedly put pressure on the project team to implement a solution as soon as possible.

There is never a perfect time to implement a new system, but too many systems are planned and implemented at the very worst time – when the existing system is creaking under the strain of increased workloads and there is not enough time to plan a replacement system. The LAS computer-aided dispatch project fell into this category. The phased implementation that was introduced did not come about through planning, but as a result of desperation.

The lure of the leading edge

Given the organizational issues affecting the LAS, combined with the poor history of industrial relations within it, it was clear the executives within the LAS saw the new system as a "silver bullet." The new system was innovative and was a "first" for the LAS. As the world's largest ambulance service, operating within London, arguably one of most influential and important capital cities of the world, the LAS executive board saw the introduction of a new IT system as a means to:

- reduce operational costs;
- reduce staffing levels;
- achieve technical innovation;
- improve industrial relations.

The management of the LAS were either naïve or misguided in thinking that the introduction of a new computer system alone would change the status quo behavior of their employees.

The design itself represented a quantum leap in technology for the LAS. Not only did it massively exceed the scope of the previously aborted project, it also exceeded the current functionality of any other existing emergency dispatch system. The LAS planned to migrate from a wholly manual operation to an almost completely automatic operation in a single phase. At the heart of the project failure was a system design which required perfect and uninterrupted feeds of data to operate – it was based on a perfect world where nothing goes wrong. The reality of the situation was very much different; people do not always do what they are told (there was certainly an element of sabotage during the implementation); technology is unreliable; and the quality of information entering the system is inaccurate or incomplete.

Inadequate risk management

From the earliest days within the project, crucial, but potentially risky, decisions were taken without any proper risk management process being performed. The choice of supplier should have sent alarm bells ringing early on, if not because of their size, because of their incredibly low bid compared to all others received. Equally, the lack of an experienced project manager or IT contract manager on the project should have been identified as a major risk on such a large project. Risk management means being brutal. LAS management should have asked themselves some very direct questions, one of which should have been "what happens if the system does not perform in the way expected?" In this case, the answer should have been "the potential loss of life".

Inadequate quality assurance

During the development and implementation of the project, it became clear that SO staff bypassed the change procedures and implemented changes on the system. More importantly, considering the planned "big-bang" implementation approach taken, it seems unbelievable that the system was never fully tested, i.e. from the logging of an emergency call to the successful transfer of the patient to hospital.

Inadequate project management

The commitment of the project team, and indeed of the LAS management and the lead supplier, cannot be doubted; they all gave their best efforts in difficult circumstances. However, the lack of adequate project management and experience within the team was a key factor in the failure to identify or recognize the significance of the many problems that would ultimately have such a dramatic effect on the outcome of the project. LAS naturally assumed that the supplier would undertake the project management role; in reality this did not happen and one of the most important governance processes within the project was left very much to chance.

▶ Planning the project: critical success factors

- Ensure that there is a sound business case for the project.

- Define the project.

- Perform a reality check on the project – is it really achievable, given the constraints of time, cost and quality?

- Gain executive support for the project.

- Build the team with the right people.

- Produce a clear plan of action.

- Identify the conditions of success for the project.

- Engage your stakeholders.

- Establish control mechanisms to track key milestones.

- Ensure that issues and risks are identified and tracked throughout the project.

- Always include time for review and revision in the plan. The plan may well require changes as a result of:
  - consultation with suppliers;
  - consultation with users;
  - contractual negotiations;
  - revision of timescales;
  - review and revision of testing plan.

- Delays in implementing projects place them at risk of being overtaken by technological change.

- It is vital that project plans are sufficiently flexible to allow for the inclusion of technological advances where appropriate.

- There is considerable benefit in developing and implementing a project in phases as opposed to a big-bang approach to systems development.

- Adopt a suitable project management methodology, but understand its strengths and weaknesses first.

▶ References

1 CCTA (The Stationery Office), *Managing Successful Projects with PRINCE2*, 1996

2 *Apollo 13*, Kennedy Space Centre Apollo 13 mission archives, NASA

3 D. Page, P. Williams and D. Boyd, *Report of the Inquiry into the London Ambulance Service*, South West Thames Regional Health Authority, February, 1993

4 M. Hougham, "London Ambulance Service computer-aided dispatch system", *International Journal of Project Management* **14** (2), 103–10

6

Project building blocks: processes

You know my methods. Apply them.

Sir Arthur Conan Doyle, *The Sign of Four* (1890)

Successful projects do not happen solely as a consequence of good fortune; they are characterized by a disciplined approach to planning, development, and deployment. It is self-evident then that an IS project will have a greater chance of success if the key processes that are identified as critical to the success of the project are identified and managed successfully throughout the lifespan of the project.

Establishing and adhering to even the most basic processes will often be sufficient to ensure that firm foundations exist for the majority of smaller and medium-sized IS projects. For larger projects that require a greater level of process knowledge, not just within the project but within the organization, process models such as the Software Engineering Institute's Capability Maturity Model must be the ultimate goal in software process management.

Project management

IS projects are inherently complex; they bring together people, processes, and technology to satisfy business objectives and deliver business benefits. Good project management helps ensure these objectives are achieved within the constraints of budget, time, and quality.

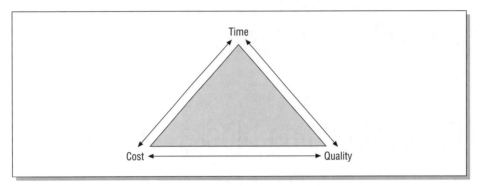

FIGURE 6.1 ■ Project constraints that must be managed within the project management process

What is project management?

Project management is responsible for planning, monitoring, and controlling the resources and activities necessary to complete a project. By adopting a suitable project management methodology, either one developed in-house or one in the public domain, such as PRINCE, project-related activities can be undertaken in a controlled manner, balancing the constraints of time, cost, and quality (Figure 6.1).

Key features of project management

All project management techniques and methodologies contain at least three basic elements:

- planning;
- monitoring;
- control.

Without planning, it is difficult to know where you want to go. Without monitoring, it is difficult to tell if where you are going is where you planned to go. Without control, it is difficult to ensure that you will be going where you planned to go. Together, these three elements are the cornerstones of project management. Through their effective application, organizations can embark upon a series of steps, the "project lifecycle," in the knowledge that they have the process in place to take them from beginning to end in a controlled and manageable fashion.

Through the application of project management, an organization can protect its investment in the project. If performed effectively, project management will ensure that the project does not run into difficulties, by providing, for example:

- identification of the times when user involvement will be required;

- division of the project into smaller, more easily planned sections;

- provision of control points where stakeholders can review progress;

- identification of the periods within the project when specific skills will be required.

If, during the project, difficulties do arise, it is the project management process that will manage changes to the project scope, budget, or timescale in order for the project to remain viable.

The project lifecycle

The series of project-related tasks that must be accomplished within an organization are commonly known as the "project lifecycle." A typical example of the project lifecycle will take the form shown in Figure 6.2. At this point, there are no specific tasks within the model that relate to an IS project – the project lifecycle, at this level at least, is generic and can be used as a template for any project.

Stages of the project lifecycle

The preparation stage concentrates on identifying and agreeing the business case for the project and a high-level plan of action and budget. Typically this stage will involve the project manager and the project or business sponsor.

The initiation phase is the point at which the project takes on a more formal role, with the selection of the project team and their briefing as to their roles and responsibilities within the project organization.

The feasibility stage will establish whether or not the project is indeed feasible, and establish key risks and conditions of success for it. Typical activities during this phase might be the identification of external resources that might be needed to supply IT products and services.

During the definition and planning phase, the separate stages that will constitute the project will be defined in detail and documented in the form of the project plan. The project manager and the core project team will co-ordinate this activity, ensuring that the plans, objectives, assumptions, dependencies, and risks

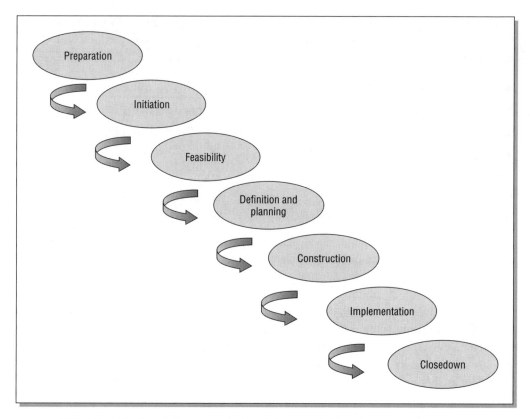

FIGURE 6.2 ■ A generic representation of the project lifecycle

identified during detailed planning are communicated to all those individuals who will be affected by the project.

During the construction phase, software, hardware, and network components will be designed, developed, and tested. The implementation phase of the project lifecycle will be the point at which the deliverables of the project, typically products and services, are deployed into a user environment.

In order to support specific IT-related activities, however, a more detailed project lifecycle is required. The majority of IS projects undertaken still adopt a traditional approach whereby a number of activities are completed in a strict sequential order. A typical plan adopting this approach is shown in Table 6.1.

The actual number and type of activities undertaken within the average IS project lifecycle will obviously be dependent upon the nature of the project but, in general terms, they all will all contain a number of tasks common to all IT projects.

TABLE 6.1 ▓ Stages within the a typical IS project lifecycle

Project stage	Duration
Feasibility	---
Systems analysis	----------
Program design	----------------
File design	-------------------------
Database design	-------------------------
Network design	--------------------------------
Coding	-------------------------------
System test	----------------
User acceptance test	--------
Implementation	-----
Post-implementation review	---

Program management

It is unfortunate that much of the training material available on the subject of project management assumes that an IS project is undertaken in glorious isolation from other projects and business activities within the organization. The reality of the situation is somewhat different; organizations seeking benefits through IT projects are likely to find themselves in one or more of the following situations:

■ multiple projects happening simultaneously;

■ geographically dispersed projects;

■ conflicting priorities and schedules across projects;

■ lack of resource management across projects;

■ changing deadlines and business objectives.

Despite the enormous impact any one of these could have on the success of an IS project, many organizations have no process in place to mitigate these risks. As a result, many organizations fail to control their projects and, subsequently, fail to realize the expected benefits from them.

What is program management?

Program management is a process that allows the organization to manage multiple projects that are dependent upon each other in pursuit of delivering business benefits. More accurately, it can be defined as the co-ordinated management of a portfolio of projects to achieve an agreed number of business objectives. This definition has several strands:

- The projects within a program are selected for inclusion: they do not just invite themselves. The existence of many projects is not evidence of a program – they must all support the program objectives.

- Projects are co-ordinated within a controlled environment. Projects should be monitored regularly to ensure continual allegiance to the program goals.

- Projects are ideally self-contained, but are mutually reliant in some regard. The program challenge is to manage those dependencies.

- A program delivers services, whereas a project delivers products. Business benefits are the primary objectives of a program.

For any organization managing a number of projects, it is clear that a business program will possess many of the components found within underlying project management structures, such as monitoring and control processes. However, there are a number of significant differences between the two:

■ Objective

Project management is a process that implements solutions and products. Program management is a process which delivers benefits through the management of a number of related projects.

■ Roles and responsibilities

Overall responsibility for the program will rest with the program manager and it will be the responsibility of each project manager within the program to report progress and issues to this individual. Whilst the individual project manager will be concerned with producing a set of deliverables within time and budget constraints, the program manager will be responsible for integrating the deliverables of each project into one overall program.

■ Affinity to other projects

Projects that are undertaken within a larger business program will often have a degree of commonality with other projects within the same program. For instance, they may run simultaneously or at least overlap with each other; they share resources, and they follow the same development and governance standards.

However, one project being canceled within the program does not necessarily cause the cancellation of the program. That is not to say projects within a program are not linked. Delays with one project often cause subsequent delays with others due to logical links between tasks in both projects.

Key features of program management

- Centralized dependency tracking. Dependencies between projects should be tracked by the program office at both a technical level (to ensure interoperability) and in relation to the deliverables exchanged between projects within the program during their lifetimes. This function achieves a key program management objective of identifying and understanding project dependencies.

- Centralized resource management. Shared resources must be tracked and managed.

- Centralized risk and issue management. Issues and risks impacting on the program must be managed proactively from within it. Mechanisms must exist for projects to raise issues and risks, and the program support office must own issues and risks which cross project boundaries.

- Centralized benefit management.

- Centralized requirements management. The program manager must take prime responsibility for identifying and establishing clear baselines for the program.

- Centralized progress tracking. The program support office must track and report progress of the program against agreed baselines for budgets and timescales. Key to this would be the need to adopt a common set of planning and management standards which would enable the communication and interpretation of progress reporting and any other shared activities.

- Challenging projects to demonstrate the workability and technical viability of their solutions.

- Providing direct assistance to projects in the form of coaching/training, short-term manpower, or an injection of specialist skills.

A framework for program management

The use of a program management methodology is something of a rarity within many organizations. Compared to the number of books dealing with the subject of project management, there are relatively few books that discuss program management in adequate detail.

Equally, it is likely that large organizations, especially consultancy providers, will adopt their own, in-house approach to program management, which will remain behind closed doors. Other organizations may have no program management process in place whatsoever.

These situations do little to provide organizations with sufficient information to enable them to plan and manage an IS program. For this reason, therefore, I have built a simple four-stage model that can be used as a basis for program management. This is shown in Figure 6.3.

Stage 1: Establishing the program

This stage identifies the wider organizational framework that must exist before one or more programs can commence. It must also examine the impact of change and the benefits to be gained as a result of business change. Key activities within this stage include:

- examination of business plans and strategies to define benefits of change;
- selecting candidate projects for the program;

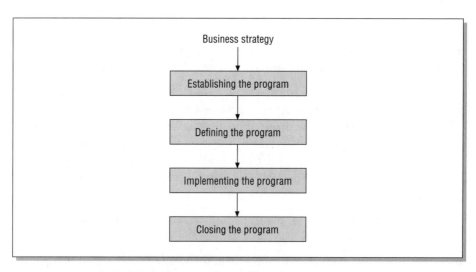

FIGURE 6.3 ■ A typical model for managing an IS program

- communication of the program grouping in support of the business case;
- appointment of the program manager.

Stage 2: Defining the program

Having established the need for the program, it is at this point that the program manager builds the controlling infrastructure from which to build the program. Key activities within this stage include:

- establish the governance for the program (rules, methods, procedures);
- communicate the program objectives to relevant stakeholders;
- develop the structure of the program;
- identify project interdependencies within the program;
- refine the business justification for the program;
- establish the benefits management process.

Stage 3: Implementing the program

This stage executes the program plans that were defined in the previous stage. It is within this phase that the projects within the program will be implemented. During this stage, feedback and control must be maintained through the use of regular checkpoints. These checkpoints must not only ensure alignment to strategic objectives, but also that benefits are being managed correctly. Key activities within this stage include:

- maintain communication channels;
- implement projects;
- ensure that business is prepared for change;
- manage benefits.

Stage 4: Closing the program

The final stage of the process examines the end-points of all plans, refining activities until all the planned benefits have been realized. Program management is likely to continue after implementation to assess the level of business change and to ensure that business benefits are met at an operational level. Key activities within this stage include:

- ensure that benefits are realized as fully as possible;
- refine the program where necessary;

- complete the benefits management process, identifying any follow-on benefits;
- ensure that lessons are learned;
- close the program down.

Risk management

An IS project, by its very nature, will contain some element of risk; this is not necessarily a bad thing, as a good project manager will see accepting and managing certain risks as an opportunity rather than a threat. Risks must be identified at all stages of a project and managed through the use of adequate risk management and risk reduction processes. Failure to adopt such processes will increase the probability that the project will not meet its specification or experience serious time/cost overruns.

The TAURUS project and the LAS computer-aided dispatch system failed through their inability to manage a number of potential risks which were identified during the project. For instance, the former adopted a particularly complex database design to try and appease the multitude of stakeholders who had a vested interest in the project, whilst the latter failed to involve key users in the development of a system which, when implemented, would dramatically change their working practices.

What is risk management?

Within an IS project, risk can be defined as any event that may jeopardize satisfying the objectives of the project. Risk management alone cannot eliminate risk altogether, but it can help avoid the risk or mitigate its impact in the event of it occurring. Risk management by definition must be a *proactive* process; assuming control of potential risks before they occur allows an agreed and disciplined response to be made to each risk.

Ignoring the risk management process condemns the project team to managing risks passively and reacting when each occurs. The management of risk throughout the lifecycle, if adhered to properly, can therefore provide a number of important benefits:

- visibility of business risks and technical risks for key stakeholders;
- the ability to concentrate resources into those areas where risks are high and to contain risks within reasonable limits;
- management of risks in a consistent and quantifiable way.

However, these benefits can only be achieved if the risk management process is performed continuously throughout the lifecycle of the project. For example, the judgement of risk should not only occur at the initiation stage of the project, but at every subsequent phase thereafter.

Risk management should also be used whenever the project team are faced with a choice of options within the project phase (such as design options following requirements capture). The selection process through which these options are adopted by the project should not be made solely on value judgements based on business and technical criteria, but should include an assessment of the risks each option poses.

The risk management process

Risk management is a process that must be introduced at the start of the project and continued until the project is completed or terminated. To ensure the acceptance and ownership of risks within the project, risk management must be included within the business case. Approval of the business case by the project sponsor is done in the knowledge of the stated risks, accepting the consequences of failing to manage known risks effectively.

For the risk management process to be effective, it requires the support of the project or program stakeholders. Effective communication throughout the risk management process is a key factor which will determine how well risks are identified and managed within the organization.

The risk management process, as shown in Figure 6.4, typically comprises six key stages, three of which comprise risk analysis, the remainder risk management.

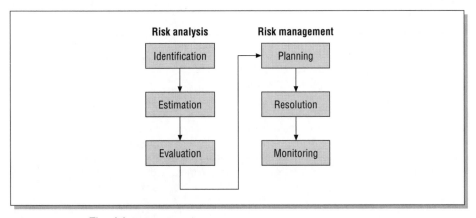

FIGURE 6.4 ▇ The risk management process

Risk analysis

Stage 1: identification

Risk identification is the most important aspect of risk management – risks that are not identified are the ones that pose the greatest threat to an IS project. All risks to the project should therefore be logged, and a popular method is to use the project risk register shown in Table 6.2 (the highlighted row denotes the risk with the greatest impact and highest probability of occurring). The results of the risk analysis process are documented in the risk register. If the project is part of a program, project risks should also be examined to assess their impact on the program. If any cross-impact is identified with another project, the risk should also be added to the other project's risk register.

Classification of risk

There are two main types of risk which can be identified for an IS project (or program).

TABLE 6.2 ■ The project risk register

Risk #	Description of risk and impact	Date raised	Probability of occurrence	Severity (1–10)	Risk category	Risk management	
						Action	By/when
1	Competitor may launch a new product at the same target market and reduce revenue by 30%.	22/02/02	Unlikely	7	Medium	Monitor competitor activity **Accept**	J. Smith
2	Contractor unable to supply sufficient resources during development phase. May delay project by 2 months.	10/01/02	Likely	3	Medium	Influence contractor Find alternative contractor Build contingency into schedule **Contingency plan**	P. Drew
3	Hardware may not be delivered in time to start testing. Contingency action will nullify this risk.	05/07/02	Likely	8	High	Contact account manager Build contingency into schedule **Reduction**	D. Kent 08/02
4	Order entry system will not be available at start of testing.	30/08/02	Almost certain	5	High	Use manual system to enter order data during testing **Reduction**	H. Small

■ **Project risk**

These risks are external to the IS project team and are associated with the project being able to deliver benefits into the organization. As business risks, they must be managed by the business sponsor or business risk manager, in conjunction with the project steering committee (if there is one). Business risks typically include:

■ leglislative activity;

■ actions of competitors;

■ the validity and viability of the business case;

■ market forces;

■ whether or not the project supports the organization's business and IT strategy;

■ political factors (public opinion, government interference);

■ The project delivering the stated requirements, but not fulfilling the customer's expectations.

■ **Project management risk**

These risks affect the ability to deliver the project within budgetary, schedule, and quality constraints. As project management risks, they are typically the responsibility of the project manager or the project risk manager and are managed on a day-to-day basis. The most common project management risks are likely to include the following:

■ People risks
  - Failure of supplier to deliver.
  - Business sector experience of supplier.
  - Inexperience of supplier development team.
  - Inexperience of project manager.
  - Inexperience of project team.
  - Contractual risks.
  - Availability of resources (such as failure to release individuals to join the project).
  - Lack of skills.
  - Relationship between customer and supplier.

■ Planning risks
  - Failure to specify all requirements.
  - Large project size.
  - Poor cost estimates.
  - Failure to specify accurate requirements.

 – Unrealistic or unachievable requirements.
 – Failure to test adequately.
 – Deliverables do not reach quality standards.

■ Technical risks
 – Development of a highly technical or complex solution.
 – Lack of technical expertise within the team.
 – Geographically dispersed development.
 – Use of leading-edge or immature technology.

Stage 2: estimation

As each risk identified has the potential to jeopardize the project, it is essential that a process is undertaken to assess how important each risk is. This process has two objectives: to assess the likelihood of the risk occurring; and to assess the severity of the impact on the project (and the business) if it occurs. A risk matrix as shown in Table 6.3 can be used to help determine the category of that risk (e.g. high, medium, or low).

Key techniques
Sensitivity analysis
Sensitivity analysis is often considered to be the simplest form of risk analysis. Essentially, it determines the effect on the project of changing one of its key variables or assumptions, such as the cost of resources or the expected profit

TABLE 6.3 ■ The project risk matrix

Severity of impact	Probability of event occurring			
	Very unlikely <10%	Unlikely 10%–50%	Likely 50%–90%	Almost certain >90%
Low (score 1–2) Minor impact on schedule, scope, and cost. No impact on benefits.	Low	Low	Low	Medium
Medium (score 3–5) Major impact on schedule, scope, and cost. Some impact on benefits.	Low	Medium	Medium	High
High (score 6–10) Major impact on schedule, scope, and cost. Major impact on benefits, project may no longer be viable.	Low	Medium	High	High

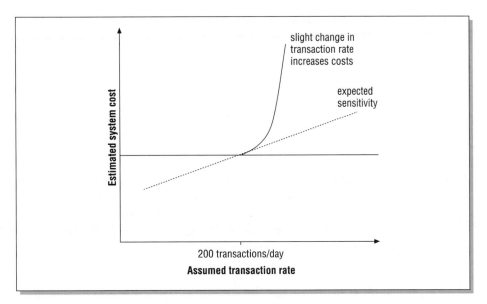

FIGURE 6.5 ▓ Using sensitivity analysis to test a key project assumption

margin. This technique is widely used within risk analysis as it quantifies how a single change to one variable can make a substantial difference to the outcome of the project.

From the example shown in Figure 6.5, the project is very sensitive, as measured against the estimated cost of the project, to a change in the assumed transaction rate of the system. In practice, sensitivity analysis is often used to test more than one variable; indeed it can be used for all identified risks in order to establish those which have a potentially high impact on the cost or timescale of the project.

Scenario analysis

Scenario analysis is a natural progression from sensitivity analysis as it identifies alternative outcomes for the project based on a number of assumptions. Like sensitivity analysis, scenario analysis often requires the project to be modeled so that it can accommodate multiple assumptions, e.g. fewer customers may not just lead to less revenue, but less cost of sales. Typically three scenarios must be modeled:

- pessimistic;

- most likely;

- optimistic.

TABLE 6.4 ■ Identifying the outcome of a project using scenario analysis

Variable	Pessimistic	Most likely	Optimistic
Development costs ($)	750,000	600,000	525,000
Delivery	3 months late	On time	On time
Payback	none	3 years	2 years

A pessimistic scenario may, for instance, assume a late delivery and cost over-run, with a slower customer usage and greater downward pressures on price. Table 6.4 shows a typical outcome of this type of risk analysis. As with sensitivity analysis, scenario analysis aims to provide decision-makers with a quantitive measure of the consequences of the project, enabling them to balance the expected benefits against the associated risks.

Monte Carlo simulation

Monte Carlo simulation is a form of probabilistic analysis that determines a probability distribution for each risk and then considers the effects of risks in combination. In essence, Monte Carlo simulation is a sampling technique that relies on the random calculation of values that fall within a specified probability distribution, often described by using three estimates: minimum (optimistic), mean (most likely), and maximum (pessimistic).

The overall outcome for the project is derived by the combination of values selected for each one of the risks. The calculation is repeated a number of times (usually between 100 and 1,000) to obtain the probability distribution of the project outcome. The diagram shown in Figure 6.6 highlights the probability distribution of finish dates for a hypothetical integration project.

Whilst the diagram is simplified from the source project data, the project that this was based on used 1,000 iterations of a Monte Carlo simulation. The actual finish date of this project was achieved within two days of the mean.

Stage 3: Evaluation

This process determines if the level of risk is acceptable or not to the project (remember, some risks may develop into opportunities). If the level of risk is not acceptable this process must help determine what actions must be taken to make it more acceptable, such as the following:

■ *Prevention*

The introduction of countermeasures which will either prevent the risk from happening or prevent it from having any impact.

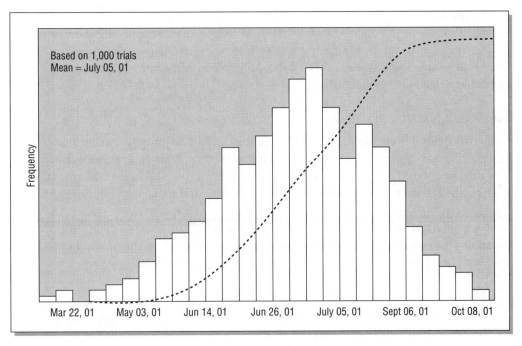

Based on 1,000 trials
Mean = July 05, 01

Frequency

Mar 22, 01   May 03, 01   Jun 14, 01   Jun 26, 01   July 05, 01   Sept 06, 01   Oct 08, 01

FIGURE 6.6 ▪ Finish date histogram for an IS integration project

■ *Reduction*

Actions taken to reduce the likelihood of the risk developing or reducing its impact to an acceptable level.

■ *Transference*

A special situation which manages the "removal" of the risk by transferring it to a third party. Insurance companies are an obvious example of such a process. However, there is a perception amongst many organizations that project risk can be mitigated by transferring the risk to a third party, such as an IT consultancy organization.

Project management risks can be managed in this way; for example, a consultancy organization taking losses for development overrun, but it will not often mitigate a *business risk*. Managing risk by providing a situation where a third party can be blamed if everything goes wrong is no way to run a project; working together to accept and manage risk is more beneficial in the long term.

■ *Contingency*

The instigation of a pre-determined procedure which comes into force when a risk occurs.

- *Acceptance*

A situation where the organization chooses to accept that the risk might occur and is prepared to accept the consequences. If this option has the full support of the project stakeholders, it may well develop into an opportunity which would not otherwise have been explored.

Risk management

Once risks have been identified and evaluated, attention must focus on controlling them. Fundamental to the risk management process is the concept of "laying tripwires." The purpose of this is two-fold: to give advanced warning that a risk is about to become an issue; and to monitor the risk reduction process applied to one or more risks, applying corrective action where necessary. In practice the tripwire is a quantitative risk factor which is set at a pre-determined level. Once in place, these tripwires must be monitored; when the quantitative risk factor exceeds an agreed threshold, contingency action must be taken.

Planning

For countermeasure actions identified during the evaluation phase, tne following planning activities should be performed:

- identify and quantify the resources needed to perform the activity;
- develop a detailed action plan;
- confirm that this is still an acceptable course of action in the light of any further information collected;
- obtain key stakeholder approval for the plan.

Resolution

Action should be taken for every risk identified within the project; the nature of that action being dependent of the category of risk that has been identified.

High risk

- Actively seek to eliminate the risk or reduce the risk.
- Actively monitor risk.
- Reassess the viability of the project before continuing further.
- Prepare a contingency plan if risk cannot be reduced and agree on the event trigger.

Medium risk

- Actively seek to eliminate the risk or reduce the risk.
- Actively monitor risk.

- Prepare a contingency plan if risk cannot be reduced and agree on the event trigger.

Low risk

- Try and eliminate the risk if cost-effective.
- Monitor risk – it may become more significant later.

Monitoring

The monitoring function within the risk management process is necessary to ensure that actions taken during the risk control process are actually happening in a way which will have the desired effect on the risk. Key activities performed within this process comprise:

- checking that planned actions are having the desired effect;
- monitoring risk early-warning systems (such as tripwires);
- modeling trends, predicting potential risks;
- reporting on the status of risk (identified from the risk log), especially on risks that have the greatest impact on the project.

Configuration management

To undertake an IS project without first establishing a process for managing project components from their development through to their retirement is likely to cause serious problems within the project. Advice given by some of the leading IT professional bodies cannot be more clear: do not engage on an IS project without first ensuring that there is a Configuration Management (CM) process in place.

Most, if not all, IS projects implement change within the organization through the development and implementation of a number of components. These represent the assets of the project, and it is the combined set of these assets that constitute the configuration.

What is configuration management?

Configuration management is the process of identifying and controlling, with the aid of change management, the assets or Configuration Items (CIs) that form the IT infrastructure for the project. Managing the status of each CI and its relationship to other CIs within the configuration will be a key function of a Configuration Management System (CMS).

Within a project, CIs are logically related and must be managed as a single entity. They may include, but are not restricted to: hardware, software (e.g. operating systems, bespoke software, packages, tools), documentation (e.g. project plans, functional specifications, test plans, requirements specifications, contracts) and data.

The primary objectives of CM are to ensure the ongoing integrity of project components, and to enable the management and security of their development and evolution. To achieve these objectives, the CM process must support the following fundamental principles:

- The configuration management team must be enpowered to make decisions and reduce bureaucracy.

- Configuration management tools and methods must not hinder development.

- Change will happen and must be managed.

- All changes must be reversible.

- Every product version or system environment must be capable of being recreated.

Configuration management should not be an optional process, and the large number of IS failures which are caused by a lack of CM processes should serve as a warning to any IS project manager. Large software development projects are particularly at risk, especially where concurrent and geographically dispersed development is undertaken, but no IS project should be undertaken without having a documented and agreed CM process.

The software Capability Maturity Model (see Chapter 9), identifies CM as a key factor in achieving software development excellence, but the reality is often much different. Configuration management is generally not understood sufficiently well within organizations, and is often regarded as an unnecessary and expensive development overhead. Indeed, studies of failed IS projects have shown that the omission of a CM process can have a detrimental effect on the success of the project.

Without a CM process, the likelihood that a serious problem will emerge somewhere within the project is high. As an example, the errors that may be discovered due to the lack of a CM process are likely to include:

- incompatibilities between software and hardware systems remaining unnoticed until testing;

- lack of source code control leading to lost changes and uncontrolled development;

- inability to audit IT development;

- inability to successfully back-out software releases;

- inability to easily and consistently assess the impact of IT change requests;

- inconsistent versions of software being used throughout the software development lifecycle;

- inability to control and co-ordinate concurrent development across multiple development teams.

The configuration management process

Configuration management, whether implemented through the use of a paper-based system or through the implementation of a software-based system, comprises five key functions.

Planning

The objective of the planning phase is to decide what level of configuration management needs to be implemented by the project and how this will be achieved. This is often the most difficult exercise that must be undertaken within the CM process.

The amount and formality of CM needed by the project depends on the type and size of the project and the environment in which the project is to be managed. Where practical, the more information that can be controlled, the better, as long as it does not place a burden on the members of the project team, especially development staff.

Configuration management exists to exercise proper control over all delivered products within an IS project and, as such, must be implemented as soon as the project starts. For projects using a rapid application development approach such as DSDM, the tight deadlines adopted within the project may not be sufficient to design and build a CM plan. In this case, existing procedures must be followed (such as problem management, incident management, version control, and change control).

Identification

Specifying and identifying all CIs to an appropriate level using an agreed naming convention.

Control

Once CM information has been introduced into the CMS, there must exist the capability to "freeze" CIs and control changes to them through an agreed authorization and approval process. CIs must be baselined and placed under formal release and version control. From the implementation of the CMS, the method used to access and modify the CI must be controlled throughout the lifecycle of the CI.

Status accounting

The recording and reporting of the current and historical status of each CI. May also include reference to planned changes for a CI.

Verification

The configuration must be verified through the use of configuration audits or reviews. There must be conformity between CI information within the configuration (such as description, specification, location, owner, serial number) and the physical state of the CI.

Introducing a configuration management system

Configuration management should be seen as a key activity that must be started as soon as formal approval for the project has been given. As with many support systems, CM can be introduced in three phases: preparation, implementation, and support.

Phase 1 – Preparation

Key tasks

- *Appoint configuration manager and team*
It is vital that every project (or program) assigns an individual who is responsible for, and owns, CM activities. Roles and responsibilities must be provided for every member of the team and, where necessary, training in CM techniques.

- *Define the scope and process*
The scope of the environment to be placed under the control of CM must be defined and agreed within the project. The initial key activity for the configuration manager is to determine the level at which CIs must be defined and at what point in the systems development lifecycle the CIs should be brought under CM control.

■ *Define and document the required features*

A comprehensive set of procedures must be produced to support the CM process; if no procedures exist they must be developed and documented. If procedures do exist, they must be reviewed and amended accordingly. In establishing the required procedures, an assessment should be made of the potential impact of any failure to properly manage the configuration. A balance must, therefore, be struck between these risks and the costs of implementing the CM processes.

As a minimum, procedures should be introduced to satisfy the following CM functions:

■ naming conventions for CIs;

■ access control for CIs;

■ issuing of CIs;

■ CM status reporting (definition, purpose, frequency, format);

■ incident and problem management;

■ change control.

■ *Select/build/install CM tools*

The requirements for the CMS must be identified and toolsets identified, evaluated, and selected. The CM tools must be installed and thoroughly tested before the CMS can be implemented. Most common CM tools are parameter-driven and the introduction of the tool into the project should be a straightforward process.

Phase 2 – Implementation

Key tasks

Training

All project members and third parties who will undertake, or have some interaction with, configuration management must understand their roles and responsibilities in the CM process. Appropriate individuals must be trained in the procedures and tools used.

Communication

The introduction and acceptance of the CM process within the project will be dependent upon how well the process is communicated to the relevant stakeholders. The communication of the CM strategy is a key role for the configuration manager and is vital in achieving the following aims:

■ emphasizing the importance and benefits of CM to both the business and IT stakeholders;

- gaining support from management and staff;

- outlining the timescales and phases for the introduction of CM;

- outlining individuals' roles and responsibilities.

In addition, the communication of the CM strategy must also raise awareness of the following related operational processes:

- change management;

- helpdesk support;

- incident and problem management;

- software control and distribution;

- network management;

- application development and support;

- IT operations;

- contingency planning;

- external suppliers and service providers.

Record the current configuration

The current configuration must be established by collecting all the necessary information about each CI within it and determining the relationships between them. To prevent integrity being compromised, this activity should be performed as quickly as possible, probably in a phased manner for discrete configurations. Configurations being baselined must be placed under change control immediately to ensure that CIs are not amended before capturing the configuration information and recording it within the CMS.

Implement the CM procedures

Once a baseline has been established, it must be considered to be under CM and change control. Any further changes to a CI must now be authorized and recorded as defined by the CM process.

Phase 3 – Support

Key tasks

Conduct configuration audits

Audits of the configuration management process must be performed regularly. It is recommended that an audit is performed a short time after the introduction of the CMS to ensure that procedures are working efficiently and effectively.

Benefits of configuration management

The implementation of an effective CM system can deliver the following benefits into an IS project:

■ Reducing development risk

IT systems are often most at risk at the point of change; if used correctly, CM can mitigate that risk. Typically, untested or incorrect versions of software are inadvertently released into a live system, often with disastrous consequences.

Through the use of status accounting it is possible to identify all changes (submitted as change requests) and corrected faults which have been applied to a specific CI. The lack of visibility of changes across a development team is one of the main reasons for CM-related software failures; the failure to identify all the components in a release is the other. This can be mitigated by baselining releases and subjecting them to strict access and change controls.

Equally, IS projects fail as a result of development staff being expected to cope with constantly changing requirements from business users. All requirements elicited during the project, even those high-level requirements identified during a feasibility study, should be introduced into the CM system and baselined as soon as possible. Communication of this CM information will ensure that all members of the project are aware of, and working towards, the same set of business requirements.

■ Control of software development environments

Development activities such as prototyping and testing often involve changes being made to a component by more than one person. It is necessary, therefore, to provide an environment which will control changes and prevent time being lost through conflicting activities. If prototyping or testing processes do not produce the expected results, there might be a need to return to a "safe" development environment of a known state before recommencing the planned processes.

■ Quantified impact analysis

It is not unknown for a system change that was originally perceived to be minor to have a catastrophic affect on the operation of the business. Configuration management allows impact analysis to be performed against any proposed changes. For instance, if a database field is changed, the development team and change approval bodies will be aware of what reports, programs, screens, and other project components will be affected as a consequence.

For this to happen, it is necessary for each database field to be recorded as a configuration item, even though the impact analysis is done at a database table level. As identified earlier during the CM planning activity, the level of granularity that is achieved within the CM system will determine the level of impact analysis that can be performed within the project; it must therefore be a project decision.

■ Supports key systems development processes

The implementation of a CMS within an organization can provide a fundamental platform to support key functions such as incident and problem management, release management, and risk management. By recording and tracking CI information, CM, in conjunction with change control, can be used to ensure that

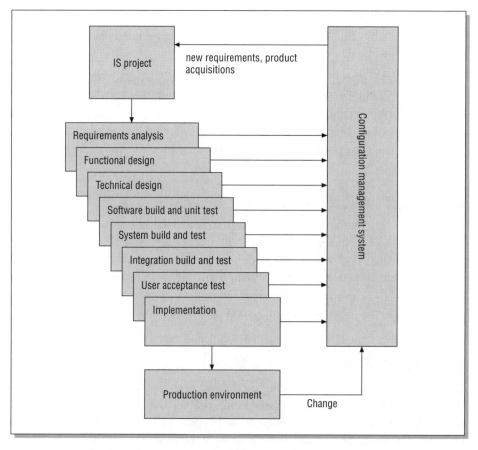

FIGURE 6.7 ■ Configuration management within the traditional approach to systems development

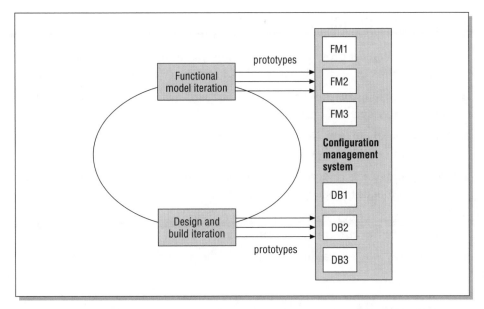

FIGURE 6.8 ▓ Configuration management within the iterative approach to systems development

changes made through the resolution of an incident or a problem are managed properly and released into the live environment in a controlled and co-ordinated manner.

To be effective, it important that the CMS supports every stage of the systems development lifecycle. Regardless of whether or not the system development methodology used supports the "traditional" model of systems development (Figure 6.7) or a model based on an iterative model designed for rapid application development (Figure 6.8), configuration management processes can be adopted.

■ Quality assurance mechanism

The CMS must contain the standards and acceptance criteria for all hardware and software which is to be used within the project. Only software that has been formally approved as having passed the appropriate quality checks should be accepted by the configuration manager into the CMS. To ensure compatibility when introducing externally purchased hardware and software with CIs in the existing configuration (excluding consumable items such as printer ribbons and paper), configuration status information such as version number and revision level can be used.

Processes: critical success factors

- Even the smallest project can benefit from planning – use a project plan to gain stakeholder ownership as well as to track activities through the project.

- Program management is essential if standards are to be maintained across related and dependent projects.

- Ensure that there is a clear and defined means of communication throughout an IS program.

- Do not attempt to undertake any project activity without first ensuring that there is a means to manage version control.

- Identifying project risks is a worthless activity unless they are managed throughout the duration of the project.

- Always review the viability of the project against the project risk register.

Further reading

N. M. Bounds and S. Dart, *CM Plans: The Beginning to your CM Solution*, Carnegie Mellon Software Engineering Institute, Pittsburgh, 1998 www.sei.cmu.edu/legacy/scm/abstracts/abscm_plans.html

CCTA (The Stationery Office), *Managing Successful Projects with PRINCE2*, 1996

ISO, *Quality Management – Guidelines for Configuration Management*, ISO, 10007:1995 www.sfs.fi/standard/scope10007.pdf (accessed 2002)

B. Ventimiglia, (1998) *'Effective software configuration management'*, *Crosstalk*, www.stsc.hill.af.mil/crosstalk/1998/feb/effectivecm.asp

7

Planning the benefits

Vorsprung durch Technik (Progress through technology)

Audi motors (advertising slogan, from 1986)

Obtaining some form of benefit, whether financial, economic or otherwise, from business investment is the sole reason for undertaking an IS project. If no benefits can be identified either prior to investment or from subsequent investments, the project should be abandoned. Activities such as project management will undoubtedly play a crucial role in meeting delivery targets but, ultimately, it is the realization of expected (and unexpected) benefits within the business that will determine project success.

In a climate of increasing business complexity and dynamism, IS project success can only be achieved by evaluating the benefits that can be expected from the investment in IT solutions. Before spending money on a project, it is first necessary to consider whether the benefits from the implementation of the project are likely to outweigh the costs of obtaining them.

Recent history suggests that without careful planning, IS projects do not deliver their expected benefits in the mechanical way expected by many stakeholders. Clearly, there is a sound case for investment appraisal.

- IS projects are very expensive, thus inviting rigorous evaluation.

- Computer systems require investment now to generate profits in the future.

- IT resources are typically scarce. Whilst hardware and capital may be available, software and managerial skills are likely to be in short supply. Priorities must be established to ensure that resource costs are directly linked to meeting business objectives.

- Organizations need to establish a level of confidence in the viability of IS projects before committing funds.

- The process of investment appraisal must be visible and auditable within the organization.

- IS projects may require significant changes within the business for them to deliver expected benefits. Investment appraisal will establish executive support and commitment from business sponsors.

- Evaluation techniques (such as payback period and cost/benefit analysis) provide a useful basis for project planning and control.

- Ongoing investment appraisal provides project managers and sponsors with the information required to make critical decisions regarding the feasibility of the project.

In order for project fundholders to assess accurately the total value of the project to the business (and therefore, be in a position to release funding if necessary), the investment appraisal process must seek to answer the following questions.

- What are the current operating costs of the existing system?

- What will it cost to operate the proposed system?

- What will it cost to develop the proposed system?

- What savings can be made from the proposed system?

- What other benefits can be realized from the proposed system?

- What will the new system's economic life be?

- What will the value of the system be at the end of its economic life?

Why do IS projects fail to deliver benefits?

■ The "automatic results" syndrome

From the number of IS projects that continue to fail around the world there must be little doubt that organizations adopting a "silver bullet" approach to IS project delivery are unlikely to achieve success. A contributory factor to this must be the misguided perception that IS projects automatically deliver business benefits. From an IT perspective, this perception is reinforced by business wrongly placing the emphasis on the implementation of a software-based system rather than on the realization of business benefits.

According to a KPMG survey,[1] 75 per cent of organizations do not know whether or not they have achieved all of the benefits claimed whilst implementing new software packages. Despite this, 89 per cent of respondents claimed their projects were either "successful" or "highly successful."

The survey for the "Profit-Focused Software Package Implementation" report was conducted using 51 organizations across a range of industry sectors. Each organization agreed to nominate one project for the survey, and the results captured suggest many organizations either achieve little or no benefits from IS investments, or do not have the processes in place to identify the benefits obtained in the first place. For instance, only 26 per cent of respondents believed benefits had been obtained and 15 per cent of respondents claimed benefits had only been "partially obtained."

■ Lack of any formal benefits management process

Such is the lack of appreciation for the need to evaluate IS investments that in a survey of 60 major organizations,[2] only 10 per cent had defined a formal process to manage the benefits on which IS investments were justified. The methods adopted by many organizations to evaluate investment in IS are notoriously inconsistent and there is little consensus of opinion as to what investment appraisal techniques should be used.

■ Assumption that benefits remain static

Benefit management, if done at all, is often only undertaken in the "post-mortem" stage of the project. Post-implementation reviews are, indeed, an opportunity for the benefits delivered by the project to be reviewed against the benefits expected from it, but they should also represent an opportunity to identify new benefits that may have surfaced throughout the project.

Identifying benefits within the structure of a post-implementation review is a useful activity; however, several surveys have shown that nearly 70 per cent of organizations have no formal justification and post-implementation review process for IS investments.

Throughout the life of an information system, the benefits realized from the project will change. Some of the original benefits stated may not occur for reasons beyond the control of the organization. Equally, additional benefits, which were not originally expected, may be identified later. Accepting the principle that benefits may change over time reinforces the need for a benefits management system to be introduced within the organization to identify and track benefits.

■ Failure to accept change may be necessary

The implementation of an IT solution is often seen as a panacea to rectify the problems experienced within the organization. As a consequence, senior management and business stakeholders often fail to understand the need to initiate change within the organization in order to realize benefits from their investment. For example, the successful implementation of an IS project may well depend on the restructuring of business units and the management structure within the organization.

■ Lack of training and education

Training and education on new systems is often performed as a minor project activity, peripheral to more important tasks, such as systems development and testing. Consequently, investment in training and education is often low and the quality of training received is poor.

Clearly, there is a risk that the investment made in an IS project will fail to return a benefit on that investment simply because training and education in new systems and processes has been inadequate. Poor training leads to mistakes being made; and as we should all know (some, I suspect, from bitter experience), mistakes cost money.

■ Implementing the project at the wrong time

Such is the expectation that a new system must be better than the existing system that there is often very little thought given to how well the system will perform within the environment where it is to be deployed. It is unfortunate then, that many IS projects are implemented when the organization is almost at breaking point. This is most likely to be as a result of the high levels of workload combined with inadequate levels of resources within the organization (which is why the new system is being introduced in the first place).

Ironically, many IS projects are implemented with high expectations for radical improvement or innovative change, but with little investment in preparation. Implementing an IS project when existing business processes are either ineffective or inefficient, or both, has a significant impact on the ability of the project to achieve the desired benefits.

In an ideal world, an IS project would only be implemented when the business is running smoothly and there is no pressure to implement a "quick and dirty" solution. Few organizations, however, are far-sighted enough or prepared to approve an IS investment that not does satisfy an immediate crisis.

■ Pressure on project managers to deliver projects on time and within budget rather than concentrating on delivering benefits into the organization

Within many organizations, project success is measured solely in terms of meeting schedule and budget constraints. It is almost laughable then, that such organizations often take the point further and declare their IS project a roaring success purely because the project was implemented *ahead* of schedule.

Of course, a project that can deliver "early winners" into the business is certainly worthy of praise, but simply delivering a project ahead of schedule is no guarantee whatsoever that the benefits expected from it will ever be achieved.

If there is no clear responsibility on an individual to deliver the benefits claimed at the start of the project, it is likely that the issue will be forgotten once the system has been implemented. That is, until the organization performs an audit of its projects and realizes that very few projects, if any, have actually delivered any measurable benefits.

In a perfect world, every IS project would include a benefits manager on the team to ensure that benefits are managed and, ultimately, realized. Alternatively, the role should be performed by another member of the team in conjunction with their own role. What is not acceptable, however, is for the role, and the responsibilities that go with it, to be omitted from the project team.

■ Over-optimistic claims made within the business case

It has been suggested by many business and finance executives that business cases placed before them are, at best, exaggerated in terms of their benefit to the organization and, at worst, a worthless piece of fiction. As an example, within one company, it became apparent that many of the business cases submitted for approval identified "revenue protection" as a key benefit; which would have been perfectly acceptable had the amount of revenue actually protected not exceeded the total revenue for the company.

Too many business cases rely on the comparison of dubious financial benefits against grossly underestimated costs. Over-optimistic claims on the savings that can be achieved, for example, in staff costs are often blindly accepted without close scrutiny of the figures presented. Equally, projects are notorious for costing more than was originally budgeted for.

■ *Basing benefits measurement on technical achievement rather than business achievement*

Obtaining measures that are solely based on IT concepts, such as "zero defects" and Mean Time Before Failure (MTBF) are of little use in measuring business benefits. Throughout the life of the project, focus must be placed on the achievement of business benefits through the effective deployment of IT.

Measuring the success of a technical implementation in isolation from how that benefit manifests itself in business terms should send warning signals to project sponsors that the project is technology-driven and not business-driven.

Establishing an SLA between the business and IT departments goes a long way towards ensuring that business benefits are protected throughout the life of the IS investment, but it must be properly planned and executed to be of any real use.

It is the purpose of an SLA to guarantee an agreed level of service for the users' business system; the requirements that will establish this agreement are typically the non-functional requirements that are collected during the requirements analysis stage of the project.

The nature of IS investments

IS projects can only deliver benefits if there is a firm understanding of what is required from the project. Once business objectives and success criteria have been established, benefits can be tracked and measured against them. However, conventional methods of investment appraisal have concentrated on purely financial techniques such as payback period and cost/benefit analysis.

Contemporary IS projects are no longer simply a means to automate manually-intensive operations, which can be evaluated purely in financial terms; IS projects seek to improve quality of service and gain competitive advantage – benefits which are much harder to evaluate. The unease with conventional methods is often reflected by the circumvention of appraisal procedures and business case justification in order to obtain project approval.

Without a clear understanding of investment appraisal techniques it is hardly surprising, therefore, to discover that for many IS projects, the identification of benefits is postponed until the post-implementation review stage.

Company Y

Facing an increased number of user-reported fault calls to their main IT helpdesk, a transit company decided to improve the reporting of service-affecting calls by the introduction of system and network management software. Proactive system management combined with automated trouble ticket creation are widely acknowledged as capable of delivering organizational benefits, such as improving customer service and maintaining customer loyalty, and there are many examples of successful projects in this area throughout the world.

The company identified the potential benefits of the project early on in the planning stages and, following a series of vendor presentations, the project team selected a suitable software package. Planning went well in the early stages of the project: a new PC was purchased for the helpdesk area and a small number of "super-users" were sent on training courses on the vendor's premises. In addition, the company paid for the vendor to customize the software to allow it to monitor the key servers and databases that supported the organization's "mission-critical" applications.

Whilst the technical specification of the system was impressive, over the next 12 months, the system was to be used less and less, eventually lying idle within the helpdesk area. The fundamental reason why the project failed to deliver any benefit to the organization was simple: the organization naturally assumed the software package (it was one of the leading helpdesk and system management tools on the market at the time) would start to, and continue to provide benefits from the minute it was implemented. At no time during the project did the organization attempt to review its existing helpdesk and system monitoring procedures to ensure that the tool would be used effectively.

The warning signs were there but went unheeded – after six months, the software consultant who had performed the initial configuration of the software returned to review the implementation as part of their support agreement.

Despite the massive changes to the IT and helpdesk infrastructure that had occurred within the organization since the system had been implemented, it became clear to the consultant that the configuration of the software had never been reviewed and amended since its installation. In his report to the management, the consultant noted that the initial configuration, in the absence of usable system metrics, was very much a "best guess" and that it should be reviewed and amended at regular intervals. The software worked on the basis of monitoring key hardware and software components and alerting helpdesk staff when specific threshold settings (such as filesystem size or database table size) were exceeded.

The consultant also noted that the helpdesk staff did not appear to use the new system. The reasons for this would soon become clear: the two super-users had left the company some weeks earlier and no one else knew how to use the system. Given the fact that the existing helpdesk staff did not even know a valid password to access the system, it was hardly surprising to discover that there was little enthusiasm for using it. Surprisingly, the helpdesk manager did nothing to encourage the use of the system within the helpdesk, despite making many of the claims for the benefits it would bring in the original business proposal.

A key factor in the failure of this project was the fact that there was a noticeable lack of commitment and involvement from business stakeholders. Indeed, the selection, installation and configuration of the software was undertaken in total isolation of the individuals who were to benefit most from it. The only time the helpdesk staff were involved in the project was when two of their team were trained in the application by the vendor.

As this project was not the only one within the organization that failed to deliver the benefits originally identified within its business case, it is surprising, therefore, to learn that the company never once conducted any form of benefits appraisal.

This case study should be of interest to many IS and business managers, as it highlights the need for benefits to be managed regardless of the size of the IS project. Software package implementation is probably the most common feature of many IS projects throughout the world and this case study should act as a lesson to us all.

Building the benefits – the benefits management process

It is the objective of investment appraisal to determine whether or not resources and finance should be committed to undertake an IS project. This is typically performed by examining the advantages such investment will bring to the organization and comparing them against the likely costs and problems associated with that investment. Identifying benefits from IS investment is by no means an easy task. Investment decisions should not be focused solely on the need to "balance the books;" they should also identify the ways in which *value can be added* through the leverage of IT.

Traditionally, benefits arising from the implementation of information systems have been stated purely in financial terms; for instance, development costs are fairly simple to estimate, based on manpower costs and equipment costs. Whilst there are many other ways to express benefits, stating them in financial terms, however, does allow direct comparisons to be made against costs.

A survey conducted by the consultancy group DMR during 1995–6 suggested that the concept of "benefits management" is unfamiliar to many organizations[3,4]. From the interviews undertaken as part of the survey, some of these organizations revealed a startling insight into corporate investment appraisal processes.

■ Investment projects are usually proposed by business champions who emerge informally; there is no formal process to identify new investment opportunities.

■ A cost/benefit analysis is performed; often in support of a business case.

- Benefits are defined primarily in terms of financial and economic returns.

- Once projects have been approved, the project management process gives priority to delivering projects on time and within budget.

Many successful organizations have realized the need to adopt methodologies to govern project management and systems development activities within an IS project. However, what is lacking in many of these organizations is the need to establish a *benefits management methodology*.

Whilst the objectives of project management and systems development methodologies are primarily focused on product delivery, the main objective of a benefits management methodology is to identify and realize the benefits that can be obtained from the delivery of these products and services into the organization.

A key assumption in realizing the benefits from an IS project is that the project itself is delivered to specification. The organization's business drivers are reflected in the business objectives for the project and, ultimately, the project specification. That is not to say, however, that the specification may not change. Benefits management should be a key force in driving change within the organization in order to achieve the expected benefits, but also to achieve the *unexpected benefits* that may have surfaced since implementation.

The only way, therefore, to ensure benefits are realized through an IS project is to align the project management, systems development and benefits management methodologies within the organization (Figure 7.1). Only through the

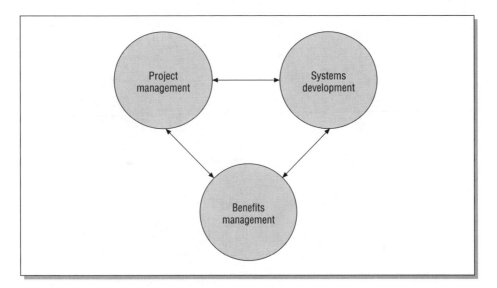

FIGURE 7.1 ▓ Aligning methodologies to manage benefits

integration of a number of tightly-coupled processes can the process of change be managed sufficiently well to ensure that systems are delivered on time and within budget, but they also deliver the benefits that are expected from them.

The benefits management lifecycle

A benefits management methodology is used to identify the potential benefits that can be realized from the project and to ensure that the activities necessary to achieve these are planned and reviewed throughout the project. Fundamental to the success of this methodology is the need to perform a number of major activities to support the benefits management process. These activities are collectively known as the benefits management lifecycle (Figure 7.2).

Identifying the benefits

During the initial investigation stage the reasons for investing in the project must be identified, regardless of whether the project will deliver a new system or amend an existing one. It is at this stage that the nature of the IS project will, to some extent, determine the type of benefits that can be realized (Table 7.1). Care

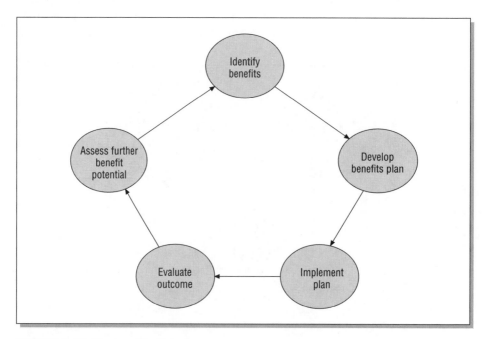

FIGURE 7.2 ■ The benefits lifecycle

TABLE 7.1 ▨ Categories of IT projects and benefits

IS project	Category of benefit	Business objective
Strategic	Business innovation or change Competitiveness	Work smarter Move into new markets
Operational	Effectiveness	Improve quality Improve service
Support	Efficiency	Save money Reduce headcount

should be taken, however, if the investment addresses a particular measure or indicator that does not support the primary objectives of the project.

If the benefits, or how to obtain them, are not clear at this stage, work must be undertaken until they are known. The identification of benefits must be closely aligned to the business objectives; each benefit must, therefore, be tested against the business objectives and critical success factors to determine its relevance.

Tangible benefits

Tangible benefits are those which can be stated in quantitative terms. A tangible benefit therefore is one that can be measured, even though it may be expressed in financial or non-financial terms.

■ Financial benefits describe business objectives in terms of revenue, contribution, profit enhancement, and cost reduction. Reductions in staff headcount as a result of automation can be measured directly through the use of financial techniques such as cost/benefit analysis.

■ Non-financial benefits describe the *value* to the organization that is directly attributable to the project, but which cannot be expressed in financial terms. These benefits are still tangible and measurable and represent business objectives such as:

- increases in operational performance measures;
- increases in process performance measures;
- increases in customer satisfaction measures;
- increases in key performance indicators.

Intangible benefits

Intangible benefits are those which are difficult to measure in a disciplined and formal way. Whilst their value to the business is often difficult to quantify, they still represent an important and often necessary return on an IS investment, such as:

- greater flexibility to respond to market forces;
- improved corporate information;
- improved operational control;
- improved customer service;
- improved use of assets;
- better control of corporate resources;
- enhanced corporate planning;
- better quality management decision-making;
- faster decision-making.

Forecasting benefits

An initial estimate of the benefits and costs of the project must be prepared during the initial stages of the benefits management plan. As the plan develops during the feasibility stage of the project, these estimates must be turned into firm forecasts and agreed with the project sponsor. Forecasts are an important and necessary feature of the benefits management process for two main reasons: they enable the project to be evaluated against other IS projects or investments; they provide information against which the post-launch performance can be measured.

Tips for forecasting benefits include:

- forecasts must be realistic;
- benefits must be matched by the costs of achieving them;
- benefits and costs must be based on the same assumptions;
- benefits and costs must be forecast for the worst case, optimum case, and the most likely outcome.

Developing the benefits management plan

A key part of the benefits management plan is to identify what tools and techniques will be needed to analyze benefits and what will be needed to deliver these benefits. A vital element of this activity will be the circumstances that must exist for benefits to be realized. It is likely that both business and IT changes will be needed and, therefore, it is important to identify the stakeholders whose support and consent will be needed.

If business change is necessary for the realization of benefits (such as restructuring of key business teams or functions) it will be important to consider its impact using techniques such as stakeholder analysis. System and physical changes (such as the need for new desks and PCs) are relatively simple to manage, especially with the help of specialist planning and training programs. Process and role changes, however, lie at the heart of the organization and are notoriously hard to manage and control.

If the organization is expecting to gain benefits from IS investment through the use of innovative methodologies, such as iterative and joint application development, significant changes to individual and team roles will be needed, as will changes to the systems development lifecycle within the organization. Clearly, training and education will be fundamental to supporting significant levels of change within the organization.

Sponsorship at the most senior level within the organization is vital to ensure that all parties are committed to ensuring the project will be a success – however that success is defined. If people are truly committed to the project, they will be more flexible about accepting a short-term disruption in the knowledge that it will reap rewards in the future. Every aspect of the new system must, therefore, have a business justification.

Managing change will be a key part of the benefits management plan. Unless there is a clear advantage to be gained through the implementation of the project, business users will resist the change and fail to support it, thus reducing far-reaching strategic projects to little more than minor operational enhancements.

Not only is it important to persuade people to accept change, they must be persuaded to support the change and be an active participant throughout the whole change process. Business users clearly have a right to know "what's in it for me?;" the benefits management process provides answers to that question.

No benefits plan is complete without at least an interim method for establishing the measures by which the benefit management process can be evaluated. It is at this point that some understanding of the term "success" must be identified; conditions of satisfaction is one popular approach. Despite difficulties in measuring benefits, every IS project should have an agreed and identifiable method for determining whether or not the project has been a success. Conditions of satisfaction are, therefore, a vital component to the benefits management plan as they represent the conditions which, if met, will enable the project to be declared a success. They need to be chosen such that they are indicative of meeting the expected project benefits. For example, they may relate to a reduction in faults or an increase in orders at a defined point in time.

Executing the benefits plan

Planning and control form a key component with project management methodologies and systems development methodologies; the same is true for the benefits management process. Monitoring the progress of the benefits plan is a vital activity that must be performed in conjunction with project management and systems development planning activities.

Many IS projects fail because there is no individual within the organization who is responsible for ensuring that benefits claimed at the start of the project are realized throughout the life of the project. It is vital that a benefits manager is appointed to the project as early as possible to ensure that importance is placed on achieving benefits as much as an achieving technical excellence and on-time project delivery.

The benefits manager and the project manager must therefore co-ordinate their activities by reviewing their respective plans to identify any issues which might affect the delivery of benefits throughout the project (unless, of course, these roles are being performed by the same individual).

Evaluating the outcome

Just as a post-implementation review must be performed once an IS project has been implemented, so too must a similar exercise be performed once the benefits plan has been implemented. The review must identify what benefits have and have not been achieved as a result of the investment. It is at this stage in the benefits lifecycle that the benefits achieved can be compared against the benefits forecast during the initial stages of the project. Reviewing the outcome of the benefits plan is a vital part of the benefits lifecycle in order to ensure that lessons learned from the investment are made available to the rest of the organization.

Stakeholder involvement in the review is important, as they must help identify what has been achieved by the business. If benefits have not been achieved they must help determine the cause and possible remedial action. One possible outcome might be to review quality procedures or systems development procedures.

Determining the potential for future benefits

The nature of IS projects is often such that it is impossible to predict all the possible benefits that may be achieved from a particular investment. Some benefits may only become apparent after the triggering of certain business events, such as strategic or operational change or simply through the passing of time.

Determining the potential for future benefits provides a means of identifying future benefits and the events that must happen to trigger those benefits. If and when such events occur (such as the acquisition of a competitor, or a change in customer attitudes), it is important to review once more what further benefits may arise.

Techniques for investment appraisal

A key requirement to realizing benefits from IS investment is the need for all benefits claimed to be measured effectively – not necessarily purely in financial terms (such as cost/benefit analysis and discounted cash flow), but measured nonetheless.

The cost/benefit analysis performed within the TAURUS project for instance, predicted that direct cost savings of £255 million ($382 million) could be achieved, with additional benefits coming in the form of risk reduction in the trading process. Intangible benefits were predicted as a result of the simplification of trading processes and the increased confidence in the UK market by overseas investors.

Sensitivity analysis is, in contrast, a non-financial technique that can be used to assess the risk of the investment by speculating upon the risks if some of the assumptions behind the benefits' forecasts are ill-founded.

Competitive forces analysis,* however, whilst not used to directly measure the benefits from IS investment, is nonetheless a useful exercise to undertake prior to IS project initiation. It works on the principle that within any organization, a number of forces exist that will affect its survival and performance. By considering each force in turn, it is possible to identify ways in which IS can assist in meeting the challenge presented by the force.

A brief overview of the more popular techniques for both financial and non-financial appraisal is discussed in Tables 7.2–7.5. These appraisal techniques, however, should only be seen as an introduction into a much larger and complex world of financial and non-financial investment appraisal which is, unfortunately, out of the scope of this book. There are luckily many good books on the subject of investment appraisal techniques and a few of my particular favorites appear at the end of the chapter.

* Based on M.E. Porter, *Competitive Strategy*[5]

TABLE 7.2 ■ The use of competitive forces analysis within an IS project

Competitive force	Implication	IS project value
Threat of new entrants	■ Additional capacity ■ Reduces prices	Create barriers to entry by building systems to control distribution channels or sources of supply
Supplier power	■ Raises costs ■ Lowers quality ■ Reduces availability	Change balance of power by building supplier multi-sourcing systems or integrating with the supplier's production systems
Customer power	■ Reduces prices ■ Raises quality ■ Greater flexibility	Increase switching costs for customer by integrating with customer's purchasing systems
Threat of substitutes	■ Price ceilings ■ Limits growth	Limit impact by cost reducing systems or use IS to support new products/markets
Extent of competitive rivalry	■ Price competition ■ Differentiate product ■ Build brand loyalty	Limit impact by cost reducing systems or use IS to add value to existing products and services

TABLE 7.3 ■ Techniques for assessing investment returns

Analysing return	Used for	Limitations	Example
Profitability analysis	Financial return of investment	■ Applies to discrete projects ■ Only suitable for measuring tangible benefits	■ Return On Capital Employed (ROCE) ■ Payback period ■ Discounted cash flow ■ Internal rate of return (IRR)
Cost/benefit analysis	■ Placing a monetary value on the cost of developing and running an IT solution and on the benefits that result from its operation ■ Traditionally used to measure tangible benefits only, but now considered as useful for measuring non-tangible benefits	Difficulties in quantifying benefits	Cost of tangible benefits = $750,000 Cost of intangible benefits = $375,000 Development costs = $300,000 Support costs = $320,000 per year Expected life of system = 10 years

TABLE 7.4 ▨ Techniques for assessing investment risks

Analysing risk	Used for	Limitations	Example
Financial-ratio projection	■ Provides a detailed view of the resources a company can measure in financial terms to assess profitability ■ Can help determine the robustness of an IS/IT strategy	Calculation of financial ration has no value in itself; it is the implications of the analysis that are important	Break-even analysis e.g. is funding available to provide the skills and equipment needed?
Sensitivity analysis	Assess project viability by testing key assumptions. Helps balance benefits against risks	Results dependent on the assumption identified and their respective values	Success of investment may be sensitive to increases in production costs
Scenario analysis	Models alternative futures for the project. Helps balance benefits against risks	Results dependent on the assumption identified and their respective values	A pessimistic outcome assumes a cost and schedule run of 30 per cent

TABLE 7.5 ▨ Techniques for assessing business effectiveness

Analysing objectives	Used for	Limitations	Example
Business objectives analysis	Assessing significance of intangible benefits	Subjective approach to measuring benefit	
Competitive forces analysis	Understanding the competitive environment of the organization in order to determine where (IS) emphasis should be placed	Developed as a framework for strategic analysis	The threat of competitors offering your customers a substitute product in a shorter timescale

▰▻ Benefits management: critical success factors

- Define "success" at the beginning of the project.
- Identify and quantify the planned benefits, and the means by which they will be tracked.
- Design the project to seek the optimum trade-off between costs, benefits, timescales, and risks.
- Only consider the project to be complete when the planned benefits are obtained rather than when the system goes "live."
- Always measure benefits against a known baseline.

- Make benefits tangible wherever possible.

- Place benefits in the wider business context.

- Acknowledge any "disbenefits" that may occur from the project; an unwanted side-effect may jeopardize future benefits.

- Ensure that all IT and business users receive appropriate training and education.

- Appraise all areas of the business on the impact of IT.

- Prepare the organization mentally and physically for change.

- Once a budget has been agreed, baseline it and forecast benefits and costs regularly.

References

1 *75% of Organizations Fail to Benefit from Software Packages* (1997), KPMG Press Office www.kprng.co.uk/services/manage/press/970729a.html (accessed 1999)

2 J.M. Ward, P. Taylor and P. Bond, "Identification, realisation and measurement of IS/IT benefits – an empirical study of current practice," in *Proceedings of the 2nd European Conference on IT Evaluation*, Henley, July, 1995

3 *Investing with Benefits in Mind* (1999), DMR Consulting Group Inc., www.dmr.com

4 J. Thorp and M. Poehner, *The Information Paradox: Realizing the Business Benefits of Information Technology*, McGraw-Hill, New York, 1999

5 M.E. Porter, *Competitive Strategy*: *Techniques for Analyzing Industries and Competitors*, Free Press, New York, 1980

Further reading

G. Johnson and K. Scholes, *Exploring Corporate Strategy*, sixth edition, Prentice Hall Europe, Harlow, 2002

J.A. Tracey, *The Fast Forward MBA in Finance*, Wiley, New York, 1996

 Part III

Design and development

It's not a bug, it's a feature

A popular adage used sarcastically to describe imperfections within an information system that do not want to be discussed.

8

Project building blocks: people

Most IS projects fail not because of technical failure, but because the people who have a vested interest in the new systems are not sufficiently involved, do not take ownership and do not contribute to the design

David Yardley

Contemporary information systems require a combination of hardware and software components in order to provide solutions that will satisfy important business objectives. It would not be unreasonable, therefore, to conclude that the success of an IS project is primarily focused upon the effective construction and deployment of technology. Indeed, the common perception held within many organizations is precisely that – the success of the *technical* aspects of the project determines the success of the project as a whole.

Considering the high incidence of project failure, even in organizations that deploy mature and proven technologies, it is evident that some of the major causes of project failure must reside in other areas within the organization, *outside* the immediate scope of IT.

Contrary to popular opinion that the success of an IS project is solely dependent upon the satisfactory completion of a technical objective, the management of people is by far one of the most important factors which will ultimately determine project success. Whilst a successful project may not necessarily be dependent upon the use of information technology, it is, however, heavily dependent upon people.

Underlying the IT industry is the science of computing. With this scientific knowledge, IT hardware and software products can be built that will process data in a specific and controlled way. Issues relating to the design, construction, and performance of these products can, therefore, be classed as "hard" issues; the problem can be stated scientifically, as can the answer. Conversely, those issues that are based not on the technology itself, but on how that technology is used to satisfy a particular need, can be classed as "soft."

In comparison, it is the hard issues that are most easily resolved within an IS project. Technical problems can be quantified and stated clearly without ambiguity, and can be resolved with the use of formal techniques, such as logic-based reasoning and mathematical computation. Soft issues, however, such as the social, organizational, and psychological aspects influencing the use of IT, cannot be resolved in the same way and pose a significant challenge for organizations undertaking IS projects.

Effective decision-making is fundamental to the success of an IS project and yet, historically, it has been an area in which business and project managers are often weak. In situations where status quo behavior within the project is compromised by internal or external events, our capacity to make good decisions is impaired. Behind every decision made lies the incentive and motivation of the decision-maker, and it is likely that any decision to adopt a specific course of action will be influenced by personal goals, financial pressures, commercial pressures, and peer-group pressures.

Clearly the behavior and motivation of people represents a significant factor in determining project success. In many of the case studies within this book, the behavior of stakeholders within the project organization has been a major cause of project failure. The LAS and TAURUS case studies in particular, clearly demonstrate that, despite the presence of significant technical problems, the events that were to bring about the failure of both projects were largely due to the failure of senior management and other key stakeholders.

IS projects are hugely dependent upon the skills and abilities of the project team, so it is somewhat surprising to discover that many project management courses and books fail to cover the subject adequately, preferring to concentrate on the "science" of planning such as task management and critical path analysis.

Project management and systems development methodologies undoubtedly provide a number of clear benefits to the project if used effectively. However, they can be responsible for introducing many risks into the project if they do not accommodate the roles, behaviors, and attitudes of those involved in the project team and the organization.

IS methodologies can never provide all the answers to organizational problems and should never be adopted without first ensuring that their weaknesses are documented and understood. If there is one weakness that the majority of IS methodologies suffer from, it is the fact that they make some dangerous assumptions regarding the behavior of individuals and groups within the project, such as:

- we all operate within a perfect world with access to perfect information;

- everyone within the organization puts group goals ahead of personal goals;

- we all share the same vision;

- we all like each other;

- we can manage our differences in a positive climate of openness and honesty;

- everyone has the appropriate skills, training, and professionalism to perform their job well;

- everyone can communicate effectively within the project;

- we share information with our subordinates, peers, and superiors;

- we all respect each other's opinion;

- we all feel empowered to disagree with decisions made by our superiors;

- we all tell the truth;

- we all behave ethically.

The human element of IS project failure

Organizational culture

■ Business and IT integration

Despite the external image of many organizations being one of partnership and synergy, the reality can be much different. Rather than having a balanced structure, with organizational functions having equal priority, it is well-known within many organizations that certain business areas command a higher status than others – an "unwritten hierarchy" in other words.

The IT function within many organizations is often seen as providing little value in comparison with other functions that directly generate revenue and profits. As a consequence, there has been little board-level representation of IT historically, and it is only recently that many organizations have decided to appoint IT directors onto the main board. Whilst this is a step in the right direction, a single board-level appointment cannot change the culture of an organization overnight and this action has done little to reduce the size of the gulf between IT and the rest of the business community.

For any IS project to be successful, especially those where the consequences of failure are enormous, one would expect senior management to play a major role in the project – at the very least, they must own the project. Unfortunately, this does not always happen and at the first sign of real trouble, experience suggests that business directors and sponsors are quick to disown the project, leaving the IT department and its director to shoulder the blame.

▬ Management style

Of all the human causes of IS project failure, working within a culture of fear or intimidation must rank fairly high. Unwritten codes of conduct and expectations of working hours that go beyond acceptable limits, combined with the fear of failure, can often create a stressful and unproductive working environment.

A management style that relies on an authoritarian approach is rarely effective within a project environment, and whilst a *laissez-faire* style of management may not be much better, it is important that management behave in a way that supports and encourages individuals and teams within the project. An overly abrasive or confrontational style of management might achieve some limited success in the short-term, but over a longer-term will only succeed in alienating the most important aspects of the project – the users and the project team.

The most visible and common form of an abrasive management style exists within those organizations where it is considered necessary to work long hours. What might have started off as a short-term approach to "improve" productivity has now become the norm, gradually alienating those who do not support the regime. Other key examples of an oppressive style include the following.

"Shoot the messenger"

For a key stakeholder under intense pressure to deliver, the arrival of a subordinate bringing news of (yet another) project slippage is often the last straw. The stakeholder has but one objective – to make it clear to his or her subordinates that bad news will not be tolerated – a task that usually involves publicly humiliating the person who dared to communicate the bad news. Expecting a team to perform well under these circumstances would be difficult, to say the least.

Whilst these actions alone may introduce risks into the project, the fact that managers adopting this practice run the risk of ignoring serious project issues must increase the probability of failure significantly. Do not for a minute, think I am exaggerating – I have witnessed the verbal humiliation of IT professionals in front of their colleagues by an IT director whose own position within the company was in jeopardy. It was not pleasant. Shortly after, the director was removed after a company audit found his strategy, approach, and behavior somewhat lacking.

"Shifting ownership of problems (don't give me problems, give me solutions)"

One of the fundamental requirements that must be met for communication to be effective is the ability to listen and to understand what is being said. For people to work together with their superiors, there must exist a climate that allows problems to be raised and discussed in an open and positive way.

If a problem is raised by a member of the project team, the problem must then become a team problem (*"we* will sort it out") rather than expecting the person who raised the problem to own and resolve it (*"you* sort it out").

"Communicating only what the boss wants to hear – a no-problem culture"

The censorship of information, particularly information which identifies serious problems within the project, is not uncommon and represents a significant contributor to project failure. The motives behind censoring information to higher levels within project organization are likely to be linked to the culture of the organization, especially those where the practice of "shoot the messenger" is commonplace.

However, it is also likely that personal motives and agendas play an important part in the censorship of information. For instance, I have known a project manager who, in the knowledge that his promotion away from the project was imminent, ensured that his project status reports sent to the business sponsor gave a healthy and positive outlook, even though a number of serious technical faults were emerging that could have had severe consequences to the success of the project.

Internal pressures to deliver

Many IT directors and IS managers often complain that they are never given sufficient time to implement effective strategies by senior business executives. Contributing to this problem must be the lack of IT representation at board level within the organization.

The pressure placed on commercial organizations to sustain high rates of growth ultimately places schedule constraints on project delivery times. The demand for "rapid" projects often means unrealistic targets are set for project managers by project sponsors or, in some cases, by sales staff, who have promised dates to key customers.

In a climate of strong pressure to deliver, there is a likelihood of making decisions which are inherently riskier than those made when there is less pressure placed on the key participants. Under such pressures, key stakeholders are likely to ignore vital warning signs or, worse, refuse to accept that there is a serious problem. The events leading up to the NASA *Challenger* disaster support this very notion. The tragedy of the space shuttle disaster was that it was preventable. The sequence of events leading up to the disaster have been widely published, but the root cause of the problem was that a potential fault had been noticed by the engineers well before the launch, but their "no-go for launch" decision was over-ruled by NASA managers who were eager to launch in front of the world's press.[1-3]

Pressures to deliver from key stakeholders within the organization also pose a significant threat to the project manager who does not have the power to directly contradict the wishes and views of the business sponsor. In many cases, the project manager, rather than being asked to plan the project and inform the sponsor of the end-date, is told the scope of the project and its implementation date by the sponsor. Even assuming the project manager informs the sponsor that the project requirements cannot be achieved within the constraints of time or budget, it is often unlikely that the sponsor's position will change.

The sponsors of the LAS project exerted incredible pressures on the project manager to introduce a new system as quickly as possible, as they themselves were being affected by far-reaching reforms within the health service.

Resistance to change

Whilst we would all like to be in a position to please everyone all of the time, circumstances often prevent us from doing so. IS projects have the capability to bring substantial benefits to the organization, but often this is done at some cost to those individuals working within it. To many users, IS projects do not bring benefits, quite the opposite in fact. For instance, the introduction of new systems can trigger redundancy and poor morale as new working practices are enforced (such as the use of electronic time recording systems).

It is within our very nature to often view change as a threat to the status quo, and this can only have a detrimental effect on the project. For example, it is not unknown for users to continue to use the old system alongside the new one, thus negating any benefits that might have been made as a result of an otherwise successful project. This might be as a result of the users' lack of trust in the new system, but in at least one real-life example, it was because they had so little work left to do, they wanted to appear busy in case someone noticed their idle hands.

Egomania

I am sure I am not the only person to have witnessed an individual, in a position of authority, drive a project through with reckless abandon, disregarding the concerns of others, in the strive to achieve their personal objectives. When meeting the implementation date becomes the only priority, people who stand in the way of progress or cannot match the pace are likely to be sacrificed along the way. Whilst this approach may work for a "one-off" business problem of truly immense proportions, it can only alienate individuals in the long-term. Should they choose to remain within of the organization, these individuals will often go to great lengths to avoid becoming involved in any further projects of this nature in the future.

Poorly performing project teams

It is not the sole objective of project management to introduce abbreviations and arcane terms such as BCWS*, "total float," or "lag" into the business vocabulary. Project management focuses on people. A cursory glance at the average project plan is likely, therefore, to identify key activities and task dependencies necessary to achieve key milestones, but equally likely to omit competency-based training and team-building practices. The chances that the plan will also identify coaching and mentoring requirements will be even slimmer.

Whilst the project plan must provide a "roadmap" to stakeholders, showing precisely how their objectives will be met, the plan must also provide details of the support infrastructure that will be required if the wider project team (including the users) are to operate effectively.

The composition of a project team is not just a problem facing IT project managers; it can also become a major problem for IT directors. When an IT project manager leaves a company it will always pose a problem, but that is nothing compared to a situation where the outgoing project manager also poaches many of the company's software team in the process. In these situations, it is likely that the IT director will be left stranded with a half-completed software development project and insufficient resources to complete it. Even with expensive advertising campaigns, it is not always possible to recruit staff of the necessary caliber to supplement the project team. Project delay is a likely outcome and if not resolved quickly, so too is the threat that the project may no longer be viable.

* Budgeted Cost of Work Scheduled

Luckily these situations still represent the exception rather than the norm. If they are to remain that way, IT directors, need to put their technology initiatives to one side for a minute and learn a few important lessons about their own staff. People are an organization's biggest asset and are often worth much more than their remuneration packages suggest. Of course, it is extremely difficult to prevent key staff from being poached at critical times to the business; the probability of it happening however, *can* be reduced by the pragmatic use of bonus and personal development schemes.

Indeed, there are many other ways of improving staff loyalty and morale, but these two schemes probably have a better chance than most – they reward hard-working staff who constantly deliver benefits into the organization and they give an important message to skilled IT staff – "you are important to the company."

The skills needed to manage people effectively are often underestimated within many organizations, which is why their projects are not the successes they should be. It is important therefore not only to consider the performance of project teams within the organization, but to ensure a supplier's project team also have the necessary personal skills to work effectively.

Clearly, there is a strong relationship between the performance of the project and the performance of the project team. Despite this, many project management methodologies still assume the project team consists of all the most competent, committed, and technically expert individuals within the organization. The reality is slightly more sobering; project managers often have little choice in the composition of their team, and are regularly confronted with many unwelcome situations such as the following:

■ The blame culture within the organization, combined with the poor man-management skills of the previous manager, has resulted in all of the best IT staff leaving the project. The project manager is therefore left with the "team from hell," whose only contribution to the project will be a negative one, such as "I told you so".

■ The new project manager has an obligation to accept inexperienced and untested IT graduates into the project, despite the fact that, without key development resources, the project milestones will be threatened.

■ The new project manager after his first week has realized why all his predecessors left the organization – the business sponsor is a ruthless accountant who neither understands nor trusts people. Communication channels are non-existent and he expects the project manager to take all the key decisions – and all the blame.

Key causes of project team weakness

Undermined motivation

Numerous studies have discovered that motivation probably has a greater impact on productivity and quality than any other factor. Despite this, its importance is still largely ignored within the project organization. Motivation is a "soft" factor and difficult to quantify, and so it is often overlooked by managers who are more comfortable using other factors which, whilst being less important, are easier to measure. Every organization knows how important motivation is; very few actually do anything about it.

Uncontrolled problem employees

Failure to deal with uncontrollable and problem employees has been the subject of a number of books, such as the *Psychology of Computer Programming*[4] and *Teamwork: What must go right; what can go wrong.*[5] The former identifies the failure to deal with "rogue" programmers as a fundamental weakness within the team, the latter is more general in nature – it identifies the failure to deal with a problem employee as (still) the most common complaint that team members have about their leaders.

At best, failure to deal with problem employees undermines the morale and motivation of the rest of the project team, at worst it just increases the turnover of good team members and ultimately damages the quality of the project. Beware of the project team member who is the "rusty musket" (doesn't work and can't be fired).

Poor working conditions

IT staff often complain bitterly about the conditions in which they must work, and for good reason. Noisy, crowded offices, a consequence of over-zealous management looking to reduce costs, do little to inspire and motivate talented professionals. Management are often quick to point out that money is less of a motivating factor than ones such as job satisfaction, job security, and workplace conditions. Not many organizations, however, ever put theory into practice. According to the authors of *Peopleware*,[6] workers who occupy noisy, crowded bays or cubicles tend to perform significantly worse than employees who occupy quiet, private offices.

A lack of training and support

The need for training is regularly overlooked in the struggle to deliver an IS project, and this can only be to the detriment of the project. Training needs for the project team must be assessed regularly, certainly during the early stages of the project and probably at key stages throughout the life of the project as well.

Adding developers late to a project

Probably the most classic of all project team mistakes is to add developers to a project that is behind schedule in the hope that the additional effort will instantly resolve the problem.

There are, however, valid exceptions to this rule; for short periods only, additional resource may help the team resolve a *specific* problem; but generally, new people subtract more productivity from existing staff than they add through their own efforts. Indeed, Fred Brooks, a well-known commentator on software development topics, once likened adding people to a late project to "pouring gasoline on a fire."[7]

The role of stakeholders in the project

Stakeholders are those people who are affected by the outcome of a project, either in a negative way or in a positive way. All those involved in the project are, therefore, stakeholders, but many of these will take no direct part in the project as team members, but will have their roles and responsibilities changed as a result.

Primary stakeholders are those individuals who are directly affected by the project and will be internal to the organization, such as users and managers. In addition to primary stakeholders, there may be external stakeholders, such as suppliers, legal bodies, and other third party organizations who are not formally involved in a project, but who may impact or be impacted by the activity.

The business sponsor of the project is likely to be the most important of all stakeholders in the project. It is the business sponsor who must provide a clear vision of the benefits that can be delivered from the project and a clear picture of the world in which these benefits can be achieved.

The business sponsor must be committed to the value of IT within the organization and to the reality that it can happen. Persistence and communication will, therefore, be valuable attributes which the sponsor may need to achieve success. In return, the IS stakeholders must become focused on business issues if they are to appreciate the project objectives.

An organization's capability to deliver competitive advantage through an IS project can often be benchmarked against the quality of the relationship that exists between the business and IT stakeholders.

Stakeholder analysis

All stakeholders within a project have the potential to influence the success of the project in some way. There may be a few key stakeholders for whom the project is of little importance, but whose involvement is critical to the success of the project. Similarly, there may be stakeholders who have the power to stop the project dead in its tracks. Understanding each stakeholder's position and stance in the project will undoubtedly, be an important activity as it is likely that their consent or finance will be needed at some point during the project.

The diagram shown in Figure 8.1 outlines a popular method for analyzing stakeholders in terms of the power they possess in comparison to the interest they have in the project. Once the key players or stakeholders have been identified, it is important to determine the "comfort zone" of each one. No two stakeholders will have exactly the same motives and incentives for the project and, as a consequence, will expect differing levels and types of information. Whilst the diagram represents a fairly simple approach to stakeholder analysis, its benefit is that it can be used to capture critical stakeholder information very quickly.

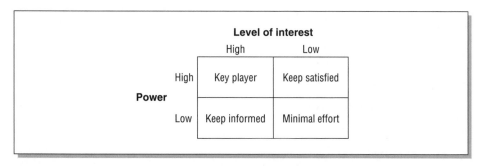

FIGURE 8.1 ■ Assessing the level of stakeholder interest

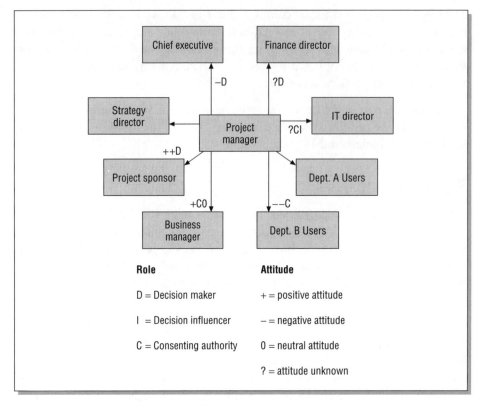

FIGURE 8.2 ▬ A typical stakeholder influence map

At a greater level of detail, it is important to analyze each stakeholder or group of stakeholders within the project to gain a greater understanding of how they can affect the project (Figure 8.2). The influence exerted by every stakeholder in the project can be determined from the assessment of the following factors:

- positive towards the project;
- negative towards the project;
- not committed one way or the other;
- a decision-*maker*;
- a decision-*influencer*;
- an individual whose consent is required for the project to succeed.

The London Stock Exchange TAURUS project

Outside the public sector, major IS project disasters are unlikely to find their way into the public domain; the demise of the TAURUS project, however, rocked London's financial institutions and was heavily reported in the pages of numerous financial publications within the UK.[8–20]

Along with the exchanges in New York and Tokyo, the London Stock Exchange (LSE) is regarded by many as one of the most important financial institutions in the world. The sheer volume of information that must pass through the LSE, in the form of share transfers, records of ownership, and dealing payments, is immense, and the scale of the business operation within the LSE cannot be underestimated.

During the 1960s the LSE realized that the existing paper-based system of share dealing, involving the registration and transfer of thousands of paper share certificates, was no longer capable of managing the current and predicted workloads. The LSE correctly forecasted that share ownership and international trading would continue to rise with the growth of the global economy. An electronic system of share ownership and transfer was, therefore, an essential part of an infrastructure that would underpin the LSE and reinforce its claim to be the most important financial center within Europe.

For over a century, two key documents have been required to hold and transfer shares in the UK; a share certificate, issued by the company to each shareholder as legal proof of ownership, and a completed stock transfer form, delivered to the company so that it can transfer the shares. Automating the paper-based system, which was itself based on antiquated practices, was considered by the LSE as early as 1966. This would involve the many members of the LSE pooling their share settlements systems, but did not receive the endorsement from banks, investors, and other stakeholders in the City of London until 1970.

The first computerized settlements system TALISMAN (Transfer Accounting Lodgement for Investors/ Stock Management for Principals) was not approved by the Council, the governing body of the LSE, until 1971. After only a year, the decision was reversed following protests from the brokerage firms who complained that a centralized system would allow the exchange to learn too much about their business and their clients.

The LSE, having failed to persuade its members of the virtues of automatic settlement, also suffered its own problems; there were many resignations as the IT department came under attack for "empire building." As a result, design of TALISMAN was halted until 1977. TALISMAN was finally introduced in 1979. Even at this early stage, the factional in-fighting within the LSE was beginning to surface. It would be the same resistance from the IT-illiterate power-brokers, the modern-day Luddites within the City, that would eventually undermine the TAURUS project.

Despite the problems, TALISMAN was, in fact, a success. Whilst not reducing the mounting costs of settlement within the LSE, it did provide some controls. It had a weakness though; it could not provide a solution to reducing the amount of paperwork needed to effect stock transfer.

In 1980, a committee known as the Powell Committee was established to find a solution to the problem. Drawing its membership from the institutional investors, stockbrokers, and bankers, custodians, and registrars, and others who were judged to have an interest in the matter, the committee rejected the idea of enhancing TALISMAN and voted for an ambitious plan to abolish paper share certificates altogether. The plan they devised was called TAURUS (the Transfer and Automatic Registration of Uncertificated Stock) and work commenced on the project in 1983.

During October 1986, the "Big Bang" took place and fundamentally changed the way in which the LSE operated. The most visible change was that seen in the trading floor which became an exclusively electronic market. This event more than any other signified the first step towards 'dematerialization'; the concept of paperless trading.

Up until Big Bang, the average number of client transactions in UK equities rarely exceeded 20,000 a day. In 1987, the first year after Big Bang, this figure soared to 50,000, partly as a result of the UK Government's privatization program. During this year, TALISMAN, still essentially a paper-based system, nearly collapsed as the privatization of many state-owned industries generated millions of share certificates. Sellers failed to deliver share certificates to market-makers, who failed to deliver them to buyers. The backlog became enormous, so much so that, at its height, there were enough unsettled transactions to occupy the system for 12 whole days. At its peak during August 1987, the value of deals being traded was £8 billion ($12 billion). The LSE's failure to provide a paperless trading system cost its members as much as £50 million ($75 million) as a result of interest charges and having to hire additional staff to manage the workload. Moreover, share buyers had up to three weeks to pay for their purchase, which increased the credit risks within the market; buyers might go bust before they paid or sellers might go bust before they delivered the shares. As some of the share deals were worth hundreds of millions of pounds – the risk of default was high, high enough to break the bank – literally.

Work on the project (dubbed TAURUS I) finally resumed in 1987, by which time the settlement backlog had cleared (helped mainly by the stock market crash in October 1987) and comprised three distinct phases:

- **Phase 1**   The abolition of paper certificates. Instead, investors would receive statements at regular intervals.

- **Phase 2**   The introduction of a rolling settlement, reducing the payment period to three days. At the time, the London exchange had a settlement period of nearly three weeks – much longer than any of its competitors. Reducing the settlement period ensured that money changed hands quicker, reducing the risk of default.

- **Phase 3**   The instantaneous transfer of money with the transfer of ownership, a process referred to as "delivery versus payment."

The failure of the LSE to control and manage the project, in terms of people, technology, and quality was to ensure that the project never got past phase 1. Whilst it was the intention of the project to replace paper share certificates, the software package used to display share prices could not be integrated with the existing TALISMAN system. By now, doubts had already begun to surface about the LSE's ability to manage major IT projects, already an existing IT project of a much smaller scope was 18 months behind schedule.

This was probably a crucial turning point in history of TAURUS I, as the system design which had been under development since 1983 was based on a large, centralised database. To handle the trillion shares issued by the 3,000 London-listed companies would have required the combined power of two IBM 3090 mainframe computers. Furthermore, to process the huge amount of data within acceptable performance limits would require 560 separate disk drives, each one being loaded to only 3 per cent of its capacity. It is not difficult to understand why, then, the proposed technical design was considered too complex to be achievable.

The LSE's decision to create a single database also came under intense pressure from the many listed companies who would have to use it. They were adamant that this solution did not take account of their vested interests in the way the exchange operated. It seemed that a great many companies were able to make money out of the inefficiences of the current trading systems and saw no benefit in changing the status quo.

Despite the many obvious problems with the project, it was not until late 1988 that the decision to abandon it was taken, based on the advice from a number of independent reviews. The reviews concluded that the estimated costs of the project, £60 million ($90 million) were too high and the technical complexity too great, raising serious questions as to its viability.

At this point the Bank of England stepped in to try and resolve the stalemate. It gave its backing to the establishment of the SISCOT Committee (Securities and Investment Steering Committee on Taurus) whose brief was to produce a proposal which would satisfy the many stakeholders with a vested interest in the project.

After deliberating over a number of possible designs for TAURUS, the committee opted for a solution which was both technically complex and expensive. Indeed, given the pioneering use of leading-edge technology it was advocating, the committee could not have chosen a more risky solution.

The solution was nothing short of a compromise to keep the key financial players locked into the project. Registrars and custodians argued against the centralization of data as they would lose revenue from the share maintenance services they provided to companies and investors. Listed companies who were in fear of the frenzy of take-overs within UK markets argued that with databases scattered all over the country they would not be able to identify the records of their shareholders. The new design for the project (dubbed TAURUS II) was based around a distributed database, with the LSE acting as the central hub. This design would allow access to the many companies involved, and would protect the interests of the powerful and influential users of the exchange.

In August 1989, the exchange appointed a consultant from Coopers & Lybrand as project director. Up to this point, the project had been run by the LSE itself. One of the first tasks he would perform would be to announce a three-month delay to the project. The planned implementation date of TAURUS would now be late 1990.

Development on TAURUS continued, with IBM contracted to design a bespoke data communications system. At the heart of the system would be a software package developed by Vista Concepts of New York, Vista's Securities Processing System (VSPS). The package was already the market leader in the lucrative securities market and had established an excellent reputation. VSPS, however, was designed for handling real-time transactions and needed extensive customization in order for it to interface with the batch processing functionality of the TALISMAN system. Development work on VSPS was split into two teams located in London and New York. The logistics of this would soon bear down the project; to make matters worse, the software development team had to cope with constantly changing requirements. The software package initially cost £1 million ($1.5 million), with a further cost of £4 million ($6 million) estimated for revisions. By the time the final curtain came down on TAURUS, these costs had risen to a staggering £14 million ($21 million), and the software was still unfinished.

During 1991 it became clear that the project had slipped many of its milestones mainly as a result of the complexity of legal and regulatory issues being imposed by the Department of Trade and Industry (DTI). The LSE originally envisaged straightforward regulations concerning the issuing and cancellation of certificates, but their discussions with the LSE resulted in a 150-page legal document. TAURUS was once again postponed until May 1992. By September 1991, there were doubts raised as to whether TAURUS could meet this new date. This delay was due to two key issues; enhancements to the existing TALISMAN system were not progressing well; it was later disclosed that this new date had not included any contingency and had been declared in an effort to expedite the software development process. After consulting the two main contractors on the project, IBM and Vista, a new target date of April 1993 was agreed for TAURUS. This decision would add another £15 million ($22.5 million) to the original budget of £50 million ($75 million).

In October 1992, integration testing was to begin with real code from IBM and Vista. By this time, however, the project had attracted the attentions of Anderson Consulting who, in a deal with the LSE, were to support all their IT systems, including TAURUS. Andersen spent the next few months reviewing the project and in December 1992 submitted their report to the finance director whom the chief executive had put in overall charge of IT at the LSE. The report highlighted serious problems with TAURUS. Their main concern noted the lack of any overall architecture for the project, concluding that such an approach seriously affected its viability.

To avoid any professional rivalry between the consultancy firms, the finance director ensured that each consultancy kept control of its respective area and appointed a consultant from Coopers & Lybrand to take charge of the technical aspects of TAURUS. The consultant ordered a full review of TAURUS, eventually predicting that TAURUS would take another three years to build, doubling the cost. On March 11, 1993, within days of the review's findings, the decision to abandon TAURUS had been taken. In announcing the cancellation of the project, the chairman of the LSE, Sir Andrew Hugh Smith, wrote that the review "revealed weaknesses which would require the testing program to be halted for at least fifteen months until the central system can perform with sufficient robustness to allow further testing with participants".[10]

The cost of failure

The original costs for TAURUS were expected to be in the region of £45 million–£50 million ($67.5 million–$75 million). The benefits case for the project expected a saving to be made in the region of £250 million ($375 million) over a 10-year period. By the end of the project, TAURUS had cost the LSE £75 million ($112.5 million) and the other companies involved between £200 million ($300 million) and £400 million ($600 million) and returned no financial benefits. Many observers concluded that the huge costs were as a result of contracting development work on a time-and-materials basis; with the suggestion that had a fixed-price contract been agreed, such cost-overruns would not have occurred.

In human terms, the consequences of failure were to be felt throughout the whole project. Most notable was the departure of the Chief Executive of the LSE, who resigned immediately. Soon to follow would be some 220 stock exchange employees and 130 contract staff, mostly from Coopers & Lybrand – the TAURUS project director since August 1989, was one of them.

Critical failure factors

Political interference

The insistence of the DTI for TAURUS to adopt the most secure method of encryption and investor protection caused problems to an already troubled project. Design and testing complexity increased as the system was effectively required to become "hacker-proof." The result was an encryption system that was so secure it was only bettered by the systems adopted by the UK Government Communications Centre (GCHQ) at Cheltenham. A consultant working on the project noted that this level of security was "totally unnecessary." The project also became bogged down with the amount of legal regulations that were being imposed upon it in order to provide a framework for TAURUS. In the previous paper-based system, share certificates were legally recognized as proof of ownership; the statements TAURUS was to produce were not.

Failure to understand the implications of the solution

The design of TAURUS was so complex, no one fully understood the implications of their actions. The DTI took more than a year to amend UK company law to recognize the automated transfer of shares.

Failure to agree requirements

From the start, TAURUS was continually dogged by the vested interests and rivalries of the many organizations who used the LSE; stockbrokers, registrars, and limited companies.

Shifting design

The project needed a stable, core architecture which had the flexibility to withstand the dynamics of the London financial markets, yet no final blueprint for the design of TAURUS was ever produced. Indeed, even at the point at which the project was cancelled, key aspects of the design were still not in place. The decision to abandon the centralized database architecture was inevitable given that the custodians and registrars essentially sabotaged the project to protect their own interests.

Technical complexity

If any one decision can be blamed for the demise of TAURUS, it was the decision to abandon the £60 million ($90 million) centralized database which would maintain records of all share-holdings in the UK stock market, in 1988. Abandoning the original centralized database design, the SISCOT committee opted for a much more technically complex architecture. At the core of this architecture, a distributed database was to be implemented, linked together by a communications network. The LSE would act as the 'hub' within this huge network, linking together over 400 sites with a different combination of computer hardware and software at each. Even for experienced IT consultancy organizations possessing large systems integration experience, this solution would represent a considerable challenge.

VSPS, the software package selected to provide online functionality, required 70 per cent rewriting. This was a daunting challenge made worse by the fragmentation of the software development team. The decision to opt for a time-and-materials contract for this development was an obvious factor in the escalation of costs, although much greater attention should have been placed on contractual issues as a whole with a development on this scale.

Poor project management

There was never any clear project plan for TAURUS. In fact, up until the first two years of its development, the project had no director. It was clear from the early stages of the project that the project director failed to focus on the overall objectives of the project – choosing instead to ensure that consensus was found amongst the LSE's members and partners. To be fair, given the number of committees which were established to manage the project (over 20), the project director's role was clearly undermined and undervalued; a case of "too many cooks in the kitchen."

Throughout the TAURUS project, sensible project management gave way to a feeling of invincibility – the curse of the "silver bullet syndrome" in many respects. Sir Andrew Hugh Smith, was quoted in the Financial Times after announcing the cancellation of TAURUS, saying ". . . there may have been an element of self-delusion," referring to the inability of the project team to recognize the threats to the project early on in its development.

Poor systems development

Despite the use of SSADM, which was a government-backed systems development methodology particularly useful for large-scale projects, key stages of the software development lifecycle were omitted or given only scant attention. SSADM is a highly prescriptive methodology; if it is used correctly, key deliverables such as requirements specifications, logical design specifications, and physical design specifications, are produced. It is these deliverables that provide the foundations for the construction of software.

Resistance to change

It would have been hard to find more resistance to the idea of automated share dealing than that displayed by the stakeholders within London's financial institutions. Brokers maintained that private shareholders would not be willing to exchange their paper share certificates for periodic statements detailing share-holdings which they might have to pay for from their broker. They argued that it would take years, possibly decades, to eliminate share certificates completely.

Failure to address quality issues

Considering the size of the project, the level of quality control adopted was extremely poor. Software engineers were allowed to develop systems without a rigid quality assurance process in place to ensure that quality standards were maintained. The fact that the project seemed to have a will of its own points to a clear lack of control at the most senior levels within the LSE. Following the appointment of a new LSE Chief Executive, there was a huge upheaval of staff within the LSE. The resulting turmoil must have had a detrimental effect on the overall management of the project and, more specifically, the management of quality within the project.

Wider testing of TAURUS, which was to involve the securities companies, was started in January 1993. Considered to be the simplest part of the test cycle, it had already fallen behind in the overall testing schedule. Of the 154 functions which were meant to have been tested during the test phase, only 50 had been completed. Even the LSE admitted testing was 'slow and patchy'.

Major events in the history of TAURUS

1979:	TALISMAN system implemented.
1981:	Stock Exchange first considers the automation of share transfer.
1986:	Big Bang leads to huge increases in trading, creating a backlog of unsettled deals. There are calls for the exchange to be closed one day a week so bills can be settled.
1987:	Taurus I is proposed – central database of all shareholdings, costing £60 million – but is abandoned in 1988 due to cost and the opposition of share registrars.
Early 1989:	Taurus II is born – based on a distributed database architecture.
August 1989:	A Coopers & Lybrand partner is appointed as project director as Taurus suffers first delay.
March 1990:	Project director sets target date – October 1991.
May 1990:	Exchange predicts TAURUS will save City of London £250 million over next 10 years.
May 1991:	Stock Exchange Chief Executive admits Taurus will not be ready until May 1992.
October 1991:	Government redrafts proposed Taurus legislation. Target date moves back to April 1993.
January 1993:	Introduction is pushed back to April 1994. Full review of TAURUS ordered.
Feb 1993:	Review concludes TAURUS will take another three years to build and costs will double.
March 1993:	Stock Exchange abandons the Taurus project. LSE Chief Executive resigns immediately; project director is dismissed.

Stakeholder conflict

It is the objective of stakeholder analysis to identify key participants in the project, the relative power or influence they possess, and their attitude towards the project. Whilst the stakeholders identified from this process are likely to share similar views on the need to achieve a broad set of objectives, the approach and timescale for achieving them is likely to be a potential source of conflict.

This is a fairly obvious example of conflict within an IS project; there will be many other situations throughout the project where the likelihood of conflict will be high, yet the warning signs will not be so obvious. A good example of this would be a situation where a project team, working over a weekend to meet a key deadline, is told the next day that the customer has changed the specification and their work will have to be repeated at a later stage.

A contemporary view of conflict within organizations suggests that, far from being a bad thing, conflict is beneficial, and indeed a necessary event. That may well be the case but, for the purposes of achieving project success, it is important to understand the key causes of conflict and possible ways to resolve it.

Key causes of conflict

Failure to identify and engage key stakeholders within the project

IS projects are likely to fail when the project team does not identify all the "real" stakeholders within the project. In the case of a large US mutual fund company, the developers had been working closely with the IT vice-president to develop a new $300 million (£200 million) software system. The vice-president was perceived by the project team to be the primary stakeholder for the project and was kept informed of progress throughout the project.

However, when the system development phase ran into problems, it drew the attention of the CEO who was, in fact, the key stakeholder in the project, even though he had not previously been involved with it. After seeing the risks involved in implementing the system, he immediately withdrew his support for the project.[21]

Clearly, in this example, little attempt had been made to identify all the key stakeholders in the project and determine who would ultimately declare whether the project was a success or not. As the principal sponsor for the project had not been kept informed of progress throughout the development stages of the project, there was little chance that full support could be given, resulting in the collapse of the project.

TABLE 8.1 ▨ A typical project status report

Key project milestone	Status	Actions
Additional funding made available for Phase 2 feasibility.	Red	Finance director must authorize funds for additional resources by next week.
Business process training completed	Amber	Requires amendments to process manual. Ongoing.
Requirements approved	Green	

Stakeholders, whilst not engaged on the day-to-day issues of the project, must be kept informed of progress as well as issues and risks which could jeopardize the project. Having said that, it is no good providing a report to the business sponsor every six months if the project is only intended to last a year.

Regardless of whether the news to report is good or bad, it is good practice to issue summarized, regular progress reports to key stakeholders, rather than to send too much information in one large report. The Red, Amber, Green (RAG) approach to monitoring the status of a project is popular amongst many IT departments, mainly due to its simplicity, brevity, and clarity.

In its most common form: "green" denotes an event that is due to complete on schedule; "amber" denotes an event that is underway and requires action to complete; "red" denotes an event that has not been completed and the project delivery schedule is now under threat – thus requiring immediate action. Whilst the RAG approach can be used to track the status of the project at any level, it is most commonly used to track the status of project milestones. An example of a "RAG" status report is shown in Table 8.1.

Conflicting objectives amongst key business stakeholders

Whilst most senior business managers are aware of the massive failure rate of IS projects within their industry and, to a lesser extent, within their organization, they do not for one minute think that it is as a result of their own incompetence or internal power struggles.

Most business managers now readily acknowledge IS projects as an enabler of change and, as a consequence, are more than willing to give their financial backing to key IS projects such as strategic data warehouse systems or Customer Relationship Management (CRM) systems, thinking they will gain competitive advantage. However, organizations rarely understand what they are taking on and, in the process of trying to capture the requirements for the project, end up in a quagmire trying to understand their own organizations. Usually, it is only the clear-sighted IT director that can thwart the stifling effects of internal bureaucracy.

During the analysis phase of one particular data-warehousing project, it suddenly became clear that the sales bonuses paid across an organization were not the same. Given the wholesale interest in this information, it was only a matter of time before it had spread across the whole of the organization's sales force. The inevitable conflict was eventually resolved, but at a large cost to the project in terms of slipped timescales and over-stretched budgets.[22] In a similar situation, an internal conflict arose as a result of two departments being convinced that they both owned the same sales list of customers.

A situation where there are two or more business sponsors disagreeing with each other is a nightmare for any IT director or project manager. They cannot take the decision for them; yet if no decision can be made, the business case for the project is severely weakened, if not compromised and rendered worthless. Unfortunately, too many IS projects fail because IT stakeholders ignore the risks, hoping that the conflict will be resolved by the time software development begins. Their mistaken belief that a technical solution will somehow resolve a major business conflict is one that is likely to have repercussions later on in the project.

Such topics rarely get a mention on project management courses and, likewise, never appear as issues in the average project plan, yet they are just as likely to stop a project in its tracks as would a major error in a packaged software solution. Any project that seeks to change the organization in some way runs the risk of generating internal conflict within the very departments it is trying to help. These conflicts cost organizations huge sums of money every year – and it is usually only the lack of honest communication with, and project transparency to, senior executives (whom we must assume, do not want to waste good money on promoting conflict and bureaucracy) that perpetuates the problem.

Excessive control exerted by the business sponsor

It is the duty of the business sponsor to empower the project manager (through business case approval and funding) to deliver the required business functionality and, ultimately, measurable benefits within agreed timescales and costs. By empowering the project manager, the business sponsor is effectively handing over the day-to-day running of the project. With an effective reporting, control, and change management framework in place, this situation is satisfactory.

Problems will invariably arise if the business sponsor asserts an excessive amount of control over the project, effectively undermining the leadership and authority of the project manager. Whilst there are many ways in which this situation can manifest itself throughout the project, the most common ones are likely to include:

- directing the work of the project team;
- engaging directly with suppliers;
- over-ruling day-to-day decisions made by the project manager.

Even when a project reaches crisis point, the project sponsor and senior management can be guilty of incompetence and negligence by refusing to listen to the project manager they themselves appointed. The behavior of senior management within the London Stock Exchange is a perfect example of how the abdication of responsibility combined with a monstrous display of arrogance can seal the fate of a project already in trouble and in need of wise leadership.

In hindsight, it is difficult to see how any project manager could have made TAURUS a success given the organizational culture of the London Stock Exchange and the failure of its senior management to listen to the advice given to them from the project team.

Ignorance in IT from the very managers and executives sponsoring IS projects must surely represent a risk to the success of the project. Whether this "technophobia" is due to Luddism or plain old age is not the issue here; what is, however, is how such behavior manifests itself within the business. A lack of faith in IT from senior business directors or sponsors can have serious consequences on their relationship with project managers and the success of the IS project as a whole. Whilst we often find the inability of senior executives within the company to master even basic IT systems, such as a desktop PC, mildly amusing – what are the consequences for an IS project if that same executive is also its business sponsor?

Key IT decisions taken independently of the business sponsor

IT program and project directors have a responsibility to deliver an agreed scope of work within the constraints of time and quality. Business sponsors empower IT through the submission and approval of a business case. This should clearly identify the roles and responsibilities for IT stakeholders to support the delivery of specific products or services.

IT program and project managers clearly have a responsibility to ensure that funding made available to their projects is utilized appropriately in the furtherance of specific business objectives. Business sponsors must be kept informed if funds are to be used by IT management for development activities that have not been approved by business fundholders. Trust and understanding are significant factors if the business sponsor is to invest heavily in IT projects; and, as we all know, trust is hard to establish and easy to lose.

Supplier management (customer's perspective)

The need to develop complex business systems within a limited amount of time and money is just one of the many contributory factors that can lead to a serious breakdown in the relationship between a customer and a third-party supplier of IT products or services. The most optimistic view of the outcome is where the two parties accept the reality that they cannot work with each other and agree to part company in a diplomatic and subdued manner. A more realistic view portrays a climate of increasing hostilities between the supplier and the customer, resulting in the inevitable legal action followed by the summoning of expert witnesses.

Project failures such as the LAS computer-aided dispatch project should act as a warning for all managers who are in a position to influence the choice of supplier. Many projects never recover from poor decisions made early on concerning the choice of supplier. Sponsors and managers, under pressure to limit budgetary spend, are sometimes too eager to chose the supplier who offers the lowest price for work, and not the one who offers the best service.

Customer management (supplier's perspective)

It is not uncommon for customers to put their suppliers under huge pressures to quote an incredibly low price for a substantial piece of development work. The supplier is now faced with a number of options, such as reducing the quality of the work, supplying more junior (and cheaper) consultants onto the project, or just taking what money is available and doing what they can (i.e. not guaranteeing to complete the project). Whilst there is an argument supporting the view that the supplier may be acting unethically in some cases, questions must also be asked regarding the behavior of the customer in this situation.

Not surprisingly one of the most common causes of conflict between the supplier and the customer arises from the much-loved, but often misunderstood fixed-price contract. Such contracts are common in projects where the systems development activity has been outsourced to a third-party supplier. The customer, determined to be in control of the development budget, draws up a contract with the supplier which is based on performance against key deliverables.

The rigid and mechanistic approach to development forced upon the supplier by the customer is a potential source of conflict as it is clear that both parties have expectations which are drastically opposed. The customer is motivated to try and include as much functionality as possible into the requirements specification for a fixed cost; the supplier, often having little or no control over activities performed by the customer, is motivated to reduce their exposure to risk.

It is often forgotten that third-party suppliers are almost completely dependent on the actions of the customer throughout the project and, as a consequence, expose themselves to a number of risks, including:

- customer delays in the decision-making process;

- reviews of plans, prototypes and specifications are slow to materialize;

- customer insistence on additional requirements;

- failure of the customer to attend planning, review and approval meetings or inability to participate fully during them;

- the customer insists on technical solutions that lengthen the schedule or impact other stages of the project;

- the customer's existing technical infrastructure is unstable or of a poor quality, resulting in reduced productivity.

The supplier, therefore, is seeking to limit the scope of the project to a level that is considered technically achievable but also commercially viable. Where the risk is acceptable, a major supplier will normally be prepared to fix the price for a series of development activities. Typical prerequisites to ensure that a commercially sound and fixed price agreement can be produced include:

- well-defined scope expressed in terms of documented requirements;

- for a 'build' piece of work an agreed solution design documented according to an agreed template;

- agreed set of deliverables supported by an agreed methodology so that deliverable document structures and expected level of detail are set at the beginning;

- agreed program or project management plans including escalation strategy, reporting formats, quality assurance, risk management, project acceptance criteria, and change management.

Stakeholder resistance

Resistance to change can take many forms within a project, and it is important to identify it as soon as possible and take appropriate action to resolve it. Stakeholder resistance can take many forms, but the more popular examples are likely to include:

- continually asking for more detail before making a decision;

- disseminating so much detailed information to the project team that no one has a chance of understanding it and making a decision based upon it;

- assuring others that the project is important, yet never allocating any time to it;

- communicating the need for realistic solutions, but dismissing every proposal as unrealistic and impractical;

- disregarding serious project issues with responses such as "I'm not surprised," effectively deflating the importance of the message;

- "head in the sand" attitude towards bad news, often demonstrated by the display of aggression towards the messenger;

- staying silent, implying that consent has not been given – the whole decision-making process within a project can be brought to a halt by a stakeholder unwilling to provide positive affirmation.

- refusing to commit staff and resources onto the project, either because they are too busy or because the project is not seen as having a higher priority than their current business assignments.

Dealing with stakeholder resistance

Stakeholder resistance is almost always characterized by the lack of effective communication, such as stalling tactics and information overload. The best approach to overcome such resistance is to employ the principles of effective communication. In particular, it is important to understand both verbal and non-verbal signals from the stakeholder. The following three-step approach is one effective method of identifying and resolving stakeholder resistance.

Step 1: Look for the warning signs

- Where the messages received from verbal communication conflict with non-verbal communication signals (body language, tone, posture, etc.), trust the non-verbal signals. Trust what you see, not what you hear, and you will gain a better understanding of the root causes prompting the resistance.

- Watch out for repetition or tell-tale phrases.

- Trust your instincts.

Step 2: Confront the stakeholder

Inform the stakeholder of the problem, using words and phrases they understand. Do not use jargon, catch-phrases or buzz-words – these can all lead to a failure to effectively communicate your problem.

Step 3: Allow the stakeholder to respond

Once the stakeholder has understood the resistance, it is crucial to stop talking and let the stakeholder respond. Do not be tempted to fill the silence with your own voice – that will let the stakeholder off the hook and will not help you resolve the fundamental problem.

Improving the human aspects of the project

Promoting effective communication

Many leading IS consultancies maintain that project management is 80 per cent communication – they are not wrong. Effective communication is a fundamental requirement within any project, and its absence will often lead to the failure of the project, even when it has a firm technical foundation.

One of the main reasons why communication is often lacking in many IS projects is that there is no time for communication to take place in an effective way. Informal methods of communication, such as discussions in the staff canteen, do have a place within organizations but, ultimately, more formal methods of communication need to be adopted within the project.

At every stage within the project, communication is required. Those individuals who repeatedly deliver success are those who are likely to possess good communication skills. Studies of management consultancy businesses have suggested that 70 per cent of individuals' time is spent communicating with others; the remaining 30 per cent being spent on problem analysis.

Other studies have found that managers spend up to 90 per cent of their time talking to other people. Time is a scarce commodity in business, and what little time is available for communication must be used effectively.

Reducing the blame culture

The need to find a scapegoat is particularly prevalent within organizations where there are clear and defined boundaries of operation between departments, especially between those departments representing the "customer" and those departments representing the "supplier."

Clearly, it is vital that customers and suppliers work together to establish a climate of trust and co-operation. Open, honest communication is a good starting point, so tell each other what you think, but be equally prepared to listen.

Personal skills training and team-building games are popular within many organizations and can help reduce the culture of blame within them. However, unless the IS methodologies used to develop projects within the business also support an anti-blame culture, the problem will manifest itself within the project framework. IS methodologies must work for an organization, otherwise they provide little benefit. Methodologies that encourage joint ownership of the problem and its subsequent resolution, such as DSDM and JAD, allow users and developers to work as a team. This helps reduce the need for the usual "safety-net" approach for the developers (and, to some extent, the users) by having a signed-off specification.

Traditionally, the signed-off specification is the final arbiter of what is or is not in the scope of the project. However, many specifications are too ambiguous and vague, allowing each party to blame the other for misinterpretations.

Joint responsibility and development help avoid this, but only if a marked change from traditional development roles and responsibilities is promoted and supported throughout the duration of the project. Through the lifecycle of the project it is important that IT and business stakeholders take responsibility for their actions – if a problem arises, it is a problem for the *team* not a problem for any one individual (although an individual may take ownership of the problem). In such circumstances, the individuals representing the business and IT functions must work together as one team and accept joint responsibility for their actions.

Building the core project team

The earlier sections of this chapter highlighted how the success of an IS project is dependent on the abilities of the people working within it. If this is true, why then do so many organizations experience problems despite recruiting the best technical experts onto their projects? One explanation might be because a group of experts working as individuals do not possess the wide range of skills and behaviors that exist within a well-formed and cohesive project team.

A project team is built to serve a specific purpose and lasts only for the duration of the project. Its importance to the project cannot be underestimated, and from the very start of the project, team roles must be identified and agreed with all the individuals involved on the project.

Key roles within the project team

For any project team to be effective, it must have the right balance of skills. If we could all choose our project "dream team" (which of course we can't because the

TABLE 8.2 ▨ The project "dream team"

Project role	Responsibility
Project director	A senior manager who is responsible for all key business activities affected by the project.
Project leader	Leads the team, stakeholders, and management and ensures that other roles within the project are assigned and carried out effectively.
Co-ordinator	Handles many of the traditional planning and control activities associated with project management.
Benefits manager	A business manager who co-ordinates key stakeholder involvement to ensure that the business takes appropriate responsibility in achieving the expected benefits.
Design authority	A business analyst who can develop a system design specification which will meet the business objectives.
Technical authority	A technical specialist who can manage development, testing and implementation of the technical solution.
Risk manager	An independent authority on identifying and mitigating risks within the project. The risk manager must be a senior figure within the project who has the power to stop it if there is a serious risk of failure – commercial or otherwise. Independent research suggests there is a strong correlation between project success and the appointment of an independent, senior manager as risk manager.

individuals we need are working on other projects), it might be similar to the one shown in Table 8.2.

The seven roles identified are those which should provide a sound platform from which the team can deliver the project; they do not, however, need to be assigned to seven different people. Clearly a key role within the project will be that of the project manager. Traditionally, that role has been one of co-ordinating activities, but in a well-performing team the project manager will be a leader, having a clear vision of how the organization can benefit from the use of IT.

If the project involves a high degree of business change, then there is a strong case for the project manager to be a business manager, rather than an IT manager. An IT manager would then assume the role of technical authority, ensuring that all IT-related activities were managed whilst establishing and maintaining key business relationships.

This is likely to be an effective partnership within the project, as it helps prevent one of the main failings of project managers recruited from IT backgrounds – they fall in love with the technology and lose sight of the project's main objectives – to deliver quantifiable benefits into the business.

It has often been said that the perfect project manager is one who lives for the project – in essence the project manager *is* the project. The project manager is a figurehead for the rest of the team and an inspiration to those within the project. The reality, of course, is often very different. High salaries are keeping the market for good project managers extremely buoyant, and it is proving increasingly difficult for organizations to retain them.

The skills shortage which continues to affect the IT profession has resulted in many skilled project managers being replaced by inexperienced and unsuitable employees who have no formal project management qualifications.

A successful project manager is someone who is prepared to stand up, make decisions, and drive the project forward; someone who is genuinely excited about changing the business for the better. At a personal level a successful project manager has the guts and determination to assume responsibility and accountability – enough at least to say, "the buck stops here." It is clear that a successful project manager possesses many competences – too numerous to mention in this book; however, a summary of the major ones must include the following:

■ Negotiation. Gets the resources required and influence senior management by negotiating cleverly.

■ Leadership. Displays classic management, teamwork, communication, and leadership ability. Ensures management commitment and a disciplined approach. Earns respect from the team rather than demanding it. Develops strategies to improve team cohesion. Identifies skills and behavior needed to enhance team performance.

■ Offers value. Raises business performance rather than simply delivering technical capability.

■ Charisma. Has the presence to establish and maintain key relationships.

■ Tenacity. When put under pressure, the project manager remains focused on the end-game. If something needs saying, it is said with conviction.

■ Business-literate. Knows how to translate and communicate IT theory into business practice.

■ Communication. Communicates goals clearly to all. Identifies and resolves conflict. Promotes and maintains ownership of project within the business. Interacts with team and stakeholders. The remote project manager who is never in the office cannot hope to build team spirit and commitment.

Training, coaching, and mentoring

Training, coaching, and mentoring are words that are unlikely to appear together on the average personal development plan or project plan. For some inexplicable reason, organizations are still likely to expect project members to acquire new skills in an *ad-hoc* way, rather than as part of an ongoing personal development program within the organization. Training undoubtedly has a cost attached, and that cost must be offset against the expected benefits the system will eventually provide.

The risks of ignoring training needs should not need to be stated; training is an investment in the organization's major asset – its employees – yet it is often considered an unnecessary expense. End-user organizations are not the sole culprits when it comes to compromising on training; some of the less ethical consultancy organizations often send their consultants out on client sites so they can "learn on the job" (often their way of empowering staff to be responsible for their own career development). The lack of training not only jeopardizes timescales for development within the project, but also the quality of that development.

There is sufficient evidence from failed IS projects to suggest that many new and inexperienced project managers are struggling to cope, often through no fault of their own. What is of more concern, however, is that organizations often do little to help.

In some of the worst IS project failures, organizations have stood aside and watched project managers suffer needlessly. These events rarely have a pleasant ending, and many of these situations result in the departure of a dedicated professional who could have been a huge asset to the organization if given a small amount of support and guidance.

Whether these project managers were misled into thinking that the project was an exercise in simplicity itself or, maybe, because they were wildly out of their depth is largely unimportant. What is important, however, is that help should be made available to those who need it. Project sponsors are right to expect good results from project managers, but whilst the managers themselves might be keen, bright, and good communicators, being thrown in at the deep end in a business-critical project does neither party any favors.

The answer is, of course, to provide project managers with access to internal mentoring or coaching schemes, especially for those who are new to the company or those who show promise, but are still relatively inexperienced. Mentors should be made available, preferably external to the manager's department, to whom the project manager can turn to for advice.

CASE STUDY

Company Z

A service company entered into a multi-million dollar agreement with a major hardware supplier and a software vendor to implement an order management system. The system was intended to replace an existing legacy system that was struggling to cope with significant increases in customer demand.

The contract awarded to the software vendor was a fixed-price contract and specified a six-month delivery time for the initial software release. The vendor was also expected to provide further enhancements by an agreed date. However, the initial release of the software significantly exceeded its planned timescale, thus impacting the delivery date for the system enhancements. By now the project was nowhere near complete, yet its development budget had been exhausted and it was significantly behind schedule.

It was at this point that an independent audit of the whole project was undertaken. The audit concluded that the project was still viable and recommended a number of actions that should be adopted by the customer. The extent to which any recommended actions were performed is not known. Shortly after, the project was abandoned.

Key project events and failure factors

■ *Roles and responsibilities*

From the start of the project it was agreed that the hardware vendor would also manage the systems integration activities for the whole project. As the vendor had previously undertaken this role for similar projects successfully, it is unclear why the IT managers within the organization decided that they could no longer allow the vendor to perform this role.

It is likely that the IT project team did not want to relinquish control of the project to an external supplier, possibly because they had serious doubts over the vendor's capability.

The consequences of this action were inevitable: the internal IT project team became the de facto systems integrator. Whilst the project team were trying to maintain ownership and control of the project, an admirable course of action in the light of events, their lack of experience in this role clearly introduced a risk into the project.

■ *Blinded by technology*

The large amount of functionality needed to support the many business requirements was to be provided by integrating a number of third-party software packages, supporting order entry, pricing, pre-sales, and forecasting. Multi-vendor package integration was, however, not a skill that the internal IT team possessed.

In comparison with their existing systems, the design of the new system was both architecturally complex and extremely sophisticated. Under the circumstances, it is highly likely, therefore, that the internal IT team became overawed with the technology at their disposal at the expense of managing their relationship with the business stakeholders.

■ Scope

The scope of requirements identified by the business was extremely ambitious to say the least.

From the audit performed on the project, it became clear that the over-ambitious requirements specification was the outcome of promises made to the business by the project team in an effort to obtain business funding. Essentially, in order to obtain full support from the business, the project team promised to deliver everything the business wanted without really understanding the consequences of their actions.

It seems likely that the project was undertaken without an effective requirements management process being in place. Given the huge list of requirements for the project, this process would have ensured that requirements were not only prioritized in terms of their business value, but also validated as correct, precise, and testable.

Considering the scope of the project and the over-ambitious timescale, it is difficult to understand why serious questions were not raised regarding the planning of the project. From a technical perspective, the project represented an exciting challenge to the IT project members. From a business perspective the scope and timescale for the project should have raised concerns over the ability of the vendors to deliver the functionality required.

■ Organizational culture

Many of the issues that affected the project were exacerbated by the behavior of senior managers within the organization who chose not to get involved in the project until it was too late. The inherent culture within the organization gave the IT project team little control over the behavior of their business counterparts, and any IT activity which was viewed as hindering the flow of the project (such as ensuring that the requirements were validated and approved by the business) was seen as negative.

■ Resistance to change

Even with clearly identifiable warning signs, such as the repeated failure to achieve major milestones within the plan, the team maintained the status quo, refusing to alter the schedule or the deliverables of the project. It did appear to many within the organization that the team viewed the late delivery of an already over-budget project as the norm and did not seek to change that view.

■ Project planning

The IT project team had overall project management responsibility and required the support and approval of the business organization in order to commit to planning and development milestones. Despite this, development started on the project without the internal IT team or the external software vendor fully understanding the complex business requirements.

■ *Risk management*

Despite all the problems that were prevalent within the project, such as insufficient testing, lack of business knowledge within the project team, lack of confidence in the software development processes of the vendor, the project plan was never amended to accommodate the risks to the project.

In mitigation of the project team, they were now so involved in what was becoming a nightmare of a situation that they were unable able to rise above the technical problems affecting the project to be able to take an overall view.

Supplier management

The flexibility and maturity of many "off-the-shelf" software packages means that they now provide either partial or complete solutions to the majority of business problems. As a result, more and more project managers are turning to third-party suppliers to develop and manage the delivery of packaged solutions into the organization. The fact that more and more systems are now developed outside the organization should not abdicate their responsibility in overseeing development work undertaken by suppliers.

Suppliers have to be managed to ensure that the organization's requirements, project standards, and other constraints are met. No supplier will understand the business and their specific requirements as well as the business themselves, so it is vital that appropriate techniques are adopted by the project manager to ensure that the supplier delivers what is expected.

The key objective of supplier management is to ensure that everyone working on the overall IS project is working towards the same goal. It is not acceptable for a supplier to change their rules of engagement and supply what they want rather than what the customer wants. The supplier management process must, therefore, impose strict standards on what is expected from the supplier and how their association with the organization in general will work in practice.

Managing the contract

The contract between the customer and supplier is a legally-binding document, and should be managed carefully throughout the three key stages of the contract process:

1 pre-contract;

2 invocation (signature);

3 during the contract.

Pre-contract

The process of inviting IT suppliers or service providers to bid for work through mechanisms such as an Invitation to Tender (ITT) or a Request for Proposal (RFP) is a broad and complex area and has many legal implications. Consequently, this subject cannot be covered fully within the scope of this book. There are, however, a few key points that should be considered when deciding to engage third-party suppliers:

■ Do be fair and open

This could be the start of a profitable and mutually beneficial relationship for both parties. Play fair and do not attempt to exploit the supplier – it may backfire and leave you in an awkward position. Once the contract has been agreed in principle, do not try and change it at the last minute to the supplier's detriment; customers who do this rarely receive full co-operation and respect from the supplier. If potential problems do emerge, raise these openly with the supplier and discuss them.

■ Do not reveal the budget

Do not provide any indication of the budget available for the project. This will only give suppliers an idea of how much to charge.

■ Do indicate there is competition

It is only fair to inform the suppliers that they will not be alone in bidding for your work; it will also encourage the supplier to provide honest and realistic prices. Do not, however, let them know who the competition is, as they might be able to use that information to their advantage.

■ Do indicate when you are available for suppliers

It is quite likely that suppliers will need to discuss certain issues and requirements with you. There is little benefit to be gained by refusing to see them, but do not let them use the meeting as an opportunity to deliver a sales pitch.

■ Allow time for suppliers to respond

The average time between issuing the ITT and receiving proposals from suppliers is usually three to six weeks. During this time there may be some queries from the supplier that will need to be handled but, apart from that, you will just have to wait. Make sure your schedule does allow time for the tendering and supplier selection process.

■ *Do not discuss the selection process*

The information sent to suppliers should indicate the schedule for the selection process, but it should not disclose any details about the selection process itself. During the tendering process, clearly indicate which requirements are "must-haves" and which one are merely "nice-to-haves."

Invocation

The basis of the contract must be a signed agreement between both parties, in which the details are clearly defined.

During detailed contract negotiation process, it is likely that events may occur that put a strain on the relationship between the customer and supplier. It is sensible, therefore, to ensure that the individual who has negotiated the contract with the supplier is not the same individual who will manage the project of which the contract forms a part.

Remember to conduct the contract dealings fairly – try and ensure that the risks, rights, and obligations are equal for both parties. Do not try and take advantage of the supplier or leave the supplier with all the responsibilities and no rights as this is hardly the basis for a long-lasting and mutually-rewarding relationship.

During the contract

Successful IS projects involving third party suppliers do not need to rely on legal and contractual conditions to ensure that both parties work together effectively. Once the contract has been signed, the customer and supplier are equal parties in it. The relationship between the customer and supplier should have been established during the supplier selection process and there should have been enough personal contact during that time to have developed reasonable expectations as to how the supplier will behave. There should be no need, therefore, to refer back to the contract once it has been signed.

The benefits of supplier management

Effective supplier management is likely to bring about the following benefits to an IS project:

■ Delivering what was expected

By managing the supplier properly, the probability that the supplier will actually deliver the system as specified by the customer increases dramatically.

Successful delivery is dependent on both parties communicating effectively and tackling issues and risks together throughout the lifecycle of the project.

■ Contained expenditure

It is not unknown for a supplier to try and sell solutions which generate the most income for themselves. Organizations that fail to control the scope and role of the supplier, often as a result of their own inadequate planning and development standards, are in effect giving the supplier a license to print money.

The causes of failure

No contract with supplier

Engaging a supplier to undertake work on the basis of an informal understanding without a formal contract being signed is asking for trouble. The quest for speed negates the need to establish a clear understanding of scope, schedule, standards, and costs.

An unreasonable contract

If the terms of the contract are unreasonable for the suppliers, then they have little incentive to work well on the project. Suppliers who are constrained by unreasonable contracts often spend more time trying to identify "get-out" clauses or ways of altering the terms at the expense of their development responsibilities.

Failure to manage the supplier's progress

Whilst the contract established between customer and supplier will have laid down the rules of engagement for the delivery of a specified piece of work, events can still take a downward turn if the supplier is just left to get on with the job. It is important to remember that the work undertaken by a supplier is only a subset of the overall project, and their progress must be monitored in the same way.

It is likely that the supplier will provide their own project manager to manage their development team, but it is not uncommon for this individual to be under the control of a project manager within the organization. This arrangement is often preferred by both parties as it provides a single point of contact for the supplier and allows their manager to identify their personal success with the success of the project as a whole.

▨▶ People: critical success factors

- Every project must have a project sponsor who can champion the project throughout the organization, both in the IT department and among end-users. A typical project sponsor would be an operating or marketing executive.

- The project manager must be empowered to take risks and make decisions. The overwhelming burden of bureaucracy that is often placed on a project can stifle enthusiasm and leadership within the project manager and the project team.

- The organizational culture must empower the project manager to say no. Too many projects overrun due to "scope-creep" – often the result of pressures being placed on the project manager by the business sponsor to include additional functionality at a late stage within the project. Project sponsors must be made aware of the impact to any changes requested during the project.

- Do not use the history of poor relations between the business and IT communities as an excuse for project failures. Be proactive and approach the other party first. Make sure the whole team possess "soft" inter-organizational and inter-personal skills. Encourage multi-departmental and multi-skilled teams incorporating staff from IT and business teams.

- If you do not have the right people on the team – hire them. If you cannot hire them, raise this as a risk.

- Establish a no-blame culture within the project.

- The board-level or executive sponsor must establish a project steering committee to provide the project manager with direct access to decision-makers.

- Do not go over budget on technology and under budget on people.

- Ensure that any systems supplier uses competent staff who are qualified for the job – preferably qualified by a third party.

▨◧ References

1 M. Chandler, (1998) *NASA Challenger Explosion: A Classic Engineering Disaster*, updated October 1998 http://energiraad.no/oring.htm (accessed 2001)

2 J. Forrest, (2002) *The Challenger Shuttle Disaster: A Failure in Decision Support System and Human Factors Management*, revised March 30, 2002, http://frontpage.hypermall.com/jforrest/challenger/challenger_sts.htm (accessed 2002)

3 M. Boisjoly, *Ethical Decisions – Morton Thiokol and the Space Shuttle Challenger Disaster*, www.onlineethics.org/essays/shuttle/telecon.html (accessed 2001)

4 G. Weinberg, *Psychology of Computer Programming*, Dorset House, New York, 1998. A classic of its time, discussing programming as an individual and team effort. Invaluable to every software development manager

5 C.E. Larson and F.M.J. LaFasto, *Teamwork: What Must go Right; What can go Wrong*, Sage, Newbury, CA, 1989

6 T. DeMarco and T. Lister, *Peopleware*, Dorset House, New York, 1987

7 F. Brooks, *Mythical Man-Month*, Addison-Wesley, Wokingham, 1975

8 R. Waters, 'Taurus system likely to miss target date,' *Financial Times*, September 16, 1991

9 A. Jack, N. Cohen, J. Gapper, M. Urri, I. Hamilton Fazey and R. Waters, 'Angry City takes stock of lost time and money', *Financial Times*, March 12, 1993

10 J. Green-Armytag, "Why Taurus was always ill-starred," *Computer Weekly*, March 18, 1993

11 R. Miles, "Death in the afternoon for Taurus," *Computing*, March 18, 1993

12 R. Peston, "Stock Exchange chief failed to tame bull," *Financial Times*, March 12, 1993

13 R. Waters, "Harsh post-mortem reveals flaws," *Financial Times*, March 19, 1993

14 R. Waters, "The plan the fell to earth," *Financial Times*, March 12, 1993

15 R. Waters, "Stock market chief quits over Taurus," *Financial Times*, March 12, 1993

16 R. Waters, "Stock exchange takes a matador to Taurus," *Financial Times*, March 11, 1993

17 R. Waters and A. Cane, "Sudden death of a runaway bull," *Financial Times*, March 19, 1993

18 J. Wilcock, "The City becomes unplugged," *The Independent on Sunday*, March 14, 1993

19 D. Hobson, (1993) "Egg on John Bull's face or Taurus and the triumph of Occam's razor," *Global Custodian*, www.assetpub.com/archive/gc/93-02gcjune/june93GC046.html (accessed 2002)

20 D. Hobson, (1991) "Taming the bull," *Global Custodian*, www.assetpub.com/archive/gc/91-01gcmarch/mar91GC114.html (accessed 2002)

21 L.J. May, (1998) Major Causes of Software Project Failure, *Crosstalk*, July 1998, http://stsc.hill.af.mil/crosstalk/1998/jul/causes.asp (accessed 2001)

22 S. Vail, "Implementation: your application has failed", *Business & Technology Data Management*, 14–17, 1998

Further reading

M. Armstrong, *How to be an Even Better Manager*, Kogan Page, London, 2000. An excellent book providing an insight into the machinations of management. Key topics include: managing people, managing activities, and developing yourself as a manager

B. Boehm, *Software Engineering Economics*, Prentice Hall, Englewood Cliffs, 1981

S. McConnell (1996) "Classic mistakes," *IEEE Software*, **13** (5), September www.constrex.com/stevemcc/ieeesoftware/bpOS.htm (accessed 2001)

R. Waterhouse (1992) "Project management: is IT it? – people skills versus computer frills," *Project*, Association of Project Managers **4** (12), 26–8

9

Managing software development

When the only tool you have is a hammer, every problem looks like a nail

Anonymous

At the heart of every project exists a process that will deliver one or more products into the organization. Within an IS project, this process is focused on software development. Software development is a fundamental activity within an IS project as it enables a set of functional requirements to be met through the development of one or more computer programs. Typically, the software development process within an IS project will be responsible for the production of one of the following software products:

- systems software – used to control computer hardware and peripheral devices attached to a computer;

- military software – such as missile guidance systems, and navigation systems;

- commercial software – such as marketing, and order management systems.

Despite the need for software development projects, the IS community does not have a good track record in successful software development. Compared to project failure rates in other industry sectors such as construction and engineering, the IS profession has a lot to learn.

Indeed, software development guru Capers Jones has attempted to quantify the problem by suggesting that if the construction industry had the same ratio of failed projects as the software industry, then half of the office buildings in the world over 30 storeys tall would be abandoned before completion, the average height of buildings in New York city would be only three storeys and there would be no skyscrapers at all.[1]

The software development lifecycle

One of the main reasons for the enormous cost overruns on many software development projects is the perception that the only costs involved are those involved with coding – the task of writing computer programs. To many project stakeholders, software development and coding are synonymous, the reality is quite different. Successful software development is the product of a set of integrated processes, more commonly known as the Software Development Life Cycle (SDLC), of which coding is just one. Of all the different approaches to the SDLC, it is the traditional or "waterfall" approach that remains in most widespread use within many organizations.

Traditional software development

To many observers, the traditional approach to software development is far too mechanical and clinical to represent the complex interactions which exist within contemporary IS projects. It comes as no surprise, therefore, that there are very few books on the subject of software development that do not openly endorse the waterfall approach.

The traditional SDLC is based on a series of eight stages which must be performed and completed in sequence (Figure 9.1). Order is important as the next step in the development process cannot be started until its predecessor has been completed.

A key weakness of this approach, and of the development methodologies that are designed to support it, such as SSADM, is the lack of feedback mechanisms within the model. For instance, the strict sequential nature of the process places significant emphasis on lengthy analysis and design phases, in the hope that these tasks will not need to be revisited later in the project. Equally, by the time the construction and testing phases are reached, it is assumed that the design of the solution is correct and technically feasible. This method of software development does not, therefore, accommodate change easily, typically because it "freezes" requirements in the early stages of the lifecycle or by ensuring that any changes made are prohibitively expensive.

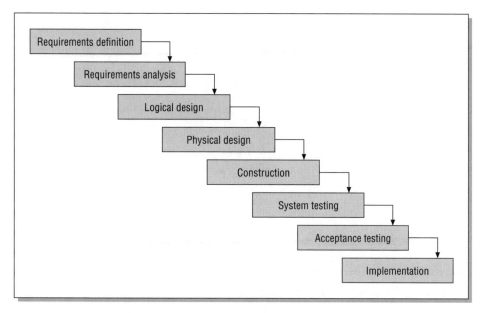

FIGURE 9.1 ▓ The traditional approach to software development

Iterative development

The use of RAD techniques and CASE (Computer-Aided Software Engineering) tools as part of a disciplined software development process is undoubtedly a popular solution to many of the problems experienced within traditional software development.

Iterative development is based upon two fundamental principles, "iterative" development and "incremental" development. Iterative development, unlike the traditional "waterfall" model of systems development, allows the development team to go back to key tasks, such as analysis, design, construction, and testing in order to refine the solution.

For example, if it is decided that the original design identified will not deliver the required functionality, the team can go back and undertake further analysis and design, effectively re-iterating their original activities (Figure 9.2). Because of this iterative approach, each step within the development process needs to be completed only enough in order to move to the next step, as it can be completed within a later iteration.

Incremental development differs from the traditional concept of a single, all-encompassing iteration by breaking down the development activity into a number of smaller iterations or "time-boxes" within the development lifecycle

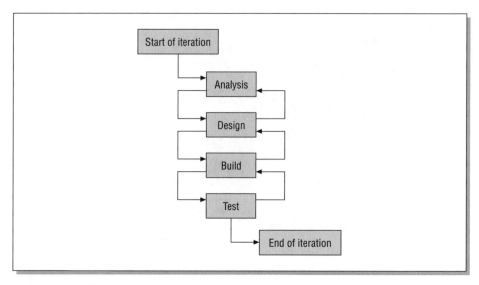

FIGURE 9.2 ■ The lifecycle of a single iteration

(Figure 9.3). Time-boxes set a deadline by which part of the system or an early version of the system will be delivered. The duration of each time-box will clearly influence the nature of the project – a time-box greater than three months is likely to be interpreted as a project phase in the traditional approach to development and focus may be lost. Equally, a time-box of two weeks may place intolerable burdens on the user community; the optimum duration for a time-box is likely to be somewhere between three and six weeks.

A key principle underpinning contemporary approaches to software development is the need for active user participation. However, whilst bringing users into the development process may seem the perfect way to ensure that systems are produced that are business-focused, techniques such as joint application design (where managers, users, and developers agree functionality) and iterative development (which promotes feedback through the development process) have also been responsible for encouraging users to request more and more functionality.

Time-boxing development keeps the demand for functionality in control by having an immovable deadline for the time-box. When the time-box has finished, so has development for that iteration. Control over user requirements can now be achieved as the only component within a time-box that is flexible is the scope of work; resources and time are fixed. This is a significant departure from traditional forms of software development, where functionality is fixed, but the time and resources needed to produce it vary enormously from stage to stage. Figure 9.4 shows how this principle relates to DSDM – a popular software development methodology supporting iterative development.

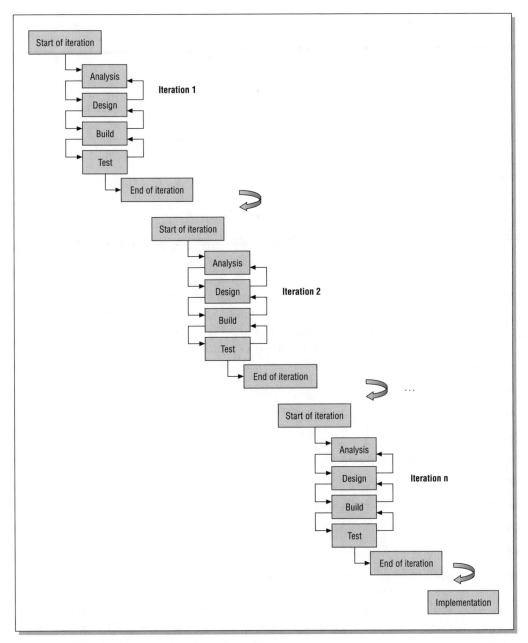

FIGURE 9.3 ▓▓▓ The iterative development lifecycle

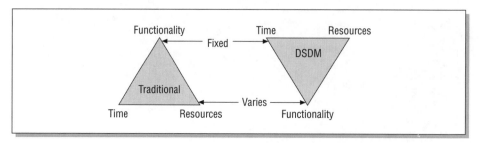

FIGURE 9.4 ■ Key differences between DSDM and traditional software development techniques

The causes of software development failure

Even with the adoption of an established software development methodology, coding activities within software projects are often approached in an *ad-hoc* fashion, in isolation from critical controlling processes such as configuration management, risk management, and release management. The software development life cycle, however, regardless of the approach used, does not, in itself, guarantee project success. This can only be achieved by ensuring that the software development process is closely aligned to other key processes within the project, namely:

■ requirements management;

■ project management;

■ defect tracking;

■ configuration management;

■ quality assurance;

■ maintaining skill and competency levels within the development team;

■ change control;

■ people management.

Few organizations have either the resources, or the will to integrate every one of these key processes into their software development lifecycle. This, however, does suggest at least one reason why the rate of IS failure is so high. Whilst the earlier chapters of the book identified many of the general factors affecting IS project success – a subset of these relate specifically to software development failure and include:

■ the lack of metrics;

■ the lack of sizing, estimating, or planning tools;

- the lack of progress reporting or design tools;
- no code inspection or defect tracking;
- informal change control;
- more than 30 per cent unstable requirements or more than 2 per cent scope-creep per month;
- excessive schedule pressure;
- poor relations with users or divisive internal politics;
- naïve senior executives;
- geographically separate development team;
- unclear management structure;
- more than 40 per cent staff attrition;
- abrupt introduction of new or radical technologies;
- incompetent or poorly-trained software development managers.

 **CASE STUDY**

Denver International Airport Baggage System

Denver International Airport (DIA) was built to replace Stapleton International Airport and was the first major airport to be built in the US since 1974.[2,3] Spread over 50 square miles (129.5 square kilometres), it had the capacity to eventually expand to 12 runways. On opening, the airport had a terminal building and three concourses, the farthest of which being about one mile (1.6 kilometres) from the terminal.

Because of the sheer size of the airport, airport planners decided that a state-of-the-art automated baggage handling system, capable of moving bags around the airport would be needed. To meet this requirement, one of the largest and most sophisticated baggage systems of its kind in the world was designed, at an estimated cost of $129 million (£86 million).

The original design for the system was extremely large and included over 17 miles of track, six miles of conveyors, 4,000 "telecarts" on which baggage would be loaded, 5,000 electric motors, 59 barcode reader arrays (used to electronically identify the destination and routing of baggage) and over 150 computers which would manage routing of traffic throughout the airport. Through the use of a high-speed baggage system, the airport expected quicker turnaround times for aircraft resulting in a better service for passengers.

Despite such a sophisticated design, the baggage system was plagued by both mechanical and software failures. In tests of the system, bags were misloaded, misrouted, or simply fell out of the telecarts, causing the system to jam. The installation of video cameras at some of the known trouble-spots documented many operational problems which included the following:

- The baggage system continued to unload bags even though they were jammed on the conveyor belt. This happened because the photo-electric sensor at this location failed to detect the pile of bags on the conveyor belt and hence did not signal the system to stop.

- The system loaded bags onto telecarts that were already full, causing bags to fall off and jam the telecart. This happened because the system lost track of which telecarts had been loaded or unloaded during a previous jam. When the system was refreshed after a jam, it failed to show that telecarts were loaded.

A question of complexity

Failures in the software system were heavily reported at the time; estimates suggested the system employed over one million lines of real-time software code, with "two to three errors per 1,000 lines of code typical".[2] At the time it was estimated that debugging software errors accounted for 25 per cent of the project's schedule or as many as 24 man-hours per error.

Troubleshooting real-time software without the aid of sophisticated software debugging tools is extremely difficult, and the need to either recreate the problem or recreate the run-time environment configuration will be a key factor in determining the success of the exercise. It appears there was little evidence of either playing a major role during the development and operation of the DIA baggage system.

As a result of problems with the baggage system, the opening of DIA was postponed. Originally due to open in October 1993, the date was initially moved to March 1994 and then to May 1994. The cost of these delays was estimated at around $1 million (£600,000) a day, of which over $500,000 (£300,000) was related to interest charges on the $3.2 billion bond issue raised by the city of Denver. In setting a "final" deadline of February 1995, DIA also introduced an alternative "conventional" baggage system at a cost of almost $61 million (£42 million) which would provide a backup service to the automated system in the event of failure.

A column in a local newspaper at the time compared DIA's baggage problems to the now-infamous AT&T switching failure incident. Problems started when a small and relatively minor software error progressed undetected through AT&T's switching system. The ripple-effect, however, produced a much larger problem which eventually swamped the main switching system and shut-down nearly 90 per cent of the company's domestic phone operations for several hours.

The global scope of failure

Whilst it may appear that the majority of software failures are to be found within Europe and North America, Asia is no stranger to IS project disasters. The new $2.2 billion (£1.5 billion) Kuala Lumpur International Airport in Malaysia suffered hours of flight delays when the airport's new "total airport management system" was unable to cope with commands entered by improperly trained staff[3].

The system combined airport-wide communications with IT, allowing airport tenants and operators to communicate and share information from a number of shared databases. When, shortly after opening, the $168 million (£112 million) central computer system failed, thousands of travelers were left stranded in its wake. The computer system controlled everything; from escalators to flight information monitors. Ticketing had to be performed manually; communication lines broke down, as did mechanical baggage systems.

Similarly, numerous problems turned the world's most expensive airport, Hong Kong's $20 billion (£13 billion) Chek Lap Kok international airport, into chaos when key computer systems failed.[5] The faulty IT systems resulted in arrivals being stranded on the tarmac due to the lack of parking gate directions being issued; passengers missing fights due to problems with the Fight Information Display System; lost and delayed luggage with baggage handling systems failing and problems reconciling baggage, which meant that baggage was loaded onto planes even though the passengers failed to board.

The day after the new airport opened, all airfreight traffic was diverted to another airport due to a bug in the freight system deleting records. The managing director of the cargo terminal was in no doubt who was to blame – the airport authority by stating that "the whole feeling we got throughout this project was the airport would open on a certain date regardless of whether we were ready or not."[6] The breakdown in operations at the airport cost the Hong Kong economy 0.35 per cent of its annual gross domestic product.

Both airport systems suffered problems which were caused by the implementation of technically-advanced IT systems combined with poor training, inadequate testing, and a failure to provide backup systems in the event of failure. In both cases, relatively minor events such as poor quality data being input into key systems eventually caused large-scale failures.

The huge cost overruns experienced by many IS projects are more likely to be incurred through the identification and resolution of programming errors rather than from the direct costs of coding. The lack of a disciplined approach to software development is clearly a significant factor affecting the success of IS projects and, to a large extent, it is a reflection of the calibre of those managing software development projects. Knowing the right approach to software development and understanding what procedures and processes must be established before the project commences are the actions of a competent and responsible software development manager.

It is not uncommon for many organizations to claim that their projects adopt de facto software development methodologies as a means of ensuring quality within their IS projects. For one thing it impresses the customer, and for another it helps promote and sustain confidence within the development team.

Despite these claims, however, many of these organizations do not possess formal procedures documenting how such a methodology should be used within their environment, nor do they have the processes necessary to ensure that the methodology is adhered to. As a consequence, many IS development projects using tried and tested methodologies are lured into a false sense of security. Software development excellence is seen as a *fait accompli* rather than from a combination of process management, project management, and the use of an effective software development methodology.

Measuring software development complexity

IS projects, regardless of their size, are complex in nature. Ensuring the success of software development activities within IS projects, therefore, requires a disciplined approach to be taken. Despite this, most organizations undertaking software development projects possess nothing more than an *ad-hoc* approach to software development, which inevitably leads to software project overruns on time and cost.

Defining software complexity

Software complexity is often considered to be proportional to the size of the development effort; it is much more. Complexity is a factor of software development that also includes:

- organizational structure – management and team roles and responsibilities must be clear and understood for reporting and control mechanisms to operate effectively;

- leading edge technology – development using costly, immature, and unproven technology;

- scope of development – managing and integrating development from multiple development teams;

- poor requirements analysis – any software develement project is inherently more complex if the full requirements are not understood and agreed beforehand;

- geographical location of team – even simple software development becomes complex if it must be co-ordinated across geographically dispersed development teams.

The need for software metrics

IS projects are inherently risky because the software development processes necessary to deliver complex functionality are, themselves, complex. What is clear, though, is that without measurement, the software development process cannot be improved. For instance, monitoring the ratio of defects found and corrected before the system is implemented into a live environment to those reported by users after implementation is just one method that fosters improvement in the software development process.

However, whilst there is a clear need to establish software quality metrics, measurement against these can only begin once a starting baseline has been identified (i.e. where are we now?). Once a baseline has been established, a software improvement plan can be introduced (i.e. how can we get to where we want to be?) and, finally, a means of achieving software development excellence can be embarked upon (i.e. what do we have to do to achieve our goals?).

The lack of accurate estimates in the software development process must not be seen, however, as just a deficiency in programming activities. Successful software development will be dependent upon program code of a known and acceptable level of quality, but it will also but will also require similar levels of excellence in documentation, design, analysis, testing, and training. Metrics must relate to people just as much as they relate to technology.

Software development metrics deal with the measurement of a software product and the process by which it is developed. Once metrics have been established they can be used in the management and control of the development process to trigger improvements such as the following:

■ Improving the consistency of software development effort (productivity)

Inconsistent productivity rates between different IS project teams may be an indication that there is no standard development process (i.e. we all produce different code to tackle the same problem) or that such a process exists and is not being followed. If development teams conform to a standard development process, productivity levels should stabilize and become more consistent.

■ Improving the quality of software produced

Poor quality software is often the main reason why many of the project's expected benefits are never realized. Software that does not perform the intended task to an agreed level of quality is all too frequent, and does nothing to bridge that gulf that so often exists between the IT and business communities. Indeed, most business managers, I suspect, would probably agree to a moderate increase in software development costs if they thought that the end result would transform their business and deliver the planned benefits.

▪ Tracking and monitoring changes in scope (scope-creep)

It is unrealistic to assume that requirements can be "frozen" at the start of an IS project – there must be an expectation that business requirements may change during the project. This in itself is not a problem; the rate at which they change in scope and complexity, however, *is* a problem.

Requirements must be measured at the end of the requirements management, design, and implementation phases of the project to obtain figures that can provide the basis for meaningful comparison. Metrics obtained for the requirements/design phase can be compared to metrics obtained once the system has been implemented. If the figure has increased, then either the project has become better defined or the project has actually grown in size. The amount of growth is an indication of how well the requirements were captured and/or communicated to the development team.

▪ Calculating the actual cost of software

Most organizations greatly underestimate the total costs involved throughout the lifecycle of a software system. Whilst initial costs include licensing and development, many organizations fail to identify costs for future enhancements and maintenance in their budgets. Software development costs, therefore, do not only represent the costs associated with the construction and deployment of a new system, but also the ongoing costs of maintaining and improving that system during its economic life.

▪ Estimating software development effort and costs

Many IS projects are identified as failing when the planning tasks associated with the project (in this case, software development activities) greatly exceed their schedule and cost estimates. One of the main causes of this failure is the use of wildly inaccurate estimates from over-ambitious or inexperienced software developers within the project.

Estimating techniques

Estimating techniques can be broken down broadly into two categories: top-down estimating and bottom-up estimating. Top-down estimates are based on the requirements of the system, whereas bottom-up requirements are based on understanding the design and size of the components within the system.

Top-down estimating

■ *Function Point Analysis*

Function Point Analysis (FPA) has been used to varying levels of success since being developed by Allan Albrecht in the mid-1970s.[7] Function Point Analysis measures software size based on the logical functionality of the system. Overall complexity of the system is derived from the number of function points the system possesses, based on, for example, the number of internal and external interfaces the system incorporates.

The benefits of using FPA, however, are now largely discredited amongst many IT professionals, but it still remains popular nevertheless.

■ *Estimating by comparison*

One of the most popular top-down techniques for estimating within many IS projects is estimating by comparison. Experience is a key factor in determining the success of IS projects, and the lack of it constitutes a serious risk to the software development process. Estimating by comparison uses information gained from previous projects (whether successful or not) to help identify meaningful estimates for future development work which is of a similar nature.

The use of past experiences to help plan future projects is a small but useful step in the larger process of defining and implementing a source of historical software development information. Once captured, this repository of information can then be used to improve the overall "maturity" of the software development process within the organization.

For this technique to be effective, however, it has to rely heavily on the skills of individuals to develop estimates based upon actual experience. This approach is similar to the use of expert judgement, although in this case the experts use existing information gained from other projects to develop the estimates.

Estimating from past experience allows an assessment to be made of the software development activity using a combination of documented and anecdotal evidence. Often used in conjunction with other techniques, estimating from experience uses information gained from previous projects to provide a baseline on which to base a more accurate estimate, such as: "How similar is this project to other completed projects?"

- Is the technology the similar?
- Is the size and format of the data similar?

- Is the architecture of the system similar?

- How similar are the functional requirements?

- What estimating methods and data values were used for these projects?

- Were they successful?

- Can I use the same estimates for this project?

For example, if a previous Java™-based development project contained 100 program units and the work to be estimated uses 50 Java program units, then it may well be expected that the programming effort required for the new project will be 50 per cent of the effort required for the completed project.

■ *Expert judgement*

The use of expert consultants or gurus remains a popular choice for many organizations wishing to benefit from the experiences gained from individuals who have performed similar work. Typically such experts are usually sourced from specialist companies external to the organization.

Bottom-up estimating

Bottom-up estimating relies on counting programs, screens, interfaces, reports, and any other delivery-focused component within the software development process. One of the most widely used bottom-up estimates is the one used to identify program size; the Lines of Code metric (LOC).

Using LOC as a rough metric, the software development team can identify the relationship between one program and another (e.g. a 2,000 line program is twice as "large" as a 1,000 line program). Whilst this may initially seem to be of little value, the LOC metric can, however, be used to calibrate subsequent estimates which have been gathered using top-down methods (and vice versa).

The LOC can be classified as a *simple* metric because it can be directly observed, as can other simple metrics, such as number of defects during unit testing or total development time for the project. A much more valuable metric that would help promote a greater understanding and assessment of the software development process is the use of *computed* or *derived* metrics.

Computed metrics are those that cannot be directly observed but are computed using other metrics. Examples of computed metrics are those commonly used for productivity, such as LOC produced per person per month (LOC/person-month), or for product quality, such as the number of defects per thousand lines of code (defects/KLOC).

Software cost estimating tools

■ *COCOMO*

COCOMO (COnstructive COst MOdel) is probably the best known and documented of all the software cost estimating tools. Being model-based, it provides three levels of use: basic, intermediate, and detailed. The detailed cost model can provide software costs that are within 20 per cent of actual values 70 per cent of the time[9,10].

When implemented, the tool provides a range on its cost, effort, and schedule estimates, from best-case to most likely, to worst-case outcomes. It also allows a planner to easily perform "what if" scenario exploration, by quickly demonstrating the effect adjusting requirements, resources, and staffing might have on predicted costs and schedules (e.g. for risk management or job bidding purposes).

■ *SPQR*

SPQR is the more popular name for the Software Productivity, Quality and Reliability model produced by Capers Jones.[8,9,10] Its basic approach is similar to that of COCOMO and is based on 20 reasonably well-defined factors and 25 less well-defined factors that influence software costs and productivity.

The model requires more than 100 responses from questions about the project to be supplied in order to formulate the parameters which must be provided to compute development costs and schedules. The manufacturers claim that SPQR can provide cost estimations that are within 15 per cent of actual values 90 per cent of the time.

Presenting the estimates

Presenting estimates for software development plays an important part in helping to set and manage expectations for the customer and other key stakeholders. Estimates, by definition, cannot be precise, but the case scenarios as shown in Table 9.1 are important for a number of reasons:

TABLE 9.1 ▨ The presentation of software development estimates

Case scenario	Development estimate
Best-case	May 15, 2003
Planned-case	June 15, 2003
Current-case	June 20, 2003
Worst-case	August 15, 2003

- They allow test estimates to be compared against each other, which may highlight important issues. For example, if the current-case and worst-case scenarios are the same, then the project has got serious problems and remedial action is necessary.

- They provide an effective means by which key target dates can be communicated to project stakeholders.

- They promote understanding and awareness of the actions stakeholders may need to take in order to move from one case scenario to another. For instance, to move from the planned-case scenario to the best-case scenario may require additional funding to be approved.

Achieving software development excellence

Over the years, the IT profession has gained a reputation for failing to meet the needs of an increasingly global business community. Indeed, the IT profession is now infamous for introducing a plethora of products, methodologies, tools, and processes which so often fail to meet the high expectations placed on them. The procurement of new software tools and methodologies is not, however, the fundamental cause of this problem. It is much more likely that this problem is caused by the failure of the organization to manage their software development process effectively.

The software Capability Maturity Model

In response to this problem, the Software Engineering Institute (SEI), operated by Carnegie Mellon University in the US, developed a model for assessing the maturity of the software processes within an organization.[11] The model, the SEI Capability Maturity Model (CMM), describes the principles and practices underlying software maturity and was developed to help software organizations improve the maturity of their software processes from *ad-hoc* chaotic processes to mature, disciplined approaches. The CMM is now a *de-facto* standard for assessing and improving software processes and has, at its core, the following fundamental concepts:

- A *software process* can be defined as a set of activities, methods, practices, and transformations that people use to develop and maintain software and its associated products (e.g. project plans, design specifications, code, test cases, and documentation). As an organization matures, the software process becomes better defined and more consistently implemented.

- *Software process capability* describes the range of results that can be expected by following a software process. If used within an organization it provides one method of predicting the most likely outcome from future software projects undertaken.

- *Software process performance* represents the actual results achieved by following a software process. Whilst software process capability focuses on expected results, software process performance focuses on results achieved.

- *Software process maturity* is the level at which the software process is performed, managed, and controlled. Maturity implies a potential for growth in capability and indicates the quality of the software process within an organization and the consistency with which it is applied to IS projects.

The CMM is organized into five levels of maturity, with each level of maturity representing a small, evolutionary step towards continuous process improvement rather than a large, revolutionary innovation. Maturity levels range from one to five (Figure 9.5) and each one comprises a set of process goals which,

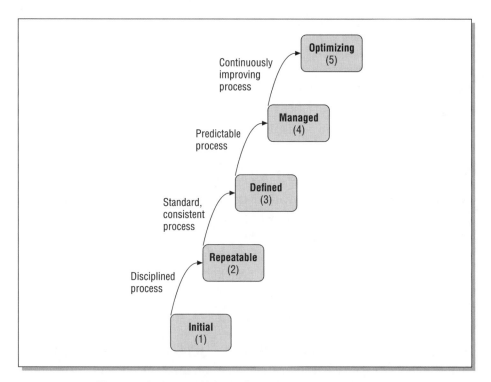

FIGURE 9.5 ▨ The maturity levels within the Capability Maturity Model

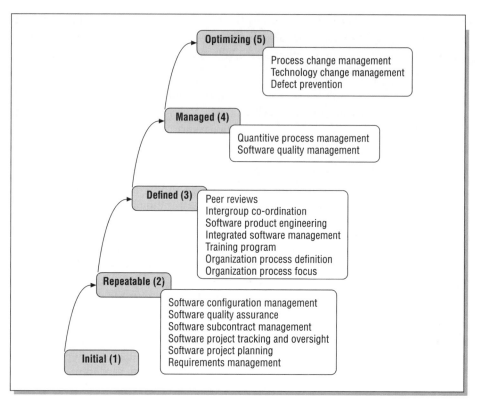

FIGURE 9.6 ■ CMM key process areas by maturity level

when satisfied, indicate that an important component of the software development process has been established.

With the exception of Level 1, each maturity level comprises a number of key process areas (Figure 9.6). Each Key Process Area (KPA) identifies the processes that an organization must focus upon to improve its software development maturity.

Level 1 – initial level

At this level, the absence of any recognized software development process characterizes development as *ad-hoc*, unordered, and occasionally even chaotic. Planning software development activities is difficult as the productivity and quality of software cannot be guaranteed, nor can the availability of the resources required to produce it.

An experienced and competent software development manager can overcome many of these problems if an exceptionally good software team are used to undertake development activities. Equally, a forceful and influential manager can probably withstand organizational pressures and short-cut the development process for a limited period.

However, when these managers and their teams leave the project, their skills leave with them. Strong individual process skills are no substitute for a mature and disciplined software development process.

Despite the *ad-hoc* nature of development processes, Level 1 organizations do deliver software that is usable, even if, through a lack of planning, the development project has exceeded its budget and timescale. At this level, IS projects experience wide variations in achieving cost, schedule, functionality, and quality targets. Success is, at best, unpredictable.

Heroic feats may, however, deliver satisfactory software into the organization, but these can only be repeated for a subsequent project if those same competent individuals are assigned onto it. Of course, selecting, hiring, developing, and retaining people are significant issues for any organization regardless of their level of maturity, but they are largely out of scope of the CMM.

Level 2 – the repeatable level

At this level basic policies for managing a software project and the procedures to implement these policies are established. Project controls to track cost, schedule, and functionality are implemented as part of the project management process.

Projects undertaken within Level 2 organizations also adopt basic software management controls. Realistic plans for new development projects can be made based on results observed from previous projects and on the requirements from the current project.

Software requirements and the software components needed to satisfy them are identified and baselined, and processes are in place to control their integrity. Equally, software product standards exist, and processes are in place to make sure they are followed. If any subcontractors form part of the project, processes are in place to establish and manage a customer–supplier relationship.

The software process capability of Level 2 organizations can be summarized as "disciplined." Sufficient processes exist to plan and track software development, creating a stable development environment. Project processes are formulated through the use of a project management system, using realistic estimates based on the performance of previous projects.

Level 3 – the defined level

At the defined level, development procedures are standardized and documented across the organization as a whole, including software development processes and management processes. At Level 3, this is referred to as the organization's standard software process.

Projects undertaken within Level 3 organizations use the organization's standard software process to develop their own approved processes unique for the project. A well-defined software process at this level is characterized by the inclusion of readiness criteria, inputs, standards, and procedures for development, verification mechanisms (such as peer reviews), outputs, and completion criteria. The use of a standard software development process throughout the organization not only provides management with good visibility of IS projects, but also allows projects to be audited and benchmarked to help improve organizational process capability.

The software process capability of Level 3 organizations can be summarized as being "standard and consistent". Software development and management activities are stable and repeatable across the organization as a whole.

Level 4 – the managed level

At the managed level, measurable quality goals are established for software products and the processes employed to create them. To help support these goals, an organizational measurement program exists to obtain productivity and quality data from all projects within the organization.

Measuring the software processes is a key element at this level and allows projects to control their products and processes by ensuring that their process performance falls within acceptable limits. A known and acceptable level of software process capability at this level allows new products and applications to be introduced into the organization as risks can be identified and managed.

The software process capability of Level 4 organizations can be summarized as being "quantifiable and predictable." Processes are measured and performance is controlled to ensure that it operates within acceptable limits. Software products are of a predictably high quality.

Level 5 – the optimizing level

At this level, the software process can defined as being continuously improving. The whole organization is focused on continuous improvement by identifying weaknesses in its processes and proactively improving them. The aim at this level is for organizations to ensure continuous improvement by obtaining quantitative feedback from processes and testing new ideas and technologies. In particular, software processes are evaluated to prevent known types of defect from recurring and lessons learned from previous projects are captured and communicated to other projects.

The software process capability of Level 5 organizations can be summarized as being "continuously improving." Level 5 organizations are continuously striving to improve their software development processes and, as a result, to improve their project successes.

▬▷ Reducing software project failures using the CMM

In 1995, an assessment was undertaken by the SEI of 440 organizations[12]; over 70 per cent were still at Level 1, whereas only a mere 1 per cent had reached Level 4 and only one organization had reached Level 5. Other surveys undertaken in Europe and North America indicate that between 85 per cent to 98 per cent of software development organizations are classed as Level 1.

Achieving software excellence is not cheap and should not be considered to be a "quick-fix" to a simple problem. It is ironic, therefore, that whilst many organizations will not invest money to make sure software development is done right the first time, there always seems to be money available to do it right a second time. These organizations should consider themselves fortunate; in a competitive market where companies win or lose customers on the strength of their products and processes, not everyone is given a second chance.

The CMM is, however, only a process-based model, and whilst it can be decomposed initially into a number of key processes, and subsequently into a number of "key practices" it can only provide information on "what" must be done. The CMM does not indicate "how" these goals should be achieved, such as the implementation of configuration management or defect tracking.

Using tools and techniques to implement the CMM

Software development techniques such as RAD combined with CASE tools can be adopted fairly easily within organizations to support many of the CMM key processes. Indeed, for organizations at the initial level of process maturity, RAD techniques, used in conjunction with project management and configuration management tools, can be introduced very easily into the organization and add value almost immediately.

CASE tools

CASE tools are automated tools that support the software development lifecycle and provide support for activities such as data modeling, functional decomposition and automatic code generation. Typically CASE tools support development over multiple platforms and operating systems, and so are most often utilized in client-server environments. Whilst specific functionality varies, the majority of CASE tools possess some or all of the following features:

- an information repository or data dictionary;
- the application of recognized software development techniques;
- project management and quality assurance;
- full systems development lifecycle support.

The use of very high-level languages such as fourth generation languages (e.g. CA-Ideal® or FOCUS®) is a form of RAD known as "generator" RAD.[13] Indeed, the use of fourth generation languages to support application development can help reduce the complexity of programming activities and reduce development times.

The main problem with these tools, however, is their lack of scalability. Generator tools are likely to improve usability, visibility, and assembly at the expense of efficiency. For example, the New Jersey Department of Motor Vehicles' registration system was written in Ideal to meet an aggressive schedule, but was so slow that at one point over one million New Jersey vehicles were driving around with unprocessed license renewals.[14]

Even when systems are constructed from larger components, such as GUI (Graphical User Interface) builders, database management systems, and distributed middleware, scalability problems remain a serious threat when such components are used in very large, distributed software environments.

The London Ambulance computer-aided dispatch system, discussed in Chapter 5, used Visual Basic to support the rapid development of key systems. Whilst other factors also played a significant part in contributing to the failure of the project, the problems encountered as a result of poor system performance were never to be resolved which ultimately led to the decision being taken to abandon the system.

It is important, therefore, for an organization to assess the impact of using iterative techniques on its culture, processes, employees, and projects. Only then can the migration from a traditional development methodology to an iterative development methodology deliver real benefits.

When CASE tools are used effectively, they support rapid, iterative design, and the rapid generation of code. In a demanding business climate where "first-to-market" delivery often takes precedence over functionality and efficiency (which can be resolved in subsequent releases), speed of delivery is likely to be an important determiner between project success and failure.

The use of CASE tools to support the software development lifecycle is generally acknowledged to provide the following benefits:

- gains in software development productivity;
- the production of high-quality software;
- reductions in maintenance costs;
- improvements in systems performance.

The successful adoption of a RAD methodology, supported by the appropriate CASE tools can, therefore, introduce a level of software process discipline and progress the maturity of an organization to CMM Level 2 or above. At this level, a disciplined process is in place, and software development methodologies such as DSDM or RUP can be used to help support the main KPAs identified within the CMM.

Both RUP and DSDM can be mapped to Level 2 of the CMM through the use of software development processes and CASE tool support. Table 9.2 provides an example of how DSDM can be mapped onto the CMM.

Reducing software development schedule failure

All software development projects are undertaken in the knowledge that the project must deliver an agreed set of products into the business within the constraints of time, cost, and quality. Software project failure is, therefore, characterized by the inability to implement an agreed set of deliverables within these constraints.

A key contributor to IS project failure is often the insistence of business stakeholders that all necessary business capability must be delivered from a single product release, resulting in excessively long development schedules. Lengthy development timescales are not in themselves a serious problem to an IS project; they do, however, represent a major risk which can affect its successful delivery.

Projects that have lengthy development timescales, frequently, as a result of using a sequential approach to software development, often fall foul of the following:

TABLE 9.2 ■ Mapping DSDM onto Level 2 of the CMM

CMM Level 2 KPA	DSDM principle	CASE requirement
Requirements management	Ambassador user role.	Requirements management tool.
Software project planning	Empowered teams. Project plans defined by delivered products rather than by completed activities.	Project management tool.
Software project tracking and oversight	Project monitoring. Communication of progress to interested parties (project team, user management, other management). Monitoring the production of deliverables and quality at the end of each time-box.	Project management tool linked to configuration management tool.
Software configuration management	Parallel working necessitates CM tool support. Functional model iterations and design and build iterations must be captured by CM system.	Configuration management tool.
Software quality assurance	Quality control enabled through inspections, reviews, dynamic testing, use of static code analysis (if tools available). Quality assurance enabled either through existing procedures or through implementing the quality plan.	Useful tools include: code analyzers, automated testing tools, audit tools, inspection tools, configuration management and requirements management tools.
Subcontract management	Achieved through vendor/purchaser relationships. DSDM "cashbox" approach to negotiating and agreeing costs.	Configuration and requirements management tools.

- loss of focus from business and IT communities ("why are we doing this?");
- gradual increase in scope ("with a bit more time we can deliver more functionality");
- users reject system for not satisfying business requirements ("we don't do that anymore");
- development costs massively exceed their budgeted targets.

Research undertaken by some of the leading consultancy organizations has identified a possible connection between the overall duration of the project and the probability that the project will experience one or more of these problems. From this research, many attempts have since been made to determine the optimum length for an IS project. A rough estimate placed on this value has generally been acknowledged to be somewhere between five and six months.

Despite the unqualified nature of this recommendation, the underlying principle should not be ignored. Projects that cannot deliver products or services into the organization within these timescales should be rigorously reviewed. Even a large and complex project should be capable of being split up into a number of smaller and inherently more manageable "sub-projects"; reducing risk whilst maintaining a phased approach to satisfying key project milestones.

Although RAD techniques can be used to reduce the schedule for a software development project, do not be misled into thinking they are a panacea to the problems associated with failing IS projects. Projects are no more easier to initiate, plan, or control just because they use iterative techniques.

In many cases, such projects may prove much more challenging than projects using traditional development techniques. This is particularly true if this is the first iterative project to be implemented within the organization; the risks are there and failure remains a possibility.

RAD techniques will almost certainly increase the risks to the project if they are implemented for the wrong reasons. A form of RAD, known appropriately as "dumb" RAD, is commonly encountered when a project sponsor sets an unrealistic and arbitrarily short deadline for a software project without first undertaking an analysis of its feasibility.

This can happen for a number of reasons, the most likely candidates being internal company politics, poor decision-making, fear of losing a vital business opportunity, or simply through over-optimism in the delivery capabilities of the project. Failed RAD projects such as those experienced by the Bank of America (Master Net), the London Stock Exchange (TAURUS) , the American Airlines consortium (CONFIRM) and Denver International Airport's baggage system are not the first, and are unlikely to be the last, RAD projects to end in disaster.[13]

Whilst meeting schedule targets is one of a number of project management success criteria, if schedule deadline is the project sponsor's critical success criterion for the project it is important that a clear and precise approach is agreed between the project sponsor and the project manager. If the software development process is managed properly, it will enable the delivery of the most valuable capability within the stated deadline. An effective approach that mitigates many of the risks inherent in this situation works as follows:

1   The customer identifies their requirements.

2   The customer identifies their longest acceptable project schedule.

3   The developers estimate the schedule for developing the requirements. For this to be accurate, a combination of expert judgement and software estimating tools should be used.

4   If this schedule can be accommodated within the project schedule, then development can proceed, otherwise:

5 The customer prioritizes their requirements.

6 The developers design a system which supports the most important requirements, thereby allowing low-priority features to be excluded if there is insufficient time left in the schedule.

7 Key functionality is developed. Further capability is added in priority order until there is no schedule time available.

Each step is critical for the approach to succeed. For example, if requirements are not prioritized and the system architecture is not flexible enough to allow features to be added or dropped, an attempt to reduce the scope of the project in order to meet the schedule is likely to run into problems. Experience should tell you that the most likely effect of this will be to push the schedule further out.

Adopting this approach also enables the risks associated with software development to be mitigated when meeting cost constraints rather than schedule constraints is identified as a project success criterion. As with the fixed-schedule approach, it is vital that requirements are captured and prioritized by business stakeholders. If these requirements can be delivered within the costs identified for the project, all well and good. If not, the most important requirements that can be satisfied within the costs are developed first (often referred to as "cash-boxing" requirements).

Planning for software excellence

Achieving software excellence by implementing new methodologies and adopting process models such as the CMM is a sound investment, but it is not a "silver bullet." New tools or methodologies often fail to deliver the benefits promised, either because the tool does not meet the requirements of the business or because insufficient planning was undertaken prior to implementation.

For example, the exaggerated claims made supporting the use of Object-Oriented Development (OOD) techniques within iterative development regimes has not halted the number of software development failures – projects using OOD techniques fail just as frequently as those using more traditional forms of development.

What is apparent is the need to understand and plan the approach by which software excellence within the organization will be achieved. Do not expect it to be a short-term technical solution to a business problem; excellence can only be achieved when people, processes, and technology are used together effectively, in support of business goals. In planning for excellence therefore, the following may act as an initial guide.

■ **Understand the environment**

Before determining or modifying a methodology for the IS project or organization, determine the nature of the problem, and the capabilities of staff, software, and hardware environments. Identify baseline measurements for size, development effort, software changes, and errors.

■ **Match the process to the environment**

Tailor processes to match the environment; use your understanding of your staff and the problem. Do not include processes that cannot be enforced.

■ **Experiment to improve the process**

Once a basic match has been made, stretch it a little. Base changes on the likelihood of improvement goals being reached – but be wary of too much change.

■ **Limit the use of leading-edge or unknown technology**

Just because other organizations have successfully used new technology is no guarantee it will work for you. Minor improvements can be made from sharing technology, but consider the risks if planning major changes based on relatively unknown technology.

Managing software development: critical success factors

- Develop and adhere to a software development plan.
- Empower the project team. Assign roles and responsibilities and ensure that each member understands the methodology and development standards.
- Minimize bureaucracy – more meetings, documentation, and management does not necessarily translate into more success.
- Establish and manage the software baseline.
- Measure progress against the plan. Use past projects for comparisons. Do not hesitate to reduce the scope of work if necessary.
- Re-estimate system size and complexity regularly. There is nothing wrong with realizing that size has been underestimated or that productivity has been overestimated. The failing would be not to define processes to detect this and take action when necessary.

■ Foster a team spirit. Communicate well and ensure that all members of the project understand their role in achieving the project goals. Help each other to overcome difficulties and celebrate successes as a unit, applauding each other along the way.

■ Control problem employees. Failure to deal with individuals who cause disruption is a common characteristic of 'problem' projects, and it is still the most common complaint teams have about their leaders. At best, failure to deal with problem employees undermines the motivation and morale of the team. At worst, it increases turnover among the good development staff and damages product quality and productivity.

■ Set reasonable goals.

■ Only implement changes after their impact has been assessed and approval obtained.

■ Do not "gold-plate" development. Implement only what is required. Lots of minor enhancements over time can cause massive schedule and cost overruns.

■ Do not relax standards in an effort to save costs.

■ Prepare three separate time and cost estimates based on past experience, software functionality, and from a formal estimating technique. Compare actual results with estimates.

■ Adopt a suitable software development methodology.

■■■ References

1 T.C. Jones, *Assessment and Control of Software Risks*, Yourdon Press, New York, 1994

2 T. Kozlowski (1994) *For your amusement: Denver International Airport DOA, Again/The art of troubleshooting* – comp.software-eng #21702, www.phenix.bnl.gov/phenix/WWW/lists/phenix-comp-1/msg00007.html (accessed 1999)

3 J. Moad, (1998) 'Grounding those high-flying IT projects,' *PC Week Online*, July 17, 1998, www.zdnet.com/pcweek/opinion/0713/17cuff.html (accessed 1999)

4 General Accounting Office, *New Denver Airport: Impact of the Delayed Baggage System* (Briefing Report, 10/14/94, GAO/RCED-95-35BR)

5 M. Scott, (1998) "HK's airport systems buckle under pressure," *Computerworld Hong Kong*, July 14, 1998, www.cw.com.hk/News/n980714003.htm (accessed 2001)

6 P.S. Dempsey, "Airport woes a wake-up call", *The Denver Business Journal*, January 11, 1999

7 D.H. Longstreet, *Fundamentals of Function Point Analysis*, Longstreet Consulting Inc., revised January 27, 1999, www.softwaremetrics.com/fpafund.htm

8 C. Jones, *Programming Productivity*, McGraw-Hill, New York, 1996

9 B.W. Boehm, *Software Engineering Economics*, Prentice Hall, Englewood Cliffs, 1981

10 B.W. Boehm, Software Engineering Economics, *IEEE Trans. Software Eng. SE-10*, 1 (January 1984), 4–12

11 Carnegie Mellon University Software Engineering Institute, *The Capability Maturity Model – Guidelines for Improving the Software Process*, Addison-Wesley Longman Inc., Englewood Cliffs, 1994

12 M. Williamson, *The Science of Software Development*, CIO, April 15, 1996, www.cio.com/archive/041596_devenpor_print.html

13 B. Boehm, *"Making RAD work for your project,"* extended version of March 1999 *IEEE Computer* column, USC, 1999

14 R. Glass, *Software Runaways*, Prentice Hall, 1998

Further reading

B.W. Boehm, *Software Engineering Economics*, Prentice Hall, 1981

F. Brooks, *The Mythical Man-Month*, Addison Wesley, Englewood Cliffs, 1975

C. Jones, *Applied Software Measurement*, McGraw-Hill, 1996

C.F. Kemerer, "An Empirical Validation of Software Cost Estimation Models," *Communications of the ACM*, **30** (5), 416–29

R.S. Pressman, *Software Engineering A Practitioner's Approach*, McGraw-Hill, 1997

10

The need for quality

Every job is a self-portrait of the person who did it. Autograph your work with excellence.

Anonymous

One of the many reasons why IS projects have failed in the past and will continue to fail in the future is that the success of the project is often measured solely by the ability of the project team to implement it within the constraints of time and cost. A logical progression of this argument identifies a situation where a successful project is considered to be one that delivers business functionality of indeterminate quality yet does not exceed the budget or schedule.

One can only contemplate what the users of a newly-implemented computer system must feel when key project stakeholders receive substantial bonuses for delivering a system, which in their view is, at best, no better than the previous system, or at worst, totally unusable. What is more disturbing, however, is that despite many projects not satisfying key business requirements, project success is still implied by referring to the system as: *better, cheaper, faster, prestigious, value-added*, and *business-critical*.

Such terms provide no value whatsoever in defining project success. The use of "value-added," for example, in describing the outcome of a project, is generally subjective, and dilutes the meaning of quality. For quality to be a meaningful attribute, objective measures must be used, against which the desired levels of quality can be measured.

What is quality?

The standard definition of quality in ISO 9000[1] refers to all those features of a product (or service) which are required by the customer.

Quality is essentially, "fit for purpose;" by definition, therefore, quality products must *conform to requirements*, whatever those requirements may be. Quality is a process, therefore, that must begin with understanding the customers' quality expectations. A new computer system that is more expensive and faster than its predecessor is not necessarily a "quality" system, as it may not match the customers' expectations and, therefore, does not conform to their requirements.

Designing and implementing a distributed, multi-node, high-availability server running "leading-edge" application software is not the way to introduce quality into an IS project if all that is needed by the business is a simple, inexpensive, easy-to-use system for processing staff sickness and expenses information.

Whilst it is clear that an IS project must deliver products or services into an organization, the "fit for purpose" definition of quality dictates that these products do not necessarily have the same quality expectations. Within an IS project, quality expectations are likely to be expressed in terms of:

- functional requirements;
- performance;
- practicability;
- security;
- compatibility;
- reliability;
- maintainability;
- expandability;
- flexibility;
- clarity;
- cost;
- delivery timescales;
- comparison to another product.

Quality can be considered as a "level of excellence" that must be agreed between the customer and the supplier. Understanding and agreeing the expectations of the customer is a key requirement for establishing an acceptable level of quality

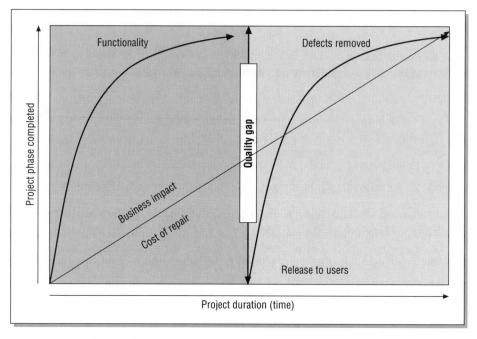

FIGURE 10.1 ▨ The quality gap

for an IS project. The business functionality delivered and its fitness for purpose, as perceived by the users, should therefore be the same. When they are not, there is a compromise in the quality of the system – the quality gap (Figure 10.1).

Inherent within an IS project will be a number of risks that have the potential to influence the size of the quality gap. Such risks will often be focused around the design and development activities of the project, such as:

- the difficulties users have in being specific about their requirements;
- the difficulties suppliers have in understanding customers' needs;
- the impact of constantly changing requirements;
- aggressive cost and schedule constraints which put pressure on IT teams to produce code that has not been fully tested;
- the inability to fully test software within a commercial environment;
- the absence or misuse of systems development methodologies.

Therefore, for an IS project to be successful, it is vital that quality processes and controls are established before the project starts. Introducing quality at a later stage not only compromises the quality of the overall project, but it is costly and often impossible to implement without causing serious disruption to the project. A Quality Management System (QMS) introduced at the start of the project lifecycle is, therefore, the most effective way to implement and maintain quality throughout the whole project.

Project quality management

Quality management must be established within the organization if IS projects undertaken within it are to meet their objectives and return some form of benefit. Quality management is a means by which the overall management activities necessary to develop a quality policy, objectives, and responsibilities can be identified and implemented. In order to be able to achieve these goals, the QMS must support the following fundamental quality processes:

- quality planning;
- quality control;
- quality assurance.

Quality planning establishes the objectives and requirements for the quality system. It is the objective of quality planning to identify which quality standards are relevant for the project (e.g. ISO 9001, BS EN 9001, EN ISO 9001, ISO 9126 and TickIT). For instance, ISO 9000-3 is a guideline for applying ISO 9001 to software development organizations. To be ISO 9001 certified, a third-party auditor must assess the quality procedures within the organization seeking certification. Certification is usually valid for about three years, after which time a complete reassessment is required. Do not assume, however, that a company quoting ISO 9001 certification must therefore be a producer of quality products – certification only indicates that documented procedures are followed.

It is important that everyone involved in the project is aware of one of the fundamental tenets of modern quality management – *quality must be planned in, not inspected in*. If you do not plan how quality standards will be met at the start of the project, you cannot hope to satisfy them through the introduction of *ad-hoc* and undisciplined quality assurance and control activities at the end of the project.

The quality planning process must also establish the cost/benefit trade-offs for the quality process. Identifying and removing defects can significantly increase the overall cost of the project, making it more expensive to build poor quality software than it is to build good quality software. Clearly, the primary benefit of meeting quality requirements is less rework, which means higher productivity, lower costs, and increased stakeholder satisfaction. The primary cost of meeting quality requirements is the expense associated with project quality management activities. It is, therefore, a fundamental concept of quality management that the benefits of managing quality must outweigh the costs involved in assuring it.

The main deliverable from the quality planning phase is the project quality plan which describes how the project team will implement its quality policy. The plan must identify the quality assurance and quality control activities that will be undertaken within the project. The project quality plan will therefore represent a subset of the overall project plan.

Project quality plans can be formal or informal in nature; highly-detailed or synoptic as long as they address the needs of the project. Typically, a quality plan will contain the following key sections:

1 **Introduction**
   a) Purpose of quality plan
   b) Scope of quality plan
   c) Deviations

2 **Project overview**
   a) Background
   b) Objectives
   c) Scope
   d) Dependencies and interfaces
   e) Assumptions
   f) Infrastructure requirements
   g) Stakeholders
   h) Stakeholder roles and responsibilities

3 **Project management**
   a) Management objectives and priorities
   b) Project monitoring and controlling processes
   c) Control of suppliers and sub-contractors
   d) Management quality checks
      – Project audits
      – Project reviews
   e) Issue and risk management

4 **Technical management**
   a) Methods, tools, and techniques
   b) Work products and reviews
   c) System and user documentation
   d) Software quality assurance plan

- – Standards and conventions
- – Product and process reviews
- – Problem reporting and corrective action
- – Tools, techniques and methods
- – Supplier software quality assurance
- e) Software configuration management plan
  - – Configuration management supporting procedures
  - – Baseline and build plan
  - – Change control process
  - – Configuration status accounting
  - – Configuration audits
  - – Tools, techniques, and methods for configuration management
  - – Supplier configuration management

Quality control is the means of ensuring that the project's deliverables satisfy the quality criteria specified for them.

Quality assurance is the means of evaluating overall project performance on a regular basis to provide confidence that the project will satisfy the relevant quality standards. To achieve this, project quality assurance must seek to:

- identify and analyze the risks to successful project outcome;

- develop the appropriate management and project controls to minimize those risks;

- monitor the project to ensure that effective management and project controls are in place;

- collect quality information which can be used to improve the quality management process and support future project planning activity.

Software quality assurance

A typical IS project has at its core, some form of software development activity. It seems sensible, therefore, to identify and manage quality within an IS project, we must first define the term 'quality' in the context of software development.

Software Quality Assurance (SQA) is the process that seeks to improve the entire systems development lifecycle by ensuring that software products, processes, standards, and procedures are followed. Fundamental to SQA is the concept of "prevention;" non-compliance is made visible to management through techniques such as inspections, audits, and reviews.

The audit is a fundamental activity performed during SQA, and its purpose is to assess current processes and products against established procedures and standards. The audit, whilst ensuring visibility of the quality process to management, also provides an indication of the quality and status of the software development activity undertaken within the organization.

Between 1992 and 1996, 533 organizations were assessed by the SEI, the owners of the CMM.[2] Of those, 62 per cent were rated at Level 1, 23 per cent at Level 2, 13 per cent at Level 3, 2 per cent at Level 4 and 0.4 per cent at Level 5. For the 62 per cent of organizations rated at Level 1, the most problematic key process area was that of software quality assurance.

The ability of the SQA process to meet its objectives will depend largely on the tools and techniques available within the organization. Whether to buy off-the-shelf tools, such as audit and inspection management tools or to develop required functionality in-house is an evaluation process that the SQA team must undertake at the first opportunity.

For the SQA process to be of benefit to the project, documented and agreed standards must first exist within the organization. Only then can the SQA process be used to measure the compliance of the project against them. Such standards might include the following:

- Documentation standards. Specify the form and content for planning, control, and product documentation (e.g. requirements specifications, development plans, product specifications, design specifications, test plans, and release plans).

- Design standards. Specify the form and content for the design activities. They provide the rules for translating software requirements into detailed design specifications (e.g. use of analysis and design methodologies, CASE tools, logical, and physical design standards).

- Coding standards. Specify the language in which the code is to be written and any restrictions which are to be upheld in its use (such as compiler options, command options, etc.). The standards must uphold language structures, style conventions (e.g. use of comments, readability) as well as rules for data structure, and interface specification, and internal code documentation.

SQA and the systems development lifecycle

Software quality assurance can be used at various phases throughout the development process to support development activities that will need to be undertaken prior to product release. At the conclusion of each phase, SQA provides management with the means to proceed to the next phase.

■ Project initiation

During project initiation, SQA should be used in both writing and reviewing the project plan to ensure that the procedures, processes, and standards used within the plan are clear, specific, and auditable. During this phase, SQA also provides the quality assurance components of the quality plan.

■ Software requirements management

During the software requirements phase, SQA ensures that requirements are complete, testable, and fully expressed in terms of functionality, reliability, performance, and usability.

■ Software design

During the preliminary and detailed software design phases, SQA must ensure that design standards are followed in accordance with the quality plan. During preliminary design, it is the role of SQA to ensure that every software functional requirement is allocated a software component that will satisfy that requirement.

Design documentation that is produced during these stages must be placed under configuration management, as must the results of design inspections. Software quality assurance must ensure that defects identified during design inspections are rectified and that changes made as a result are incorporated into the design.

■ Software construction

During this phase, SQA plays a key role in managing the development of software and design components through the use of configuration management. In particular, SQA will ensure that the status of every component is known and that non-conformances and corrective actions identified against these components are managed properly.

■ Software integration and test

During this phase SQA plays a key role in managing the testing of all deliverable items. All tests must be conducted in accordance with the test plan and non-conformances must be reported and resolved. Software quality assurance must ensure that test reports are complete and correct before ultimately certifying that the components under test (software and documentation) are ready for release.

Using SQA to support verification and validation

Software verification is the means by which software products and processes can be evaluated during their evolution. Typically, software validation involves actual testing and is conducted once verification has been completed. Software quality assurance ensures Verification and Validation (V&V) activities by monitoring technical reviews, inspections and walkthroughs. Whilst it is the role of the SQA team to monitor V&V activities to ensure that they are properly conducted and documented, SQA must also ensure that any actions which result from this are assigned, documented, scheduled, and tracked.

Inspections

Inspections are a proven technique for achieving quality by detecting and correcting product defects within the software development lifecycle. Typically, these defects are likely to be present within specifications, design, code, and testing components.

Inspections must have clear and agreed objectives and to be implemented, require a formal team structure. An inspection team will, however, only inspect work produced by another team. The inspection process can operate against almost any component within the project, the most likely ones including:

- plans;
- objectives;
- requirements;
- designs;
- psuedo-code;
- test cases;
- standards documentation;
- user documentation;
- system documentation;
- maintenance documentation.

Since being introduced in the 1970s at IBM by Michael Fagan,[3] inspections have helped numerous organizations improve the quality of their software development by detecting defects early and preventing them from migrating into subsequent lifecycle activities.

Software inspections have evolved over many years and can now be considered a mature process for improving quality. In CMM terms, software inspections are a rigorous form of process review, which represent a key process area at Level 3. Whilst defect *detection* is a process that ranges from Level 1 to Level 5 within the CMM, defect *prevention* is a characteristic of a highly-mature organization and thus only exists at Level 5 of the model.

With management support, inspections can quickly improve the quality of the product from "chaos" (defined as 20 or more major defects per Unit of Inspection Work or UIW) to relative cleanliness (defined as two or fewer major defects per UIW at exit), within a year. Software documentation on the British Aerospace Eurofighter Project, for example, originally containing more than 20 defects per UIW, was reduced to containing between 1 and 1.5 defects per UIW within 18 months.[4]

Historical cost/benefit analysis for inspections is also impressive. Despite operational costs in implementing inspections, some organizations have achieved a Return On Investment (ROI) ratio of 13:1, by reducing rework costs at later stages in the development lifecycle. Clearly the investment made in undertaking inspections can deliver real benefits into the project. It is through inspections that defects are detected early, and by preventing their leakage into subsequent development phases, the higher cost of later detection and rework can be eliminated (Figure 10.2).

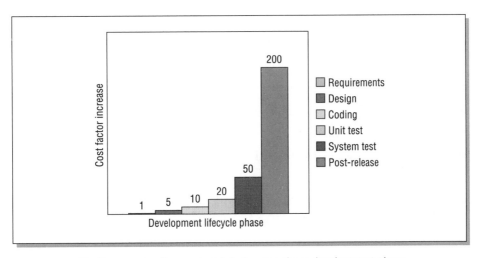

FIGURE 10.2 ▨ The comparative cost of defect removal per development phase

Fundamental concepts of inspections

■ Inspections are not just about checking source code. Requirements and design documentation contribute 40 and 60 per cent respectively to code defects.

■ Inspect as early as possible in the systems development lifecycle – requirements and design, preferably earlier at the contractual and management planning stages.

■ Make sure there are excellent standards to identify defective practices.

■ Give inspection team leaders proper training, subsequent coaching, certification, and statistical follow-up. If necessary, remove their "license" to inspect.

Walkthroughs

Walkthroughs are basically informal meetings in which the objective of the meeting is to evaluate whatever is brought into it. Whilst being a form of peer review, little or no preparation is expected.

Inspections differ from walkthroughs in many ways, probably the most significant difference being that there is a formal process for identifying defects in inspection material. Data gathered during an inspection (such as number and rate of defects identified) will be analyzed to make improvements to the whole software development process. Unlike walkthroughs, inspections will also possess the following characteristics:

■ trained inspection leaders (moderators);

■ specialized roles during inspections;

■ use of specialized checklist to inspect different document types;

■ formal entry and exit criteria for inspections;

■ formal criteria for repeating inspections;

■ pareto analysis for identifying error-prone components;

■ devices to remove individual criticism;

■ formal rework phase;

■ formal follow-up phase where all rework is completed before allowing documents to be used further;

■ clear encouragement of the team spirit to improve quality;

■ explicit recognition that defects occur and must be fixed as early as possible in the development process.

Formal test monitoring

Software quality assurance ensures that formal software testing, such as acceptance testing, is performed in accordance with agreed standards and procedures. Through SQA, testing documentation is reviewed for completeness and adherence to standards. A typical documentation review would have as inputs: test plans; test procedures; test specifications; and test reports.

During testing, SQA provides a monitoring role and ensures that non-conformances are managed before approving system readiness. In order to support formal test monitoring within the project, SQA will ensure that:

- test procedures are testing the software in accordance with the test plans;
- test procedures are verifiable;
- the correct version of the software is being tested (by monitoring CM activity);
- test procedures are followed;
- non-conformances (any incident not expected during testing) are recorded;
- test reports are accurate and complete;
- regression testing is performed to prove non-conformances have been corrected;
- resolution of all non-conformances takes place before delivery.

Total Quality Management

Total Quality Management (TQM) is a principle that is designed to enable an organization to gain competitive advantage by striving for the goal of 100 per cent customer satisfaction. To achieve this goal, a process of continuous improvement must be established and supported by all those individuals within the organization.

Within any organization, the successful implementation of TQM will require, at a minimum, the following activities to be undertaken:

- senior management must establish a program of continuous quality improvement standards;
- the introduction of established standards and structured methodologies;
- reducing time-to-delivery through the use of CASE tools;
- meeting budgetary constraints by improving staff productivity;

- managing the systems development process with project management tools and techniques;

- monitoring quality attainment and striving to improve the level of quality achieved.

Adopting TQM within an organization undertaking IS projects results in defect-free computer systems ("zero-defects") that meet users' current requirements and adapt easily to meet their future needs and expectations. Continuous improvement in the systems development process removes the quality gap by improving quality, reducing defects, meeting user requirements, and involving all users within the quality process.

Within a TQM environment, a number of factors will have a significant impact on the success of an IS project undertaken within it, namely:

- adopting TQM philosophy for carrying out day-to-day activities;

- understanding users' needs and satisfying their requirements;

- continuous quality improvement of systems by streamlining the development process using project and process management techniques;

- placing emphasis on teamwork and encouraging the participation of users, developers and managers;

- training, development programs, and continuing professional education for users and IS personnel;

- encouraging compliance with open and proprietary standards;

- developing strategies that will achieve quality goals for IS projects, both in the short-term and in the longer-term;

- managing and measuring staff performance and promotion.

As the aim of the CMM is to help organizations improve the maturity of their software development process, it is, therefore, an application of the process management concepts of TQM (Figure 10.3). In other words, the CMM is a subset of TQM. Customer satisfaction, the goal of TQM, can therefore be partly met if the CMM is used effectively within the organization.

The benefits of TQM

The successful implementation of TQM within organizations undertaking IS projects enables a wide range of stakeholders to benefit from inclusive quality

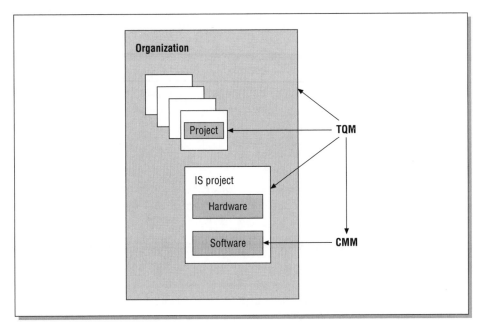

FIGURE 10.3 ▨ The scope of the CMM within a TQM environment

processes. IT staff, management and users, therefore, can all contribute to and benefit from, the adoption of TQM within an organization, even though TQM is often measured by the level of user satisfaction achieved.

TQM produces quality software that has very few, or even zero, defects. The number of defects found is likely to be small due to the involvement of the user throughout the development lifecycle. TQM achieves these impressive targets by ensuring that the following events are performed throughout the project:

- meeting user requirements;
- improving communication with users;
- achieving a clear definition of the problems and requirements;
- minimizing defects in the final releases of software;
- delivering projects on-time and within budget;
- delivering systems that are maintainable and flexible;
- reducing the number of design changes.

CASE STUDY

Intel

A classic lesson for all companies, especially those operating in technology markets, is that the performance of the product is second to the *perception* of that performance as viewed by the customer. Equally, an organization that has a reputation for quality, often achieved through established and successful branding, must also behave in a manner consistent with its positioning in the market, as this case study will demonstrate.

In 1995, Intel, the acknowledged market leader in microprocessor sales, suffered widespread public humiliation when a "minor" problem with their Pentium microprocessor snowballed into a major public relations disaster.[5,6]

In June 1994, Intel testers discovered an error in the Pentium chip, but nevertheless, took the decision not to inform their customers, as so few people would be affected. During the same month, Dr. Thomas R. Nicely, a professor of mathematics at Lynchburg College, Virginia, USA, independently discovered a bug in the maths co-processor that caused Pentium-based PCs to slightly miscalculate mathematical divisions using five significant digits or more. After contacting Intel to bring the problem to their attention, Intel merely confirmed that it knew of the problem and took no further action.

Still concerned, the professor posted a now famous e-mail to his friends and colleagues. This e-mail would be subsequently copied and forwarded throughout the world. One of the recipients of that e-mail was Andrew Schulman, author of *Unauthorized Windows 95*. He then passed it onto a software company that produced number-crunching software, to confirm the error. They did and, as a result, forwarded Dr. Nicely's e-mail not just to their own customers, but to Intel and major software houses, such as Microsoft, Borland, and Metaware.

Within days the e-mail appeared on Internet newsgroups throughout the world, and it was only a matter of time before the mainstream press had picked up the story. Media coverage on CNN and in the *New York Times* fuelled rumours that Intel's Pentium chip had a design flaw that made it unreliable. By November, despite the news spreading onto business and investment newsgroups on the Internet, Intel still claimed there was no problem, even though some independent software experts had produced a 'fix' for the error.

Finally, in late November, Intel's CEO posted a reply onto an Internet newsgroup confirming that Intel had, in fact, known about the problem since June, but went on to state that the error was so insignificant it would only occur "once in nine billion floating point divisions." The implication was that the vast majority of Pentium users would be unaffected by the problem, although some concern was expressed for a small number of users who were involved in "heavy-duty scientific work."

At this point, an offer by Intel to replace any flawed Pentium chips would have probably signalled an end to the fiasco. Instead, Intel duly set up a freephone number from which customers could seek advice from an expert. If the expert confirmed the user was at risk from the fault, the company would replace their chip at no cost. Unfortunately for Intel, this was very much a case of "too little, too late," and jokes about Intel's quality began to surface, such as: "At Intel, quality is job 0.999999998." Similarly, in a *New York Times* story about the New Jersey Nets basketball team, the headline was "Mentally speaking, Nets are Pentiums."

By December, now six months since the problem had been discovered, Intel was still suffering widespread criticism from just about every source. In a further attempt to manage the crisis, the company ran a full-page advertisement in several newspapers. In it, the CEO and several other executives apologized, not for the fault in the Pentium chip, but in the way the crisis had been handled. Pentium chips would now be replaced on request.

During the crisis, the Intel share price dropped 5 per cent and major distributors such as IBM announced they would halt the production of Pentium-based products until the defect in the chip had been corrected. Not surprisingly, these events had a significant impact on Intel sales channels. Indeed, sales in non-Pentium machines steadily rose within large business markets as well as domestic markets around the world.

The cost of non-conformance to quality could not have been greater for Intel. Measuring the cost objectively, Intel were forced to reduce the cost of the Pentium chips by up to 40 per cent and had to bear the costs of over $420 million (£280 million) to cover the cost of recall and the operational costs in staffing the support telephone helplines. More significant, however, were the costs to Intel that could not so easily be measured.

In establishing their brand recognition, Intel had spent millions of dollars. The slogan "Intel Inside" was universally acknowledged by its customers as a benchmark for quality. The "minor" chip defect and the mismanagement of subsequent events ensured that their customers would now question that "quality" for a long time after the original problem had been resolved. Today, Intel posts all known flaws on the Internet.

 ## Barriers to quality

The resolution of non-conformances produced as a consequence of IS development activities is regularly perceived to be one of the most important stages within an IS project. When serious exceptions and deviations from the norm arise, management are likely to demonstrate their full support and co-operation in an effort to limit the consequences of failure. It is also likely that visibility of this process within the project is often extremely high.

The crisis has, in fact, mobilized all the resources within the organization in an effort to resolve it as quickly as possible. As a consequence, emergency funding will be released; a project "war-room" will be established to provide a focal point for the operation and the heroic feats of those most directly involved will be broadcast throughout the organization as a shining example to others. In time, those individuals identified as being key to the resolution of the crisis are likely to receive some form of reward and recognition for their efforts.

Fixing major problems that occur towards the end of the project when pressure to deliver will be high is likely to attract management support in ways never before experienced on the project. Such actions often beg the question from the project team, "where were they during the rest of the project, when we needed their support?"

Preventing the problems from occurring in the first place, however, is unlikely to attract the attentions of management, nor trigger performance-related rewards or bonuses. If the strive for quality is managed in this way within the organization, it does not provide much incentive for IS project managers to appreciate the need to adopt effective quality standards. Within project quality circles and forums, there is a popular story that embraces this theme very well, and it goes something like this.

In Ancient China, there was a family of healers, one of whom was known throughout the land employed as a physician to the Great Lord. This physician was asked which of this family was the most skilful healer. He replied:

"I tend to the sick and dying with drastic and dramatic treatments, and on occasion someone is cured and my name gets out among the lords."

"My elder brother cures sickness just when it begins to take root, and his skills are known among the local peasants and neighbours."

"My eldest brother is able to sense the spirit of sickness and eradicate it before it takes form. His name is unknown outside our home."

The eldest brother in the parable, provides an excellent analogy for the skill of an inspection team. Their skill may not be acknowledged readily, but they are extremely valuable to the success of software development activities within the organization. The economic case for quality through inspection should never be underestimated – bug prevention is far more cost-effective than bug detection.

▪▶ Quality: critical success factors

- Quality must be planned at the start of the project, not an afterthought.
- Remember the adage – if you can't measure it, you can't manage it.
- The quality goal must be to get things right, first time, every time.
- Quality costs – but the consequences of failure will cost more.
- Once you have achieved a certain level of quality ensure that you can maintain it. Quality is still important even when the inspectors and auditors have gone home.

References

1   International Organization for Standardization, www.iso.ch

2   Software Engineering Institute, Carnegie Mellon University, *Software Engineering, measurement and Analysis published maturity levels*, www.sei.cmu.edu (accessed 2002)

3   M. Fagan, (1976), "Design and Code Inspections to Reduce Errors in Program Development," *IBM Systems Journal*, **15** (3), 182–211

4   T. Gilb, *Planning to Get the Most Out of Inspection*, Software Quality Professional, **2**: 2, March, 2000, www.asq.org/pub/sqp/past/vol2_issue2/gilb.html (accessed 2001)

5   M. Ritson, *Intel's Pentium Blunder*, Business Life, May, 2001, 27

6   V. Emery, *A Learning Experience: The Pentium Chip Story*, www.brunel.ac.uk/ ~csstbmo/distanceLearning/networkedorgs/handouts/intel.html (accessed 2002)

Further reading

R.G. Ebenau and S.H. Strauss, *Software Inspection Process*, McGraw-Hill, New York, 1994

T. Gilb and D. Graham, *Software Inspection*, Addison-Wesley Longman, London, 1993

 Part IV

Project delivery

Readiness is all

William Shakespeare, *Hamlet*

11

The importance of testing

Quod erat demonstrandum (Which was to be proved)

Euclid *c.300 BC*, Latin translation of the Greek of *Elementa* bk. 1 and *Passim*.

Following the failure of the London Ambulance Service computer-aided dispatch system, claims were made that lives were lost as a result of management incompetence.* Whilst there were serious errors of judgement made by senior management within the LAS, the single fault which led to the system becoming inoperable was, in fact, a minor programming error. Three weeks previously, a programmer had inadvertently left program code in the system that caused a small amount of server memory to be used up and not released each time a vehicle was mobilized. Over a three-week period, this had gradually consumed all available memory, causing the system to crash.

During 1999, Microsoft warned users of its Windows 95 and 98 operating systems that after exactly 49.7 days of continuous operation, their computers may "stop responding."[1] According to the company's own press release, the problem was caused by a fault within the timing algorithm and, although publishing a fix for the problem, the company cautioned users that the software fix had not yet been completely tested and should only be downloaded by users affected by the problem.

---

* These claims were eventually withdrawn after a subsequent investigation.

Regardless of size, complexity, or budget, there is enough evidence stemming from failed IS projects to suggest that computer-based systems are as likely to fail from relatively simple programming errors as they are from complex software development problems. Indeed, the technological advancement of the organization often counts for nothing in the defence against even the most simple of software development errors.

In October 1999, the $125 million (£83.3 million) NASA Mars Climate Orbiter spacecraft was assumed lost in space due to a simple data conversion error. A subsequent investigation concluded that engineers had forgotten to convert data expressed in English Imperial units to their metric equivalent during development. For a system that cost so much, one might well ask how much of that multi-million dollar investment was spent on testing.

Why do application systems fail?

As projects approach their implementation date, many project managers face the ultimate test; they must ask their development teams whether or not the system should be released into a live environment. As the most likely responses to this question may range from worried expressions to awkward silences, it is hardly a good omen from which to establish a level of confidence in the system. Research undertaken by Reasoning, a software testing tool vendor, on this very subject may provide us with a few reasons why we should ensure systems are tested effectively:[2]

- Up to 66 per cent of all system crashes are caused by exception failures;

- Software re-engineering projects have found programmers routinely make three errors for every 100 modifications they make, regardless of their programming experience. Typical errors include: omissions, modifying code that should not be changed, and making incorrect changes. If an application comprising 1,000,000 lines of code required 2,000 lines to be changed, 60 errors would remain or be introduced. Experience shows that 5 per cent of errors are 'showstoppers' and another 20 per cent cause a major impact to the project;

- Basic testing typically reduces errors by 30 per cent. Software inspection plus testing reduces errors by 72 per cent.

If the project manager is faced with a situation where the development team's answer to the question of product deployment is either "no," or even worse, "I don't know," the manager has to make a simple choice. That choice must be whether or not to proceed with the deployment of the product into a user environment, even though it has not been fully tested. Information collected from IS project failures strongly suggests that managers in this situation choose to accept the risks and give their approval for the system to be released into a user environment. The consequences of such an approach do not need to be spelled out.

Computer system failure occurs when the operation of one or more sub-systems that constitute the system (such as hardware, software, and network components) does not fall within acceptable levels of quality. Within the software development lifecycle, however, the causes of application development failure can generally be thought of as belonging to one of four broad categories.

Programming errors

Programming remains a complex and largely manual task, and the probability that errors will be introduced into it, either through negligence or, indeed, through sabotage, is a distinct possibility. Experience has shown that mistakes are most likely to be made when important and complex activities are performed under adverse pressures. It should come as no surprise that projects that are struggling to meet their schedules are often the ones that are most likely to experience some form of programming error.

One of the warning signs for a project in serious trouble is the need for development staff to work extended hours, often long into the night, every night. For a very limited period only, combined with the offer of personal incentives, this can save a project and can actually increase the satisfaction levels of those in the team. Abuse of this regime, however, will lead to a marked drop in morale amongst development staff and a sharp decline in productivity. More importantly, it is likely to trigger an immediate drop in standards, providing an opportunity for serious errors to be introduced into the software development process.

The majority of programming errors can often be identified and resolved through techniques such as inspections and peer reviews. More subtle programming errors such as memory leakage and runtime errors, however, are much harder to identify.

Testing for programming errors is an important activity that should be performed within the project as a whole. This means, therefore, that testing for programming errors should not just be limited to checking source code produced from within the "internal" project team; applications that use components developed by third parties must also be tested.

Software complexity

The complexity of an IT system can be defined by a number of factors, such as system architecture (its systems, interfaces, and data feeds) as well as its size. Relatively new software development techniques, such as object-oriented development, especially if undertaken in the absence of formal software development processes, can add little benefit to a project whilst increasing the complexity factor significantly. Whilst the initial choice of software component is undoubtedly important, so too is the way in which that component is used.

Vague and misleading user requirements

Without a clear requirements specification, the likelihood that assumptions may need to be made in order for the project to proceed is high. Design and development activities must, therefore, be undertaken in an *ad-hoc* manner, without the confidence that what is being built is, indeed, what is actually required.

The outcome of this situation is inevitable; program code, whilst syntactically correct (in the sense it has been compiled, interpreted or "desk-checked" to remove syntax errors), does not satisfy business requirements. In other words, the internal logic of the program code does not support the business functionality and constraints identified by the users.

A project manager under pressure to deliver is likely to determine the implementation date for the project purely on the proportion of requirements that have been coded. Indeed, this can be an effective measure if used correctly. There is of course, a fundamental weakness in the unconditional acceptance of this as a measure of project completion. Whilst a project with 90 per cent of its requirements coded may seem to be near completion, this figure means little unless it is also known *how well* those requirements have been met.

Projects whose requirements are not clear, complete and above all, testable, stand little chance of success. The proportion of requirements coded and tested is clearly, a key project metric, but it is also an important testing metric. If the requirement cannot be tested, there cannot be a guarantee that the requirement has been satisfied correctly. For example, a testable requirement may be stated as:

The user must enter their previously-assigned password to gain access to the system.

The test for this requirement should be fairly obvious and easy to perform, but concern must be raised regarding requirements that cannot be tested so easily, such as:

The system must be user-friendly;
The system must be responsive;
The system must be robust.

Changing software requirements

Users and business sponsors do not necessarily appreciate the impact of change on a system under development. New business functionality that is introduced into the software development process constitutes a risk to the project, however small it may be. Undoubtedly, there will be individuals within both groups who do understand the impact of change, and request it anyway.

Irrespective of the business reasons for doing so, accepting changes without first establishing a process to manage those changes correctly (which may mean refusing to accept new changes once a system has reached a certain level of development) increases the potential for application failure in a number of ways:

- development staff may need to reschedule key tasks at short notice;
- existing tasks may be reduced in priority;
- additional changes are not integrated properly into the existing application code;
- the development team may lose track of the current "version" of the application and incorporate the wrong changes into it;
- the impact of the change may only surface much later in the project.

The case for testing

Testing is the means by which quality is assessed. Despite the obvious benefits for testing within the project, in reality, it is likely to represent a one-off activity performed once programming activities have ceased, in isolation from all other aspects of the development lifecycle. Testing must not be considered as an "afterthought" to development; it is a vital process that must be integrated throughout the entire systems development lifecycle.

Successful project managers are those who undertake testing as part of the project, undertaking a test program that focuses on the identification and elimination of defects. Undertaking a comprehensive program of tests, in conjunction with design and development, delivers clear benefits into the organization – product quality can be assessed relatively early in the project and corrective action taken whilst the costs for doing so are small. Even a small investment in testing can deliver enormous rewards for organizations: quality improvements can be identified and undertaken which will enable them to deliver their business strategy and achieve their stated objectives.

Despite the rationale for testing, many IS projects still fail to deliver any return on their investment as a consequence of their failure to test throughout the project. One can only question the rationale behind investing often substantial sums of money in new computer systems without protecting that investment against the risks which are associated with software development projects.

Testing is a crucial activity that must be performed in conjunction with software development; one cannot exist without the other. Application failure and, ultimately, IS project failure occurs when the relationship between these two processes is broken, often because the pressure to deliver overwhelms the need to perform actions based on rational thought and process discipline.

The origins of testing failure

■ Testing takes time and costs money

In order to deliver business functionality, project sponsors must invest money to engage application development resources. Whilst supporting development activities with funding, many project sponsors, however, view testing as a task that provides few benefits, yet consumes huge sums of money. Such views do little to ensure that testing activities receive an adequate level of funding within IS projects.

■ The lack of importance placed on comprehensive testing

The lack of importance placed on testing by project managers under pressure to deliver from their business sponsors goes some way in explaining why the effort allocated to testing within a project plan is often reduced to a bare minimum. In the desire to deliver systems quickly, the consequences of this approach are severe.

If serious problems arise at the end of the development stage (when most of the allocated budget has been spent), then it is unlikely that these can be resolved without significantly increasing the budget or slipping the project timescales. It is ironic, therefore, that whilst project schedules are likely to be extended for development activities, they are equally likely to be truncated for testing activities.

■ Project deemed too small to warrant testing

Whilst it is easy to criticize massive IS projects that have failed due to a lack of testing, let us not forget that for every massive IS project disaster, many more smaller projects fail for exactly the same reason. Testing is not a luxury only afforded to projects in which huge sums of money have been invested; even a small project to install a new software package should undertake an adequate level of testing.

Extensive testing may not be necessary for every project, but in determining the level of testing necessary, the overriding concern must be the impact of errors, not the size of the project.

■ Testing cannot test everything

To test every program statement within an application to a level where there is 100 per cent certainty that the code is "error-free" is practically impossible within a commercial environment. Testing can only prove the *presence* of bugs, not the absence of bugs, and so can only ever provide an agreed level of confidence in a system.

It is rarely possible to test every possible aspect of an application, every combination of events (such as what-if scenarios?), every dependency, and anything else that *may* go wrong. If there is one thing we *can* be sure of, however, it is the fact that there will never be sufficient time to test everything. The only option available to the project, therefore, is to adopt the principles of risk management to determine what *must* be tested:

- What functionality is most important to achieve the project's objectives?
- What functionality is most visible to the user?
- What functionality has the greatest impact on safety?
- What functionality has the greatest financial impact?
- What functionality is considered most important by the customer?
- What parts of the code are complex, and thus prone to errors?
- What parts of the application do the developers think carry the highest risk?
- What kind of problems would cause the most adverse publicity?
- What tests have the best high-risk-coverage to time-required ratio?

■ Lack of business ownership and involvement

I am still genuinely astonished at the lack of ownership and involvement many key business stakeholders and users have in the testing process. The benefits to be gained from testing are severely diminished when, through the lack of ownership and commitment from business stakeholders, testing becomes less of a business activity, and more of an IT activity, using IT resources.

A major international organization recently developed an IS program to consolidate its products and services throughout its global markets. At the end of its user acceptance testing phase it became clear that a major business area had not taken part in testing. The failure of the project to complete their testing satisfactorily had a serious impact on the organization's delivery program and ultimately led to the postponement of a strategic IS program.

The objectives of testing

It is the objective of testing to provide a level of confidence in the system being tested. This confidence can be expressed in four main ways:

- That the technical aspects of the system meet the required operational and functional expectations;

- That the system will operate as required and ultimately deliver the benefits that were identified within the original business case for the project;

- That management will be able to execute the business strategy;

- That the financial investment in the project or program will be protected. If the case for testing cannot be undertaken to build confidence in the other three categories it must, at least, be undertaken to protect the financial investment in the system. If this does not happen, the commercial risks to the project may be too great for the project to be considered a viable proposition. It is worth remembering that the minor software error that was at the heart of the European Space Agency's Ariane 5 rocket explosion, resulted in an estimated uninsured loss of $500,000 million (£333,000 million).

The scope of testing

Testing represents one of the many software quality assurance processes that exist at Level 2 of the CMM. However, the testing process itself can be divided into a number of different categories, based on the objectives of each test. Some tests will be necessary to ensure that functional requirements are met (i.e. what the system must do), others will ensure that the non-functional requirements are met (i.e. how well the system must perform).

In order for the system to perform as expected, therefore, four categories of testing are required: reliability tests; functionality tests; application performance tests; and volume tests. Overlooking just one category in the testing process can result in the introduction of a system which will not meet the quality standards set by the users and deliver little or no benefit into the organization.

Key testing categories

Reliability

Users have little patience for an application that constantly stalls, crashes or behaves in an unexpected manner. Common sense dictates, therefore, that the reliability of a system must be assured before undertaking other types of testing, such as functionality or performance testing. If you cannot guarantee the system will be available for more than a few minutes, there is not much point in testing the response time of key functionality within it.

Functionality

The purpose of functionality testing is to ensure that the application meets the requirements established for it. For example, testing the functionality of an order processing system would ensure that the correct products are shipped to the correct customers and that the correct account is billed. It might also ensure that tests to check credit limits, delivery times, and minimum stock limits are set correctly.

Application performance

Once application or system functionality has been established, focus must then be placed on the ability of the system to meet its performance requirements. Whilst the user of the system might be fairly confident that it provides the capability to perform a business function, such as order processing, this confidence may be lost if it takes an intolerably long time to complete the operation.

There is enough information available from failed software development projects to suggest that any interactive system that takes minutes to perform a simple operation is likely to be unacceptable to the users of that system. Application performance, behind functionality, is a key requirement within organizations seeking benefits from IS projects, yet it is a feature of a system that can be compromised for many reasons:

- system architecture (such as number of data sources, interfaces, transformations);
- choice and use of software (Visual Basic for instance, would not be a good choice of software for a high-performance, real-time application);
- choice and use of hardware (e.g. processor speed, CPU utilization, memory usage);
- network bandwidth and utilization (e.g. is there a network bottleneck within the system?);

- complex functionality (e.g. does the system perform a high number of complex business operations that have not been taken into account?).

Volume

The performance of the overall system must be tested to ensure that there is no degradation in service when the system is fully loaded with work. Volume (or "stress") testing is performed by emulating actual user work within the system and scaling it upwards to understand the impact an increased workload on the performance of the system. Confidence can then be established that the system will not only cope with the current business workload, but with any future workload (such as a twofold increase in the transactions processed per day).

Most stress testing, especially when performed using automated testing tools, will often continue past the stated maximum loading to identify at what point the system will cease to operate in an acceptable manner – the "break-point." How soon that break-point will be reached must be known to all the project stakeholders.

The lack of testing performed during the development of Hong Kong's new international airport was identified as a major contributor to the failure of its computerized information systems. Volume testing was performed on the system, simulating only 10,000 transactions, even though the expected number of transactions was nearer 70,000. When the system went live, the increased volume of data being processed by a limited number of database tables caused a number of bottlenecks in the system due to application "deadlocks."

 CASE STUDY

The lessons of Ariane 5

On 4 June 1996, the maiden flight of the Ariane 5 launcher ended in failure. Approximately 40 seconds after launch, at an altitude of about 3,700 m (12,139 ft), the vehicle veered off its flight path, broke up, and exploded. Media reports at the time indicated that the amount lost was half a billion dollars – all of which was uninsured.[3,4]

A preliminary investigation of flight data was established by the CNES (French National Center for Space Studies) and the European Space Agency shortly after the incident to determine the possible cause of the failure. The investigation discovered the backup Inertial Reference System (IRS) had failed, followed immediately by the failure of the active IRS, leading the investigation to concentrate on the flight control system and, more specifically, the IRS as being the source of the failure.

In simple terms, the IRS measures the attitude of the launcher and its movements in space. Each IRS has its own internal computer which is used to calculate angles and velocities, providing data which is then sent to the launcher's onboard computer. The IRS is, therefore, in the true sense of the word, "mission-critical."

To provide continuity in the case of IRS failure, there are, in fact, two IRS components, working in parallel, each having identical hardware and software. The active IRS is therefore protected by its "hot" backup, which is continually updated by the active IRS. In the event of a problem, control can be passed from the active IRS to the backup IRS, provided that the unit is functioning correctly.

This case study is particularly useful in highlighting the need for thorough testing; the component that failed was, in fact, not in use at the time. Around 36 seconds after launch, the computer in the active IRS shutdown as it encountered an exception in a mathematical calculation. As the error had not been expected, there was no error-handling routine to trap it. The system specification for the IRS states that in the event of such an event, the context of the failure should be stored in the processor memory and the IRS system should be shutdown.

Fail-safe routines within the onboard computer automatically attempted to switch to the backup IRS, but failed because the unit had already ceased working during the previous data cycle (72 milliseconds), for exactly the same reason. Further investigation revealed the error which caused the IRS units to shutdown was nothing more than a data exception error caused from the conversion of a 64-bit floating point value to a 16-bit signed integer value. One of the values used within the computation that caused the error represented the trajectory of the launcher; the value was unexpectedly high because the trajectory of Ariane 5 differs from that of its predecessor, Ariane 4, the source of the software module.

What must have been more disappointing to the project's financiers was the fact that the error occurred in a software module that serves no purpose once the launcher has lifted-off. Normally, the alignment function within the IRS is stopped just before lift-off, but in the unlikely event of a hold in the countdown to launch, resetting the IRS could take several hours in earlier versions of Ariane. It is for this reason alone that the program routine continues for about 40 seconds after lift-off. This timing sequence was a requirement for Ariane 4, but was not required for Ariane 5.

The causes of software development failure

IS project failures such as the London Ambulance Service computer-aided dispatch system and the London Stock Exchange's TAURUS project were heavily criticized for the incompetence of their management. This was not the case for the Ariane 5 project disaster. From the content of the full report, there is every indication that the software development process was carefully managed and the acknowledgment that industry-standard practices were adopted throughout the project.

The report also acknowledges the fact that systematic documentation, validation, and management process were in place, but it is clear that within the project, validation and verification procedures were compromised. Indeed, the Inquiry Board did make a number of recommendations to improve the process. One of these was the need to test the whole system rather than just parts of it (the IRS was tested separately from the flight software).

This case study, more than any other, highlights the risk of not being able to test everything. It also demonstrates the risks associated with failing to manage the reuse of software components within a complex systems development environment.

During the testing of the IRS system, it was widely recognized that failed arithmetic conversions were a possible cause of error. To determine the vulnerability of "unprotected" code (code that could generate an exception), an analysis was performed on every operation that could generate an operand error. This process duly "protected" four out of the seven variables that were identified as high risk.

Because of an earlier decision taken within the project, conditions that could not arise were not tested, and so three variables were left unchecked. Unfortunately, the fatal exception within the IRS units occurred among the three variables that were not monitored and not the four that were.

The decision to reuse the 10-year old software from the Ariane 4 launcher in Ariane 5 was not in itself a poor decision. What is unforgivable is the fact that the quality assurance process within the project did not discover that the Ariane 5 software did not require some of the Ariane 4 routines that it called.

The development team's decision to reuse software is a laudable one; object and component-based development methodologies that are in use today rely heavily upon that very concept. However, software reuse has its risks, even if the software itself is designed to be reused. To automatically assume that a software component that operates normally within one system can be migrated into another (slightly different) system and operate normally is inviting disaster. It is the objective of integration and regression testing to ensure that such events do not generate problems, yet it is unclear to what extent this activity was performed against the various software components within the project.

Conclusion

It was the requirement to shut the IRS processor down that finally proved fatal for Ariane 5. It is not feasible to restart an IRS once it has been shutdown as it is too difficult to recalculate the attitude of the launcher. Once shutdown, therefore, an IRS is effectively useless.

Although the failure of this mission was ultimately due to a software design error, mechanisms could have been introduced to mitigate this type of problem. For instance, the computers within the IRS could have continued to provide their "best guess" on the required atitude information. What is disturbing, though, is why a software error should be allowed to, or even required to, cause a processor to halt within a mission-critical system.

In redundant systems, there is always a risk that software errors produced in the active components will automatically propagate the backup components. In the case of Ariane 5, both IRS units ran the same software that resulted in the shutdown of two "healthy" and critical pieces of equipment.

Making the investment count: iteration

There is a particularly fine maxim on testing and that is, if something is going to fail, make sure it fails *quickly*. The economics on which this is based on are fairly simple and widely acknowledged by successful software development managers: the cost of recovery from software failure rises dramatically throughout the development lifecycle. Therefore, the sooner the failure is identified, the greater the chances of resolving it within budgeted development targets.

If the classic "waterfall" method for systems development is used within an IS project, development and testing phases are undertaken sequentially. A common criticism of this approach is that it no longer reflects contemporary opinion on software design, construction, and testing. However, there is a much more significant drawback – a great deal of risk exists within the project until the final stages of testing (Figure 11.1).

Throughout the majority of the project, the development team will have a fairly comfortable ride; there is little user involvement and most of that is spent producing documentation. Only during user acceptance testing do users become heavily involved within the project, at which point the problems arising from testing throw the project into chaos. Through the use of the "waterfall" approach

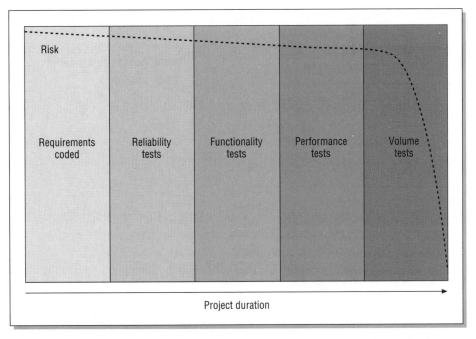

FIGURE 11.1 The level of risk present within the classic approach to software development

to systems development, no one in the project can be confident that the system will work until very late in the software development process.

The obvious answer to this problem is to identify defects as early as possible within the software development lifecycle. Using this approach, errors introduced during the project's design and development phases can be identified by early and continual testing whilst keeping rework costs to a minimum.

An iterative approach to development supports this concept by acknowledging that there are many unknowns, and therefore risks, at the outset of the project. Serious issues are therefore addressed very early on within the development lifecycle, enabling them to be dealt with more quickly. Compare this to the traditional approach to software development, where large risks to the project remain up to, and including, the final stages. Undertaking any rework at this stage is costly and often performed by teams under huge pressures to deliver on time – which is a major reason why so many 'good' IS projects fail.

Iterative development reduces risk of failure by not only testing early in the development lifecycle, but testing with every iteration (Figure 11.2). Through

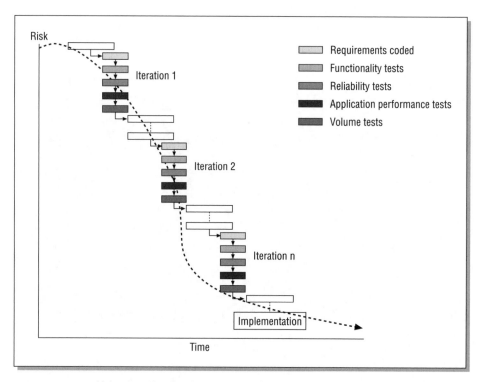

FIGURE 11.2 ▪ Using iterative development to reduce development risk

this approach defects are removed as features are implemented, allowing testing of the application to be completed shortly after the last features have been coded.

Making the investment count: testing tools

Testing is a fundamental part of the development process as it is a means to protect the investment made in software development. Despite this, many organizations still fail to deliver a return on their investment simply because testing is seen as time-consuming, expensive, and not worthy of adequate funding. Testing is not cheap, nor is it a quick process, and substantial funding alone will not guarantee that the testing process itself will be successful.

A key factor contributing to the failure of testing is that complex software systems, regardless of size, are extremely difficult to test manually. As a consequence, a lengthy exercise will be needed in order to determine just how much of the application has been tested, and more importantly, how much of the application has *not* been tested. One of the main concerns with this approach, however, is that the majority of manual testing can only ever be *reactive*. In practice, when a manual test is performed, the development team can do little apart from sit back and wait for the system or component to fail. All these factors are likely to contribute to the overall length of time needed to test new computer systems.

No matter how good a project's requirements are, testing against those requirements cannot answer the question: *what has not been tested?* Testing tools can help solve this problem in a cost-effective way by combining the benefits of requirements coverage tools with those from code coverage tools. For instance, even when an application behaves normally under test conditions, a large proportion of the underlying code remains untested. Examples of commonly untested code include exception-handling routines, error conditions and little-used logic paths within the application. Fundamental to the testing process must be the ability to identify what percentage of the code has been tested and what specific functions or lines of code have not been executed.

Whilst the purchase of specialist testing tools represents a major investment in the testing capability of the project, that investment can be justified by the fact that these tools can be used by almost everyone within the software development team throughout the duration of the project. A successful test program, therefore, will be one where automated testing tools can be used effectively by the following individuals:

- Developers and software engineers can benefit from tools that proactively identify memory errors and leaks, highlight unexecuted code, and pinpoint potential bottlenecks within their code.

- Testers, as well as performing requirements coverage tests, can also use functional testing tools to record and playback test scripts which can be used for regression testing and load testing purposes.

- Project managers can use testing tools to measure actual progress against planned progress whilst measuring quality levels throughout the operation. Helping identify the rate at which defects are found and resolved will provide important metrics for triggering exit criteria for testing, either between each iteration of development, each testing phase, or the testing process as a whole.

The testing process

Regardless of the systems development methodology used for development, the testing process can be viewed as a program comprising three key stages: test preparation; test construction; and test execution. A typical test program is shown in Figure 11.3.

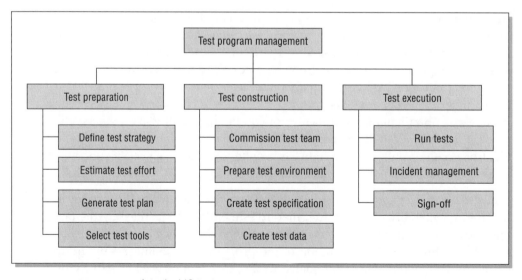

FIGURE 11.3 ■ A typical IS test program

Test program management

Test program management initiates the test program and continues to manage and control the test process until sign-off has been completed. It is the objective of test program management to deliver the following:

- an activity plan showing tasks, owner, resources, risks, assumptions, issues, dependencies, and milestones – this establishes control within the program and provides stakeholders with visibility of the test process;
- a progress report on the activity, issues and risks – promoting confidence and awareness;
- an overall management structure that will deliver testing activities and tasks;
- management of Assumptions, Risks, Issues and Dependencies (ARID).

Test preparation

The key objective of the test preparation phase is to identify the nature and duration of tests required. The main deliverable from this phase will be the creation and approval of a test strategy. It is the purpose of the test strategy to identify what must be performed, by whom, in order for testing to be complete. The test strategy must clearly state the entry criteria for the tests (what must happen *before* testing can commence) and exit criteria (what must happen for testing to complete).

Typical entry criteria will include some or all of the following:

- obtain test requirements;
- obtain budget and schedule requirements;
- identify development and testing resources (including system users);
- identify relevant project processes and standards (such as configuration management, requirements management, change control, risk management);
- identify relevant project development metrics (e.g. defects/lines of code);
- document goals and critical success factors;
- identify high-risk functions;
- set testing priorities – the higher the risk, the higher the testing priority;
- determine scope and limitations of tests (any application testing areas deemed outside the scope of tests must go through risk management process – it is not unknown for project managers to dispense with user acceptance testing in an effort to meet project implementation deadlines);

- identify tests to be performed (e.g. unit, system, integration, security, performance, load, regression, user acceptance, etc.);

- identify training requirements;

- identify test sites;

- determine software testing tool requirements (record/playback tools, code analyzers, stress testing software, runtime checkers);

- identify acceptance criteria;

- identify retest criteria;

- produce test strategy;

- sign-off test preparation phase.

Given the complexity of many IS projects and the knowledge that it is not commercially viable to test everything, a common problem faced by many IS managers is knowing when to *stop* testing. The answer, of course, is when the exit criteria have been met. Exit criteria may be based on absolute metrics or on more general, but equally measurable, events. Typical exit criteria are likely, therefore, to include:

- reaching a deadline (release deadline, testing deadlines, etc.);

- test cases completed with a specific pass rate;

- the depletion of test budgets;

- the coverage of code, functionality, and requirements reaches an agreed level;

- the rate of errors found during testing drops below an agreed level.

Test construction

If the test design preparation can be said to lay the foundations of testing, the construction phase involves building the visible structure of the testing activities. Typical activities in this phase are likely to include:

- confirm test environments;

- update test plan;

- plan test environments;

- produce testing documentation;

- create test environments (for hardware, software, and network systems) and ensure that these are added to the configuration within the configuration management system;

- ensure that all software components of the environments are recorded in the configuration management system;
- create test specifications (test scripts and test cases);
- create automated test specifications (automated test scripts and test data);
- create procedures to load, backup, and restore data needed to run critical tests;
- sign-off test construction phase.

Test execution

It is important that the activities within the test execution phase start as soon as possible. Indeed, tests can be performed as soon as there is a component ready for testing. The whole purpose of testing is to find defects, so it is better that they are found now before the users find them later.

During this phase, the activities necessary to actually test the product are performed, either manually, automatically, or through a combination of both. It is during this phase that tests will be executed to identify defects by a combination of test approaches:

- code checking (e.g. desk-checking, code analysis, and coverage analysis);
- observation (what has actually happened?);
- system outputs (screens, reports, files, etc.);
- test script output.

Test execution, like any new activity will suffer from its own problems so it is important to initially execute a series of tests to ensure that there are no problems with the test process itself. Once this has been completed, the test process can be executed. Successful execution of a typical test process is likely to generate a number of events which will need careful management. Typical test events are likely to include the following:

- Incidents. These will be produced for a variety of problems, of which errors in the system under test will only form a part;
- Recording information. Test logs should be created for all tests, particularly if the test was not completed successfully. Once the fervour of testing is complete, it must be possible to audit what actually happened;
- Negativity. Testing itself does not create the problems that it finds. A "no-blame" needs to be encouraged to facilitate the solution to incidents – the ultimate goal of testing.

- Disruption. Testing is enormously dependent on many other activities so it is highly probable that testing will suffer serious disruption at some point within the project. Be prepared for change and ensure that it is managed through a formal change control process.

- Approval. The test execution phase must be signed-off, possibly with the inclusion of caveats if necessary, by key project stakeholders.

Fundamental to every test must be an understanding of what has been tested, such as the amount of functionality tested or the amount of code analyzed. This will be an important measure in determining what has not been tested. Only through significant planning before this stage, and discipline during this stage of testing can confidence be gained. For example the following information must be obtained and recorded throughout the test execution phase:

- the tracking and recording of errors found;

- the tracking and recording of changes made to the system under test (using change control and configuration management systems);

- the tracking and recording of changes made to the development and production systems as a result of changes made during testing (using change control and configuration management systems);

- the severity of errors identified – are there any "show-stoppers?";

- the versions of all applications, modules, and systems tested;

- detailed descriptions of each error;

- documentation used during test (user guides, test scripts, etc.) and their version numbers (people may be using "draft" copies).

Making the transition from testing to product release

The average IS project plan is likely to identify testing as the last major activity prior to the implementation of a new system. However, as many, otherwise well-planned IS projects run into trouble *after* testing has been completed, it is clear that the implementation phase of the project is of much greater importance and significance than generally thought.

On completion of testing, the project team will be under significant pressure to satisfy the most important delivery milestone within the project plan, the release of the product into a user environment. It is at this point that the implementation phase of the project is often abandoned in a formal sense and, in the rush to achieve the delivery milestone, what was once called "implementation" now becomes "product release." The consequence is often disastrous – focus is wrongly placed on immediate product delivery rather than planning the implementation activities necessary to ensure that the product is released into a well-prepared and business-ready environment.

It is no coincidence, therefore, that the title for this section of the book uses the term, *transition*, rather than its more common counterpart, *implementation*. The transition phase of a project, in my opinion, more accurately reflects the main purpose of the final phase in the project plan – to migrate the software product into a user environment. The change, however, is purely in name, and the final phase of the project should remain a critical period for the entire project team. Once the product has been delivered to the customer, there will almost certainly be events that occur that require either: the deployment of further product releases; corrective action to fix minor problems; or the addition of features that were originally planned but subsequently postponed.

The process of migrating the software product into a user domain can start as soon as there is a product baseline mature enough to be deployed. Typically this will be when some usable subset of the system has been tested to an acceptable level of quality and when all necessary user documentation is available.

It is unlikely, however, that the transition from testing to final product release will be completed as a single, sequential event. With different project events requiring different delivery outcomes, it is much more likely that several iterations of this phase may be required, each one releasing a product into the user domain, until the final product baseline is achieved (Figure 11.4). At this point, the principal objectives of system implementation will have been satisfied, namely:

- achieving user self-supportability;

- agreement from stakeholders that all deployment baselines have been met and satisfied according to the project success criteria;

- reaching the final product baseline as quickly and as economically as possible.

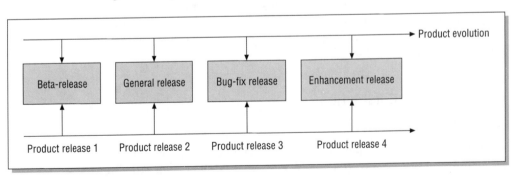

FIGURE 11.4 ▓ The transition from testing to final product release

TABLE 11.1 ■ Deployment activities that may be performed prior to product release

Deployment activity
Beta-testing
Parallel operation with existing system
Conversion of operational databases
Agreeing the product maintenance schedule
Establishing user support procedures
User training
Producing external release of product
Product packaging and distribution
Updating product/sales manuals and corporate web-sites
Providing user documentation
Formal/contractual acceptance of the product

In order to achieve these objectives, a number of deployment activities may need to be performed within this phase of the project, a summary of which is shown in Table 11.1. Whilst many of these activities will be performed during the final phase of the project, it is likely that many of them will have been planned in the earlier phases.

The required number of activities actually performed, however, will be dependent upon the complexity of the transition phase of the project. A new release of a relatively small product into a small business team may only comprise a few simple activities; the deployment of a global financial services system would obviously be much more complex to manage and require a greater number of activities to be undertaken.

Key deployment activities

Beta-testing

Software testing that is performed within the software vendor's premises is an activity often referred to as "alpha" testing. However, it is likely that any organization that has developed a new product which is to be released into an external market will want to release the product to a small sample of their customers first. For example, if the product has been developed by a software vendor, the vendor will be eager to test the performance and functionality of the product when it is implemented on a customer's premises, using the customer's own hardware.

This activity is commonly referred to as "beta-testing," and involves a sample of users being supplied with a pre-release version of the product to test – a "beta-release" of the product. Whilst beta-testing clearly provides a level of comfort for the product supplier, it is also popular amongst their customers for many reasons, including:

- being able to preview the software before general release;
- the satisfaction of finding software bugs;
- providing feedback to the vendor, making the software better as a result;
- contributing to the evolution of the product through discussion and feedback.

User training

Whilst a large sample of users may have been trained in order to participate in user acceptance testing, now is the time to ensure that *all* users have been trained in both the new system and any new business procedures that may be required to support it. Key training activities will be dependent upon the complexity and scope of the project, but are likely to include:

- developing online training guides;
- distributing user guides, process guides, and installation manuals;
- the completion of user training sessions; adopting a "train-the-trainer" scheme;
- ensuring that all users have been provided with operational user accounts and passwords.

Helpdesk support

Once the system has become operational, all users must be supported on an ongoing basis. If a helpdesk facility already exists within the organization, current procedures may need to be amended to include new product details. If no formal helpdesk facility currently exists, some arrangement must be made to ensure that user problems are handled and resolved in an effective way.

Regardless of the size and scope of the helpdesk facility within the organization, a number of key activities must be undertaken in order to provide an agreed level of user support, such as:

■ determine call logging and call escalation procedures;

■ ensure that all users are aware of support procedures and contact numbers;

■ determine out-of-hours support procedures if required;

■ identifying and training "super-users" who can provide immediate support to users.

Whilst we all tend to view helpdesks as providing a number of common support functions within the organization, they do in fact differ from each other in many respects. It is vital, therefore, that users are made aware of the structure and operation of the helpdesk they will be using as soon as possible before product release.

In general terms, there are two main types of helpdesk: a non-intelligent helpdesk (call forwarding) and an intelligent helpdesk (call resolution). The former purely logs user calls and passes them onto call management and call resolution teams; the latter attempts to offer the resolution of calls in the first instance (first-line support) before passing onto a call management and resolution team (second-line support). Most helpdesk procedures are based around a hierarchy of support to ensure that a fault call is handled by the most appropriate individual or team. A summary of a typical helpdesk support hierarchy found within many organizations is shown in Table 11.2.

TABLE 11.2 ■ A typical IS service support hierarchy

Service support level	Key activities and responsibilities
1	Super-user support. How-to support and standard defined workarounds to service issues. No code changes are performed at this level.
2	Developing and defining solutions and workarounds that are dependent upon user configuration changes, access changes or using different logical paths through the application.
3	Technical resolution of service issues requiring amendments to restore the live service; configuration changes that affect multiple users; data management (unload/reload/restore, etc.); service patch implementation; version upgrades.
4	Support for enhancements or functional changes related to approved change requests

Conversion of operational databases

Data sources that are to be referenced by the live system will need to be populated with valid and referentially complete information prior to product release. Product information that has been used for user acceptance testing must, therefore, be extracted from test systems and databases and uploaded into their production equivalents.

Whilst capacity planning and data sizing activities will have already been performed during the design and development stages of the project, additional checks should also be made upon the population of production database systems to ensure that there is adequate online and offline storage capacity to support operational business systems. Key database conversion activities will be dependent upon the complexity and scope of the project, but are likely to include:

- database reorganization and maintenance;
- archive management;
- database backup and recovery procedures;
- the transfer of code and data from rest environments and production environments.

Parallel operation with existing systems

The release of a completely new product into an organization poses few problems in comparison to the release of a system intended to replace one or more existing systems. Legacy or "heritage" systems will be, by definition, an integral part of the technical infrastructure of the organization and simply switching them off prior to the implementation of the new system may be neither a simple nor safe activity. If existing systems have interfaces into many other local and remote systems, a period of transition may be required, in order to implement a new system safely into the business without jeopardizing business operations.

Parallel operation enables a new system to be run alongside an existing one in order to gain confidence in two key areas. First, that the users are satisfied the new system is performing as well as the existing system and second, to ensure that all the necessary business and technical activities that need to be in place at the point of full system cutover are underway.

Whilst parallel operation can provide obvious benefits to more complex product releases, it is in itself a complex activity, and so must be planned and executed well if it is not to cause disruption to business activities. The duration and scope of parallel operation will be dependent upon the specific nature of the project, but that aside, key activities to support a parallel operation are likely to include:

- establishing new system or business procedures to support parallel operation;
- agreeing the schedule to decommission existing systems;
- building temporary "data bridges" between systems where necessary to ensure that integration is not compromised with the introduction of the new system.

UK Passport Agency

In April 1991, the United Kingdom Passport Agency was established as the Executive Agency of the Home Office. Its main aim was to provide passport services for British nationals in the UK promptly and economically, through its offices in Belfast, Glasgow, Liverpool, London, Newport, and Peterborough.

In July 1997, Siemens Business Services, the German systems supplier, was awarded the contract to provide and install a new passport processing system. The system was required for two main reasons:

- the existing system was relatively old and was not Year 2000 compliant.
- new functionality for providing greater security over the issuing of passports was needed.

Five weeks after deploying the system to the Liverpool office, the Passport Agency was only handling 6,200 passports a week, against the planned target of 30,000. This key performance indicator should have raised serious doubts as to the capability and performance of the new system. Rather than investigating the problem, the agency decided to continue with its implementation plan and subsequently deployed the system to its Newport office.[5,6,7,8]

By June 1999, the delays in processing passports had continued to increase dramatically. The average time to process a passport application had now reached 50 working days, slower in fact, than the agency's manual systems. According to a spokesman for the Public and Commercial Services Union (PCS), under the old system, each passport examiner was clearing 100 passports a day. In the new system they were clearing only 35. At the height of the delays in processing passport applications, a backlog of more than 500,000 passport applications was created – 10 times greater than normal. In a desperate effort to process this huge backlog, the Home Office granted free two-year extensions to passports.

Since the passport chaos during the summer of 1999, the fundamental causes of failure have never been agreed. The National Audit Office (NAO) report into the failure identifies problems with the data entry process and the accuracy of scanning hand-written forms. The poor print quality of the system was also identified as a contributory factor in this process.

Key failure factors

- Insufficient time was allocated to ensure that staff understood how to use the new technology and new business procedures.

- New legislation requiring children under 16 years of age to have their own passports had been introduced, resulting in an excessive demand for child passports during the summer period.

- Insufficient contingency planning. There was no fall-back plan in the event of implementation not going according to the plan.

- Too much focus on meeting implementation schedules at the expense of resolving major problems raised as a consequence. Even though the pilot implementation at Liverpool had identified serious performance and scalability issues, the implementation continued as normal, deploying the system to the Newport passport office, compounding the problems even further.

- The failure to communicate effectively with the public and the media. The Passport Agency failed to manage the expectations of customers, who lost confidence in the Agency after the delays became public. As a result, there was a significant increase in the number of applications and enquiries made.

- The Agency was too reliant on simple solutions to cope with the increased demand, such as expecting staff and managers to work longer hours.

Key dates

- July 1996 Passport Agency decided to introduce the digital passport to increase security, replace their existing computer system and improve their efficiency.

- June/July 1997 Passport Agency awarded a contract to Siemens Business Services.

- October 5, 1998 New IT system and outsourced procedures introduced to Agency's Liverpool office.

- November 9, 1998 Passport Agency Management Board decided to roll-out new system and procedures to the Newport office.

- November 16, 1998 New system introduced to Newport office.

- November 18, 1998 Passport Agency Management Board decided to postpone introduction of new system.

- February/March 1999 Home Office expressed serious concern at developing situation. Action plan agreed.

- May 1999 Free two-year extensions to recently expired passports offered to public queuing at passport offices.

- Late June/early July 1999 Emergency measures introduced, including free passport extensions at post offices and call center established.

Cost of failure

It is estimated that the cost of measures taken by the Passport Agency to resolve the failures during the year from October 1998 was in the region of $18.9 million (£12.6 million), including £6 million ($9 million) for additional staffing. Almost 500 holidaymakers missed their planned departure dates and, as a result, over $241,500 (£161,000) was paid out in compensation. Shortly after the situation was resolved, the Passport Agency announced the rise in the cost of obtaining a UK passport.

Have the lessons been learned?

On February 15, 2001, the Home Office announced that they were to abandon the Asylum computer project.[7] The project was initiated to reduce the backlog of asylum cases, standing at 66,000 by replacing much of the time-consuming paperwork that was needed to process asylum cases.

The Immigration and Nationality Directorate's (IND) casework application program was at the heart of a complex IT initiative and business process contract signed with Siemens Business Services in April 1996 for implementation in October 1998. The contract was worth £77 million ($115 million). Since the system went live, however, it has been dogged by problems.

▶ Testing: critical success factors

- Test early and test often.

- Ensure that every test is repeatable – it is the only way to prove that the errors identified during previous testing phases have been removed.

- Integrate application development and testing processes as much as possible.

- Develop a testing methodology throughout the organization. You will be able to test applications in a consistent manner and measure success uniformly.

- Define your expected results from testing before you start.

- Define entry and exit criteria for each type of test.

- Use a mixture of tests (such as regression, system, unit, and user acceptance).

- Review the test process as it happens and inspect the results. Early detection of errors will save costs in the long term.

- Understand the reasons *why* you are testing and ensure that you can define them in business terms. It will help you develop and execute a more focused test plan.

- Do not forget to plan for the transition of software into a user environment. The desire to implement as soon as possible after testing is likely to be at the expense of a well-documented and agreed implementation plan.

References

1   S. Miles, (1999) Windows may crash after 49.7 days (March 2, 1999), CNET **News.com** http://news.com.com/2100-1040-222391.html?tag=bplst (accessed 2001)

2   F. Redmill, (1998) "Why systems go up in smoke," *The Computer Bulletin*, Series V, **1** (5) 26–8

3   *Ariane 5 – Flight 501 Failure.* Report by the Inquiry Board, July 19, 1996, Paris

4   J.M. Jézéquel and B. Meyer (1997) "Design by Contract: The Lessons of Ariane," *IEEE Computer*, January, 1997 **30** (2), 129–30

5   *The Passport Delays of Summer 1999, Select Committee on Public Accounts Twenty-Fourth Report*, House of Commons, UK, 1999

6   *The United Kingdom Passport Agency: the Passport Delays of Summer 1999*, National Audit Office Press Notice, October, 1999

7   D. White, "UK abandons troubled immigration computer project," *Financial Times*, February 15, 2001

8   J. Sanchez, (1999) "Siemens blamed for U.K. passport fiasco," *Computerworld Hong Kong*, www.cw.com.hk/Features/f990702001.htm (accessed 2002)

Further reading

T. Gilb, *Principles of Software Engineering Management*, Addison-Wesley, 1988

B. Littlewood and L. Lorenzo Strigini, "The risks of software," *Scientific American*, November, 1992, 62–75

W. Royce, *Software Project Management – A Unified Approach*, Addison-Wesley Longman, 1999

G. Walker, *IT Problem Management*, Prentice Hall, 2001. An excellent book on the subject of SLA management and establishing a "service center" within the organization

12

Learning the lessons

The man who makes no mistakes does not usually make anything
Edward John Phelps (1822–1900)

The consequences of IS project failure often extend far beyond the immediate failure of a business system. Most notable are the legal, financial, and commercial implications of failure, which cannot be ignored, and the significant amount of unwelcome publicity these events inevitably generate.

The benefits of being able to achieve a capability where IS project success is repeatable should, therefore, be a fundamental driver within the organization, reflected in its vision and values. Concerns within the organization must be raised, therefore, when the only aspects of project delivery most likely to be reproduced are those which contribute the most to project failure.

Regardless of project size, complexity, scope, and other issues which have the potential to affect every IS project, there are some organizations for whom these factors pose little or no threat. The one characteristic that differentiates these organizations from others for whom IS project success is still the exception rather than the rule is their ability to learn lessons from project failure. We all make mistakes, and as long we learn from them, that is no bad thing. Fear of making a mistake should not prevent us from performing our work.

Clearly, the need to learn from our mistakes represents a significant challenge in changing the culture of IS project failure. The individuals who are most likely to meet this challenge will be those who are not only aware of the causes of project failure, but who are able to spot the warning signs of potential failure and take corrective action before it jeopardizes the project.

Project failure factors

Previous chapters of this book have attempted to identify the possible causes of IS project failure, through the use of case study material, statistical analysis, and observation. Based on this knowledge, the probability that one or more of the project failure factors shown in Table 12.1 will be experienced at some stage throughout the project is high.

Whilst each factor has the potential to affect the outcome of an IS project, the probability of project failure from the presence of a single factor is likely to be low. The situation is somewhat different if multiple failure factors are experienced throughout the project.

TABLE 12.1 ■ The factors influencing project failure

Technical failure	Human failure	Process failure
■ Lure of the leading edge	■ Lack of executive support	■ Absence of any project management methodology
■ Poor technical design	■ Lack of leadership	
■ Technical solution to a non-technical problem	■ Uncommitted project team	■ Absence of any systems development methodology
	■ Dysfunctional project team	■ Absence of any benefits management methodology
■ Dependence on software packages to satisfy requirements	■ Failure to manage third parties	
	■ Lack of a project 'champion'	■ Lack of quality management methodology
	■ Lack of project ownership	
■ Lack of tools throughout development lifecycle	■ Stakeholder conflict	■ Failure to identify and mitigate project risks
■ Technology-led development	■ Resistance to change	
	■ Hostile organizational culture	■ Failure to manage requirements
	■ Inexperienced project managers	■ Lengthy project timescales
	■ Lack of business justification	■ Insufficient testing
	■ Unclear or ambiguous business priorities	■ "Big-bang" approach to computerization
	■ Lack of user training	
	■ Misaligned stakeholder motivation	

▶ Learning the lessons – 20 ways to reduce IS project failure

The information contained within this chapter is not merely a hypothetical comment on how to prevent project failure; it represents constructive advice based on information gained from IS project reviews undertaken in both the public and private sectors.

Learning the lessons from project failure is a necessary part of the continuous improvement process that must be established if high levels of quality are to be achieved and maintained throughout the organization. Whilst this book has discussed IS project failure in some detail, this section identifies the key lessons which, if heeded, will increase the chances of achieving your goal – successful IT project delivery.

Lesson 1 – manage user expectations

It is vital that the project stakeholders are clear from the outset what is being delivered (and what is *not* being delivered). Involvement from key users will be vital in order to ensure that their requirements are captured and that business ownership is established as early as possible within the project.

Many Year 2000 compliance projects suffered a backlash from their respective user communities when the users of the "new" systems realized they would still be constrained by many of the problems they had experienced with the previous systems. The scope of many millennium projects was limited to meeting the requirements of regulatory and safety bodies, there would be no additional business functionality. Unfortunately, this was not always communicated throughout the organization. It was inevitable then that the expectations of many users, especially those who were aware of the costs of remediating these systems, were shattered at a time when user involvement was critical.

Comments from project reviews

Users were expecting performance gains from the system and, while performance was ultimately improved, an agreed expectation had not been discussed or managed with the users. Performance gains were never part of the project scope, but the expectations arose and needed to be carefully managed, pointing back to a clear and unambiguous project scope.

It was important to manage the users' expectations since the information previously received by them had been, at best, limited. The users needed to be hand-held and feedback from them was often hard to gain. Key users need to be identified at the start of the project and time made available by them to "own" the needs for their departments and the responsibility to provide/verify information and to commit their resources as required. The belief of the users was often one of IT owning the project and their requirements.

Lesson 2 – The project specification must take into account the needs of the business and the requirements of the users

There are two concepts to be understood here. First, projects are conceived and grow from identifiable and measurable business needs. Clear objectives identified at the beginning of an IS project can soon become blurred as the project progresses, a characteristic of projects that have excessively long timescales for delivery.

End-users must be identified before the project commences so that their needs are taken into account fully during the design and development of IS projects. It is important that the users understand very early on in the project that they have responsibilities and actions to help the project succeed. Their needs form a vital part of the analysis and design stages of the project, and a close partnership needs to be established with them if the project is to succeed.

Once requirements have been captured, they should be baselined, introduced into a configuration management system and placed under change control. If requirements are changed or added, impact analysis against the project must be performed and the project plan amended accordingly.

For organizations that develop software incrementally and iteratively, requirements for each software release should be frozen and a mechanism established to allow a new high-priority requirement to be added to the development baseline.

Second, the project specification must be focused on business requirements and not technical solutions. A business requirement that identifies, for example, the need for system interfaces and packaged software solutions is a clear indication that the project is IT-led and not business-led. It is important, therefore, to focus on business relevance when obtaining approval for the project, even if, technically, the solution may already be clear.

Comments from a project review

It is important that the users understand very early on in the project that they have responsibilities and actions to help the project succeed. A partnership needs to be established with the users to achieve the delivery of key user responsibilities. The project manager must define the tasks within the project that the users have to fulfill and seek to gain genuine buy-in from all interested parties. It is helpful to establish terms of reference for users, as well as project team members.

Lesson 3 – Measure and assess the scale and complexity of the project before committing resources (keep a grip on reality)

It is an unfortunate consequence of the power and capability of technology that it makes organizations believe that what was once impossible is now not only possible, but easily achievable. In the early stages of the project, this is often manifested by wild claims being made over the project's potential benefits, combined with a massive scope and an overly-optimistic but dangerously simplistic project plan.

Before you rush off and fully engage suppliers, users, and other stakeholders in the project, make sure the project is itself achievable. In particular determine whether:

■ the proposed timetable for the project is realistic;

■ the business case for the project is sound;

■ the solution is technically feasible.

The scale and complexity of IS projects will be a determining factor in project success. Both introduce major risks into the project, and steps must, therefore, be taken to minimize these risks as much as possible. Primarily, the level of technical uncertainty or technical innovation within an IS project, combined with the scope of the project, must be assessed prior to the release of funds.

The failures of the London Ambulance Service's computer-aided dispatch system and Denver Airport's revolutionary baggage handling system should send clear warning signals to business and IT managers alike. Both projects failed to appreciate the technical complexity of their proposed systems and consequently failed to manage the obvious design risks.

The London Ambulance Service was eager to respond to meet the challenges rising from changes to the National Health Service by introducing an innovative and technically advanced system in a very short timescale. Unfortunately, in their desire to improve their corporate image they failed to respect the inherent risks of what they were doing and paid the price.

It is evident that the lure of the "leading-edge" often compromises rational argument and business justification within organizations who are desperate to "lead the way" in their respective industry sectors. When the inevitable happens and the project runs into difficulties, the belief that the project can overcome any challenge that prevents the system from being implemented is reinforced for much the same reason. In some cases this has led to managers even refusing to acknowledge the presence of serious issues within the project.

Extracts from project reviews

Nobody was brave enough to stand up and say, this system doesn't make sense. (The TAURUS monitoring group[1])

There may have been an element of "self-delusion" [among the TAURUS project team] (Sir Andrew Hugh Smith, chairman of the stock exchange, announcing the cancellation of the project, as reported in the Financial Times, 1993)[2]

Lesson 4 – IS projects cannot be introduced in isolation from wider changes to the organization

Introducing technology into the organization will not, on its own, solve a business problem. Even so, there is still an expectation within many organizations that the introduction of a new IT system will result in precisely that. If the necessary changes within the organization are not made prior to project delivery, it is more likely that the introduction of IT systems into the organization will fail to deliver any benefits whatsoever.

The deployment of IT is not an end in itself. It is vital that training costs and schedules are included within the project plan to ensure that staff know how to use and maintain the system. Without proper training, it is unlikely that the full benefits potential of the IS investment will ever be realized; more importantly, a lack of training may introduce commercial and operational risks into the project which may ultimately threaten its long-term viability.

The implementation of new IT systems must be accompanied by the provision of training commensurate with the level of business change and technological advancement. Effective training may take some time and managers must ensure that they understand the impact the introduction of new systems will have on operational procedures.

The London Ambulance Service case study highlights the consequences of implementing a new IT system without first analyzing the impact of the system from a business perspective. For change to be successful, it must be managed effectively – and that means dealing with people and resolving issues through discussion and consultation.

By introducing state-of-the-art technology, the LAS management clearly thought that they could introduce much-needed change into the organization. They failed because they did not consider how that technology might affect the roles and responsibilities of the very people who would need to use it.

Comment from a project review

Recent restructuring within the business unit led to uncertainty regarding the program roles and responsibilities.

Lesson 5 – A clear and visible project management structure is fundamental to the project

All projects must be established around an effective and visible project management structure. Within that structure must exist clearly defined roles, responsibilities, and accountabilities. Formal reporting structures and lines of communication to senior management must be established at the start of the project and continue up to project closedown.

Comments from project reviews

The initiation of the project, prior to our involvement, did not have any clear or visible project deliverables. Additionally the project team and the responsibilities of individuals within it were not defined. A substantial amount of time was spent assessing the amount of resources that were required, and in defining the project's business & technical deliverables.

There was no formal project framework in place for the project prior to pick-up. Specifications, deliverables, roles, responsibilities, etc. were not clearly defined from the outset. Such a situation requires significant effort to overcome.

There was a lack of program governance, including business requirements and program plans . . .

Prior to product release, everyone within the project team must be aware of the stakeholder approval process. They must know who is going to sign what off and when.

The way in which the project was progressed was unlikely to achieve a positive outcome – alarm bells should have been ringing with the project manager at an earlier stage. Closer monitoring and tighter controls would have revealed that the project was iterating around and not progressing towards a positive outcome. It is vital that the project manager has a realistic plan, a viable approach and a means to closely monitor actual progression against the plan.

Lesson 6 – Take care of people first

Never forget that it is people who are the single most important factor in achieving project success. Personal development programs must work alongside the project management framework within organizations to provide the mechanisms for training, performance appraisals, assignments, and career development. Highly-motivated and skilled staff are an organization's most valuable asset and the key to successful IS projects.

Lesson 7 – Accept risk, but manage it closely

Successful implementation of IT systems calls for creative thinking supported by effective risk management. Risks are inherent in IS projects and, whilst it is true that success often comes to those who are prepared to take risks, it is equally true that failure lies in wait for those who do not manage risks effectively.

Risk-taking and innovation are valuable strengths in achieving competitive advantage, but are very much dependent on an organizational culture where such activities are encouraged and supported. Above all, it is vital to ensure that any business risks taken must be closely linked to the achievement of objectives.

Extracts from project reviews

The element of risk on the project was significantly high, given that there was an unknown quantity in respect of the third party involved, an immovable end date (set by an external regulatory body) and prior concerns raised by the third party in respect of the amount of work required exceeding the time available. Given this the project sponsors had an unrealistic expectation of a successful, on-time and on-budget delivery.

The implementation of the billing system during the project severely affected its progression. These effects should have been investigated and a re-planning activity should have been undertaken. Furthermore the area of risk analysis (and subsequent risk management) should have been revisited. Any unplanned events must be analysed to assess their impact upon the project. There should then follow actions to reassess the baseline and amend the plan accordingly.

Although the [UK Passport] Agency transferred the risk associated with the design and delivery of the new computer system to their private sector partners . . . the significant risk associated with ensuring continuity and quality of service remained with the Agency. As a result, the Agency incurred additional costs of £12.6 million in an effort to maintain services . . .[3]

Lesson 8 – Always review the viability of the project

Projects should not proceed without first establishing a sound business case for doing so. Within the business case for the project, there should be a firm understanding of the investment appraisal of the project and an analysis of the risks that may prevent or diminish the delivery of benefits.

Once the project has been initiated, it is vital that the conditions on which success is dependent are constantly monitored. Change can affect the project in many ways, regardless of whether that change is internal to the project, or external. The impact of change may well render the original investment appraisal obsolete.

Equally, the viability of the project should be reviewed at key stages throughout its lifecycle, especially when decisions are taken which may alter the objectives on which the project was built. The business case should, therefore, be a constant source of reference throughout the project. If the project is deemed to be in serious difficulties, with little chance of it delivering the expected benefits its viability and continued funding must be reviewed at the earliest opportunity.

Do not be afraid to terminate the project if the benefits case for the investment no longer holds true. If the decision is taken to terminate the project, do not let the procedure become a long-winded and drawn out affair. Abandon the project and move forward – making sure you learn some valuable lessons in the process. A key factor in the cost of a failed project is often the length of time taken to stop it. If you are in any doubt as to the viability of the project, stop development and audit the project. If this cannot be performed within the organization, seek advice from outside consultants. Additional costs will be incurred but, ultimately, they may save you from financial and commercial disaster.

Lesson 9 – Manage external suppliers

It is of paramount importance that formal terms of reference are established for all external suppliers to ensure that the exact scope of their work is clear and unambiguous. In particular, attention should be paid to the quality management systems of the supplier to ensure that they are adequate and can be assessed within existing quality systems.

There are considerable risks in relying too much on assurances made by contractors that the system can be delivered and not having sufficient involvement with them when the project experiences problems. The key lesson must be to develop close relationships with suppliers, but avoid undue reliance on them. At all times, customers must retain ownership of the project and its progress.

Control must be established firmly during the procurement process and must continue throughout the project. From a number of the projects examined within this book, it is clear that the capabilities and financial standing of external suppliers must be reviewed as part of the procurement and tendering process.

Comments from project reviews

The third party were effectively engaged by the department, but only after a lot of misspent time on another business program and so were presented as a "fait accompli" and not as a potential supplier. It soon became clear that they were not a quality solutions provider, but it was too late to take corrective action without impacting the project.

The fact that the third party had failed to demonstrate effective communication skills during previous correspondence should have been a warning that their quality of delivery may be less than that required. This led to delays in achieving an effective specification (and increased use of technical and user resource to produce a specification) and an ultimate impact to the delivery of the system.

We are already 900 supplier-man-days over budget; we should have managed them more closely.

Lesson 10 – Invest in quality

The introduction of quality systems is not cheap; quality standards, assurance processes, tools and training will all contribute towards the cost of quality. For business and IT managers under pressure to deliver systems into the business as soon as possible, quality is often sacrificed in the hope that delivery times can be reduced. Whilst skimping on quality may appear to ease schedule pressure in the short term, in the longer term, the failure to invest in quality significantly diminishes the return on investment for the project.

The lack of testing and defect prevention is still one of the main contributors to IS project failure. Testing should not be seen as a single activity that must be completed before the project can be implemented, but as a program of tests that, when complete, will provide the confidence to plan the release of the product. It is important to remember that the objective of testing is not just to ensure technical governance, it is also to protect the financial investment made by the customer.

The failure of the Ariane 5 project, resulting in an uninsured loss of $500,000 million (£333,000 million) should be a lesson to us all. Despite seemingly good management and technical standards, the failure of computer systems on board the launcher was triggered by an error caused by reusing software from an earlier system without fully testing its impact on the existing software components.

Lesson 11 – Always have a contingency plan

Fundamental to the risk management process is the need to identify and manage risks within the project. This is particularly important for organizations who outsource the delivery of IS projects to third party organizations because it is likely that risks which are left unmanaged by the supplier will transfer back to the customer with disastrous consequences.

Business and IT stakeholders must, therefore, develop contingency plans that can be implemented in the event that the risk of non-delivery actually happens. Some consideration should also be made concerning possible compensation payments to customers who may suffer from a degraded service or reduced business efficiency.

Extract from a project review

I decided not to put any contingencies into the timetable because I wanted to drive it through. Now I'm changing tack. (TAURUS project director in defending the original implementation plan against critics)[4]

Lesson 12 – Ensure that senior management are involved throughout the project

Senior management have a crucial role to play in championing the successful development of IT systems. Decisions regarding IS projects must be treated as business decisions rather than technical ones, and have the full support of senior management. There is no point in having a formal control structure within the organization if senior management do little more than to rubber stamp decisions made at lower levels within the organization. Senior management must accept they have a responsibility to track and control the project.

Lesson 13 – The project must have a clear owner who is accountable for its success

Whilst executive ownership of IS projects is vital to their success, there is considerable evidence to suggest that this is either weak or non-existent. There must, above all, be a single, strong owner for the project, especially where a number of parties have a vested interest in its outcome. The TAURUS project suffered from a lack of clear and authoritative ownership at the highest level. The consequence was that control of the project was "shared" amongst a large number of committees and third-party stakeholders. Throughout the project, compromises were made in order to please everyone with the ultimate consequence of satisfying no one. The project represented a classic failure case of "design by committee."

Lesson 14 – Ensure that all new software development projects adopt processes that satisfy at least Level 2 of the software Capability Maturity Model

Achieving software excellence takes time and costs money, but do not use this as an excuse for doing nothing about it. Building poor-quality systems will ultimately cost more than building high-quality systems. As an absolute minimum, processes that support a basic level of configuration management, requirements management, software quality assurance, and project planning must be adopted within the project. Do not rely on the dedication and expertise of your development staff to deliver the project – if they leave, your project will suffer.

Lesson 15 – Always perform a post-implementation review and publish the findings

The post-implementation review is a vital process that must be undertaken if lessons are to be learned from the project. Despite the clear benefits such a process can deliver there are very few organizations who perform post-implementation reviews in a formal and structured way.

The consequences of failing to perform a post-implementation review are simple: the organization and, more specifically, the people within it are denied the opportunity to learn from their mistakes. A post-implementation review is designed to establish how well the project has met its business objectives. The scope of the review should, therefore, cover all aspects of the project, such as: business objectives, user expectations, user satisfaction, predicted benefits, technical requirements, supplier management, and quality assurance.

The post-implementation review is often the final task to appear in an IS project plan and is often added in the knowledge that it signifies the end of the project. This, in many ways, is the reason why the benefits of the review are never realized; the task itself is seen as a 'terminating' activity rather than an 'initiating' activity.

Whilst the post-implementation review might well signify the end of development and implementation activities, there is still one remaining deliverable from the project, the post-implementation review report. The failure of organizations to learn the lessons from project failure is often simply because the post-implementation review is never analyzed and used to improve future projects. Crucial information gained from suppliers, customers, developers, management, and users is, more often than not, filed away in the project document repository, never to be used again.

Lesson 16 – Project management experience and leadership remain important

Successfully delivering an IS project is not just about producing a project plan and writing reports; it is about dealing with people, handling conflict, negotiating, and influencing others within the organization.

Successful projects are characterized by individuals who lead rather than manage. A good leader earns respect and is rewarded by working with a team who will "go the extra mile." In return, a good leader will display courage, common sense, authority, and charisma. IS projects are likely to encounter difficulties along the way and having a good, strong leader at the helm may just be enough to turn a potentially doomed project into a successful one. It is often said of a good project manager, "the people who work for you should admire and respect you and your boss should think you're insane".

Even an experienced project manager with strong leadership qualities may still not be able to save a project that does not have executive support and business ownership. A good project manager will, however, be able to recognize the warning signs early enough in the project to take an appropriate course of action. Inexperience is often the reason why many project managers become so entangled with minor events that they fail to spot the serious issues which have the potential to jeopardize the whole project.

The use of experienced project managers is essential for ensuring that IS projects are delivered on time and within budget. Project management is a skill that takes time to master and is not something that can be learnt "on the job." If organizations are to improve the success of their projects they must invest in project management training schemes and develop an effective standard project management framework.

Business and IT staff should not be promoted into project management roles solely on the basis of their technical or commercial abilities. For those individuals who show a genuine desire to deliver successful projects into the organization, a combination of training and mentoring schemes must be established within the organization to support their career aspirations – to the benefit of both the individual and the organization.

Lesson 17 – Audit your projects

Audits provide the means to check and enforce quality standards across IS programs and projects. Audits also provide visibility of potential problems and ultimately can be used to protect organizations from commercial risk. The consultant from Coopers & Lybrand who was brought in to manage the technical aspects of the TAURUS project ordered a full review of the project as a matter of principle. It was on the basis of this review that the project was finally abandoned, albeit three years later.

Lesson 18 – Ensure that financial controls are in place

Once budgets for project phases and deliverables have been developed, a reporting framework should be implemented to enable the actual costs, variances, and estimated costs to completion to be identified for each project activity.

Extract from a project review

There was a clear lack of cross-functional reporting and monitoring framework for managing the program budget against deliverables . . .

Lesson 19 – Build trust through open and effective communication

Effective communication is fundamental to the success of an IS project. When communication fails, it is also likely to have a corresponding and detrimental impact on the project. Effective communication has one key objective – to enable information to be exchanged and understood between individuals or groups. It is the open and honest exchange of information that allows rapport, trust, ownership, and approval to be established and maintained throughout the project.

Whilst the widespread use of e-mail as the primary means of communication within many organizations is a welcome factor, you cannot plan and control IS projects via e-mail. Managers who send out a huge list of activities, roles, responsibilities, and milestones to an unsuspecting and uninformed audience via e-mail in the hope that this will "get the job done quickly" are very much mistaken.

Human contact is vital if communication is to be effective. Face-to-face meetings with project stakeholders and team members should be encouraged wherever possible. Combining verbal and non-verbal communication within your meetings will ensure that the information is not only exchanged, but understood.

Above all, do not forget to listen to those around you. Creating a culture of openness where employees feel comfortable expressing their views is no use whatsoever if those with whom they are communicating do not take the trouble to listen to what is being said. The TAURUS monitoring group only met for 90 minutes every month, clearly insufficient considering the size and complexity of the project.

Lesson 20 – Above all, realize that we are only human and mistakes will be made

Whilst there may be fears that computers will one day rule our lives, it is somewhat reassuring to know that the awesome power of computer technology is nothing compared to the ability of a human being to make a mistake. Indeed, there are many cybernetic experts who would probably argue that this is only characteristic that differentiates us from our silicon counterparts.

Of course, the point of the matter is not that we make mistakes (although reducing their regularity would be no bad thing) – it is the fact that we do not include the possibility of them happening in our reasoning and, as a consequence, fail to manage such events when they do happen.

It is important to remember that no one individual or team is more important than the project itself. Humility is a virtue that differentiates those who consistently fail from those who learn from their mistakes. Indeed, humility is arguably the most important virtue for those engaged in projects consuming large amounts of investors' money.

Extract from a project review

For the project to be successful the managers and staff need to be open about mistakes and failures, to learn from them, be willing to expose their work to review by peers and have the capacity to accept responsibility themselves for the work that they and their staff do. (An independent report on the Performing Right Society's PROMS project that lost nearly £16 million.)

The potential for long-term project success

It would be an injustice to conclude this book without making reference to at least some of the IS projects that have been successful.

The following success stories indicate that, whilst significant challenges do remain for those undertaking IS projects, success can be achieved. Some organizations "get it right first time" and should be applauded; others have the will and humility to learn from their mistakes – an action which, in itself, deserves credit.

The London Ambulance Service

Following the collapse of the computer-aided dispatch system in 1992, the LAS initiated a strategic change program, with the emphasis firmly placed on improving patient care. In 1997, the LAS won the British Computer Society's Information Systems Management Excellence Award for its new control room, radio, telephone, and command and control computer system which were commissioned in 1996. More importantly, there is now a strong belief by the new LAS management that IT systems are no longer about computers, but about the people who have to use them.

The UK Passport Agency

Following the severe delays experienced by members of the public during the introduction of a new system during 1999, the Home Office and Passport Agency assured the Public Accounts Committee that there would be no recurrence of the problems. A wide-ranging program of improvements has since been established within the Agency, which has signaled the delivery of a number of substantial improvements, in particular:

- the balance between cost and quality of service has been fundamentally re-focused;
- the acceptance that political and reputational risk cannot be transferred;
- joint efficiency initiatives with the supplier – sharing savings through process and technological improvements;
- the introduction of adequate risk management and contingency planning processes;
- "vital-signs" reporting to ministers on business plan targets;
- creation of a communications strategy (based on the need to communicate to the public through a variety of means).

Barclays

On October 10, 1994, Barclays bank successfully implemented a massive £110 million ($165 million) IS project. The project was one of the largest in Europe and certainly the biggest project Barclays had ever been involved in. The risks were significant, but the "safe" option would have added tens of millions to the project costs and eliminated the potential benefits from the system.

The project proved to be a huge success, mainly as a result of the company directors ensuring that the project risks were shared between themselves and their supplier. They had stated that their supplier would not be paid if the system failed to go live. As if this was not a big enough incentive, the bank gave their supplier another – if the system did not work well, they would never again work for the organization.

▪▪◖ ◗ References

1   R. Waters and A. Cane, "Sudden death of a runaway bull," *Financial Times*, March 19, 1993

2   R. Waters, "Stock market chief quits over Taurus," *Financial Times*, March 12, 1993

3   *The Passport Delays of Summer 1999*, Select Committee on Public Accounts, Twenty-Fourth Report, House of Commons, UK, 1999

4   R. Waters, "Taurus settlement system likely to miss target date," *Financial Times*, September 16, 1991

Appendix 1

IS Project stage failure: initiation	Early warning symptoms	Corrective action
Over-ambitious project	■ Complex, far-reaching requirements combined with a "big-bang" approach to implementation. ■ Massive list of requirements. ■ Limited understanding of all the issues and risks affecting the project. ■ Wildly optimistic and immeasurable benefit claims. ■ Arbitrary estimates for timescales, effort, and cost.	■ Measure potential benefits. ■ Assess scope and requirements against strategic objectives. ■ Consider breaking project down into a number of smaller projects with limited scope and deliverables. ■ Consider rapid application techniques to deliver most important requirements first. ■ Undertake a feasibility study.
Lack of ownership	■ Project initiated without clear objectives or benefits. ■ Project not aligned to any business strategy or IT strategy. ■ No identification of business stakeholders. ■ No user involvement. ■ Lack of a justifiable business case. ■ Funding priorities unclear.	■ Ensure that the project plan and PID are distributed to key stakeholders for approval. ■ Ensure that the objectives of the project are clear to all stakeholders and members of the project team. ■ Rank projects. Award project points based on criteria such as operational or strategic benefit. ■ Make project managers spend time with the business so they can understand business issues and how they affect the project. ■ Ensure that financial and commercial benefits for the project have been made. ■ Ensure that business measures of success have been identified and measurement processes planned. ■ Ensure that conditions of satisfaction have been agreed with the project sponsor.

▶

IS Project stage failure: initiation	Early warning symptoms	Corrective action
Technology-led development	■ Failure to relate proposed technology to business objectives and benefits. ■ Poorly defined business case. ■ Limited user involvement. ■ Failure to appreciate the need for business change as well as IT development. ■ Too much faith in technology to solve business problems. ■ Allowing IT salespeople and account managers to influence staff and management during meetings.	■ Ensure that there is a justifiable business case before initiating the project. ■ Ensure that there is a process for tracking the benefits predicted. ■ Only believe benefits claims by IT salespeople and account managers if they can be measured and are relevant to the project. Be wary of wild claims often made by IT salespersons, such as "increases staff productivity." ■ Ensure that the requirements specification is written in business terms.
Failure to capture and prioritize requirements	■ Lack of business involvement in providing and approving requirements. ■ Huge list of requirements produced with no indication of their importance.	■ Ensure that business stakeholders provide resources for requirements capture and analysis. ■ Ensure that business stakeholders own task to prioritize requirements.
Failure to resolve stakeholder conflict	■ Design by committee. ■ Rational choices for design and development are compromised by much riskier options. ■ Key stakeholder input withheld. ■ Failure to agree requirements among stakeholders.	■ Ensure the project has a clear and strong owner. ■ Undertake stakeholder analysis to determine power and influence of stakeholders. ■ Manage stakeholder risks. ■ Monitor viability of project closely.

Project stage failure: planning	Early warning symptoms	Corrective action
Inexperienced project manager/lack of leadership	■ Poor team morale. ■ Lack of direction. ■ Failure of project manager to establish and maintain support from stakeholders within organization. ■ Lack of reporting and control structures.	■ Assign an experienced project manager to establish the project whilst providing a coaching/mentoring role to the existing project manager. ■ Establish a training program for project managers with additional support from mentoring and coaching.
Lack of executive support	■ Lack of accountability. ■ Frequent dismissal of problems. ■ Failure to own business issues. ■ Infrequent contact with project manager. ■ 'Pass the buck' approach to problems. ■ Lack of ownership of problems. ■ "Head in the sand" attitude.	■ Raise the issue with the relevant business sponsor, if necessary escalate to the project/program steering committee. ■ Increase visibility and profile of project. ■ Get a clear understanding of the business priorities for IT projects from the board. If the board have no clear strategy and priorities, present your own.
Poor communication	■ Hostile culture. ■ "Us and them" attitude within organization. ■ Failure to understand each side's arguments. ■ Objectives and requirements misinterpreted.	■ Increase face-to-face communication if possible. ■ Hold regular meetings (with a clear agenda and time limit). ■ Develop project/program communication strategy. ■ Promote a culture of openness within the organization.
Inadequate project planning	■ Lack of project plan. ■ Failure to identify risks and assumptions. ■ Poor understanding of project within business community. ■ Agressive schedule. ■ Poor understanding of project within team.	■ Ensure that there is a sound business case for the project. ■ Define the project. ■ Perform a reality check on the project – is it really achievable, given the constraints of time, cost and quality? ■ Gain executive support for the project. ■ Build the team with the right people. ■ Produce a clear plan of action. ■ Identify the conditions of success for the project. ■ Engage your stakeholders. ■ Establish control mechanisms to track key milestones.

▶

Project stage failure: planning	Early warning symptoms	Corrective action
Loss of focus on business benefits	■ Obsession with meeting timescales at the expense of delivering benefits and obtaining user satisfaction. ■ Lack of project success factors (as opposed to project management success factors). ■ Lack of investment appraisal methodology.	■ Ensure that focus is on the project. ■ Establish and gain acceptance of the conditions of success for the project. ■ Ensure that benefits are identified in business terms. ■ Ensure that there is a mechanism for tracking benefits throughout the project.
Unrealistic timescales	■ Milestones repeatedly missed. ■ Longer working hours needed to keep on schedule. ■ Scope of work cannot be achieved within the timescales. ■ Failure to amend plan in light of risks and issues.	■ Short-term: try and improve morale using bonus system rather than assign additional resource to the project. ■ Longer-term: assign additional staff to the project/reduce scope/extend schedule. ■ Seek expert opinon.

Project stage failure: analysis and development	Early warning symptoms	Corrective action
Lack of support from business	■ Failure to attend meetings. ■ Reluctance to commit resources. ■ Reluctance to offer information. ■ Limited user involvement. ■ Reluctance to own business issues.	■ Ensure that stakeholders are given the opportunity to provide input early in the project. ■ Ensure that stakeholders accept ownership of the project actions. ■ Ensure that stakeholders understand the limitations of the project (what the project is not supposed to do). ■ Ensure that stakeholders understand which of their requirements are included in the project. ■ Inform business sponsor of potential risks caused by lack of business involvement. ■ Hold a "commitment meeting" where stakeholders are asked to declare their commitment to the project by signing a commitment charter.

Project stage failure: analysis and development	Early warning symptoms	Corrective action
Project viability compromised	■ Major change in business objectives. ■ Major increase in project scope. ■ Major decrease in project funding. ■ Major decrease in delivery timescales. ■ Increase in unmitigated risks. ■ Organizational changes. ■ High staff turnover.	■ Regularly review the project's viability (for instance, when the project moves from one stage to another). ■ Identify "abort" criteria for project at the start of the project (from the project risk log). Monitor the risk log and any other events that trigger the decision to abort the project. ■ Ensure that the project has the full support from senior management – you may need it to terminate the project.
Lack of team motivation	■ Loss of initial drive and enthusiasm displayed at start of project. ■ Uncertainty within team. ■ Diminishing interest in project outcome. ■ Lack of drive to achieve targets.	■ Reward staff with bonuses or holidays when milestones have been passed. ■ Take the team away from the office for an "away-day." Get the team to set the agenda. If possible stay overnight so the team can have a well-earned break.
Failure to recognize warning signs and acknowledge problems	■ "Shoot the messenger" behavior. ■ Denial that problems exist. ■ Failure of management to own problems – excessive delegation. ■ Transferring blame to a "scapegoat." ■ Continually good press being distributed when you know things aren't going to plan.	■ Ensure that open and honest communication is adopted. ■ Ensure that management reporting structure is established and adhered to. ■ Adopt "open-door" policy for individuals to raise issues with project management; critical evaluation must be encouraged. ■ Introduce anonymous reporting system.
Lack of risk management	■ Failure to identify and react to unplanned events. ■ Little effort in actively managing risks. ■ Little or no understanding of events which may jeopardize the project.	■ Introduce risk management into the project. Identify each risk, the severity of the risk, probability of occurrence, the financial cost of the risk and how to mitigate it. ■ Produce a contingency plan.
Inadequate testing	■ Absence of test plan. ■ Lack of business involvement. ■ Duration of testing activities curtailed due to schedule pressure. ■ Excessive amount of time spent "fire-fighting" problems.	■ Develop test plan/program early on and distribute it for approval. ■ Ensure that testing has the support of management (executive sign-off for the test plan will help). ■ If you need more time to test – ask for it. Do not prematurely end testing as you will almost certainly suffer the consequences.

Project stage failure: implementation	Early warning symptoms	Corrective action
Failure to meet service level agreement (SLA) for new IT system	■ Failure to identify and budget for ongoing support costs. ■ Implementing project at a time when the organization cannot cope with new systems.	■ Plan and implement training programs for all technical and helpdesk staff. ■ Ensure that there is sufficient time for users and IT staff to familiarize themselves with the system before the cutover date.
Lack of training	■ Training program reduced or abandoned to ease schedule pressures. ■ Little user interest in system. ■ System not used correctly. ■ High number of user-reported errors during testing and implementation. ■ Lack of training program. ■ Failure to budget for training costs.	■ Resist pressure to implement a system without completing the training program – highlight business risks and IT support limitations. ■ Introduce "refresher" training if timescales slip. ■ Consider alternative training schemes (such as CBT) as well as traditional classroom-based training.
Failure to learn from mistakes	■ Failure to undertake a post-implementation review. ■ Little importance placed on outcome of post-implementation review. ■ Post-implementation review seen in a negative sense. ■ No 'best-practice' procedures available,	■ Ensure that outcome from post-implementation review is documented and distributed to all parties concerned. ■ Establish a function (with the project support office or program office) that is responsible for establishing best practice. Their main responsibility will be to process the deliverables from the post-implementation review and ensure that the information is used to improve standards and procedures for future projects.
Failure to meet business requirements	■ Failure to involve users in the project. ■ Vague or high-level requirements not refined and validated during design and development phases. ■ Little alignment between business requirements and system components needed to satisfy them. ■ Little alignment between project requirements and corporate strategy and goals. ■ Failure to manage user expectation. ■ Users' unfamiliarity with system. ■ Project not considered as important by business.	■ Set up an account team as a link between IT and the user, responsible for going into the business and keeping IT in line with the business direction. ■ Manage user expectations throughout the project. ■ Ensure requirements are approved by project sponsor. ■ Develop and implement a change control process to manage new requirements and make sure it has the approval of user managers and the business sponsor.

Project stage failure: implementation	Early warning symptoms	Corrective action
		■ Control expectations – state up front what the project will deliver and how it will be delivered. Make sure the users understand what the project will not be delivering.
		■ Spend time in the end-user environment to see the problems they experience with IT.
		■ Improve the education for the first-line support and helpdesks, so they can answer problems first time.
		■ Deliver what you promise.
Lack of ownership and accountability by management combined with the failure to take tough, unpleasant decisions when necessary	■ Project managers move onto different projects just before implementation. ■ An inexperienced project manager is appointed to the project. This person will become the scapegoat if plans backfire. ■ Project sponsors move to different positions within the company and relinquish all responsibility and control. ■ An external agency is recruited to take unpleasant decisions.	■ Promote and support a culture where failure is tolerated as long as lessons are learned. ■ Promote and support a culture that advocates risk-taking and allows managers to rise to the challenge without fear of reprisal if events do not turn out as planned. ■ Through communication and training, instill leadership and commitment in those who have project responsibilities. ■ Ensure that the board and senior executives maintain control over projects – and those who lead them.
Failure to deliver business benefits	■ Changing business needs and processes. ■ Failure to react quickly enough to the demands of the organization. ■ Excessive planning and development timescales. ■ Failure to review investment appraisal and expected benefits (financial or otherwise) throughout the lifecycle of the project.	■ Adopt an incremental rather than "big-bang" approach, with regular milestones, each delivering an auditable business benefit. If there is no alternative to the "big-bang" approach, ensure the project deliverables can be satisfied in the timescales allocated to the project. ■ Ensure that project management, systems development, and benefits management methodologies are aligned. ■ Ensure that business unit and corporate goals are communicated and understood within the organization.

Appendix 2

The project healthcheck

Project planning

- Does the project have a clear, unambiguous vision statement or mission statement?

- Do all team members believe the vision is realistic?

- Does the project have a business case that details the business benefit and how the benefit will be measured?

- If new and unproven technology is to be used on the project can a prototype be produced to assess the feasibility of the solution?

- Does the project have a detailed, written specification of what the software is supposed to do?

- Did the project team interview people who will actually use the software early in the project and continue to involve them throughout the project?

- Does the project use a documented software development methodology?

- Is that methodology understood in the context of the project?

- Were the schedule and budget estimates officially updated at the end of the most recently completed phase?

- Does the project have detailed, approved architecture requirements and design specifications?

- Does the project have a detailed, written quality assurance plan that requires design and code reviews in addition to system testing?

- Does the project have a detailed, staged software delivery plan, which describes the stages in which the software will be designed, implemented and delivered?

- Does the project's plan include time for public holidays, annual leave, sick days, and ongoing training, and are resources allocated at less than 100 per cent?

- Have the project plan and schedule been approved by the development team, the quality assurance team, and the technical writing team – in other words, the people responsible for doing the work?
- Has the project plan been approved by key business stakeholders?

Project management

- Has a single, key executive who has decision-making authority been made responsible for the project, and does the project have that person's active support?
- Does the project manager's workload allow him or her to devote an adequate amount of time to the project?
- Does the project have well-defined, detailed milestones that are considered to be either 100 per cent done or 100 per cent not done?
- Can a project stakeholder easily find out which of these milestones have been completed?
- Does the project have a feedback channel by which project members can anonymously report problems to their own managers and senior managers?
- Does the project have a written plan for controlling changes to the software's specification?
- Does the project have a change control board that has final authority to accept or reject proposed changes?
- Are planning materials and status information for the project – including effort and schedule estimates, task assignments, and progress compared to the plan thus far – available to every team member?
- Is all source code placed under automated revision control?
- Does the project environment include the basic tools needed to complete the project, including defect tracking software, source code control, and project management software?
- Is there a detailed plan (including critical path, time, schedules, milestones, manpower requirements, etc.) for the duration of the project?
- Is there is a detailed budget for the project throughout the project lifecycle?
- Have key personnel needs (i.e. who and when) been understood and specified in the project plan?
- Have slack time or resources been introduced into the plan so that can they be used in other areas during emergencies?

- Are project tasks well managed?
- Are there contingency plans in case the project is off schedule or off budget?
- Do the project team members understand their role?

Risk management

- Does the project plan articulate a list of current risks to the project? Has the list been updated recently?
- Is there a process in place for reviewing and updating project risks?
- Does the project have a risk manager who is responsible for identifying emerging risks to the project?
- If the project uses subcontractors, does it have a plan for managing each subcontract organization and a single person in charge of each one?
- Has the project plan been updated in light of the project risks?

People management

- Does the project team have all the technical expertise needed to complete the project?
- Does the project team have expertise with the business environment in which the software will operate?
- Does the project have a technical leader capable of leading the project successfully?
- Are there enough people to do all the work required?
- Does everyone work well together?
- Is the level of training planned for the project sufficient to meet the training requirements of those involved within it?
- Is each person committed to the project?
- Are all the project stakeholders and their impact on the project known to the project team?
- Does everyone involved in the project think it will be a success? If not why not?
- Does the project team feel under pressure to undertake tasks they know will compromise their own professional standards?

 # Glossary

Acceptance testing

Testing undertaken by an independent team to ensure that the developed system meets all the requirements originally stated. User acceptance testing a form of acceptance testing in which the system is tested by those individuals who will have to use it.

ARID

Assumptions, Risks, Issues, Dependencies. A popular mnemonic used to identify some of the important concepts of project planning.

Baseline

The identification and management of a set of components in a known state.

Benefits

The business reason for undertaking an IS project (e.g. quantified increases in revenue, decreases in costs, reductions in working capital and/or increases in performance that occur directly as a result of a project.)

Big-bang implementation

The term used to describe an implementation where the scope of system functionality is high and more significantly, delivered all at the same time.

Business case

The definition and justification for undertaking (or for continuing) a project or program. The business case defines the financial and other benefits which the project is expected to realize together with the scope, deliverables, resources needed, risks, schedule, and overall approach. A business case may request authorization for a part of a project only (e.g. for the feasibility stage of the project) or for the entire project.

Business champion

An individual within the business who possesses the will, charisma, and tenacity to drive through business change.

Business driver

A strategic business desire that will typically require a significant amount of effort to fulfill (e.g. the need to sell to new markets).

Business program

A set of closely related and interdependent projects and organizational activities undertaken to realize the benefits identified from a business plan or strategy.

Business sponsor

The business sponsor identifies the need for an IS project or program and communicates that to the organization through a business case. The business sponsor is essentially the owner and the 'champion' of the project, providing the funding to empower the appropriate IT resources necessary to deliver the stated business benefits. See also *Project sponsor*.

CBT

Computer-based training.

CCTA

Central Computing and Telecommunications Agency. The CCTA established the PRINCE methodology on behalf of the British government. The CCTA have now become the Office of Government Commerce (OGC) who own the PRINCE trademark.

Change management

The formal process through which changes to the project plan are introduced and approved. Not to be confused with the management of change.

CM

Configuration Management. A discipline, normally supported by software tools, which provides precise control over a project's assets.

CMM

Capability Maturity Model. A process-based model used to assess the maturity of the software development process within an organization, introduced by Carnegie Mellon University in the US.

CMS

Configuration Management System. A system designed to support the configuration management procedures within an organization.

COCOMO
COnstructive COst MOdel. A model that can be used to estimate software development effort, costs, and schedules – originally published in 1981.

Constraint
Defined restriction or limitation imposed on a project. These can often pose a risk to a project.

Contingency plan
Plan of action to minimize or negate the adverse effects of a risk should it occur.

COTS
Commercial Off-The-Shelf. Software or hardware products that are ready for use and on sale to the general public. COTS products are designed to be implemented easily into existing systems without the need for customization.

Critical success factors
Elements of work that, if completed successfully, will satisfy a goal or objective.

Deliverable
Output produced by the project in the process of meeting the project objectives, e.g. a report or product. Each key deliverable should be identified within the planning stages of the project and represented in the project plan by a milestone.

Dependency
A constraint on the sequence and timing of activities in a project. Activities may be dependent on other activities within the same project (internal dependency) or on activities/deliverables from other projects (inter-dependency).

DSDM
Dynamic Systems Development Methodology. A non-proprietary rapid application development methodology developed and maintained by the DSDM Consortium.

Exception failure
An unexpected condition that causes a program to fail. Common situations that can cause data exceptions are: empty data files; values outside expected limits; insufficient memory; and bad data from another program.

Expert witness

An independent IT specialist whose expert knowledge is used to support statements made by one party who are bringing legal proceedings against another.

FPA

Function Point Analysis. A method of measuring software size and complexity, devised by IBM in 1977.

GUI

Graphical User Interface. A program interface designed to be more user-friendly through the use of graphics. A GUI negates the need to enter program commands directly into the computer system (a command-line interface).

Hot backup

A hot backup is a specific type of redundant backup which can instantly assume control over all system tasks from the main system without any operational impact. This is only possible by constantly keeping the data and processes in both systems synchronized.

See *Redundant backup*.

ISO 9001

An international standard for quality assurance.

ISO 9126

An international standard for software quality.

Issue

A risk that since being identified has occurred. A risk is an event that *may* occur – when it does, it becomes an issue.

Iterative development

A contrasting approach to the traditional "waterfall" systems development lifecycle that allows key stages in the development lifecycle to be reworked during a number of iterations, refining the solution after each iteration. JAD and RAD are two techniques used within iterative development.

ITT

Invitation To Tender. A formal request made to a supplier inviting them to tender for a contracted piece of work.

JAD

Joint Application Development. Often assumed (incorrectly) to be synonymous with *RAD*. JAD is a powerful technique that can be used on RAD projects which brings together all project stakeholders into a forum from which decisions can be made which are mutually acceptable. JAD workshops deliver benefits by increasing the speed of the decision-making process, increasing ownership, and increasing productivity.

KPI

Key Performance Indicator. A business performance measures which can be used to evaluate the success of a specific course of action. For example, a key performance indicator used to evaluate the efficiency of a Customer Relationship Management (CRM) system might be the length of time it takes to log an initial customer call.

Management of change

A term often used to describe the process of transforming an organization from one state to another. Not to be confused with *change management*, which is a technique used on projects to ensure that changes to the project schedule, scope, benefits, and cost are managed properly.

Milestone

A significant event (often representing the start of a stage, key review point or significant deliverable) which is used to monitor progress at a summary level. For planning purposes milestones are activities of zero duration.

MITP

Managing Implementation of the Total Project. A proprietary project management methodology developed by IBM.

MOSCOW

A popular technique used to prioritize requirements against business needs.

MTBF

Mean Time Before Failure. An indicator used to measure the resilience of computer hardware.

OGC

Office of Government Commerce. A UK government agency that provides help and guidance to other departments, agencies, and public bodies on the efficient and effective use of IT to deliver business objectives.

OOD

Object-Oriented Development. A class of programming languages and techniques based on the concept of an "object."

OPEN

Object-oriented Process, Environment and Notation. A systems development framework particularly suited to object-oriented development.

Opportunity

The opposite of a risk. An opportunity is a possibility to enhance project benefits.

PID

Project Initiation Document. A document outlining the management approach and justification for the project. Typically, a PID will identify objectives, assumptions, risks, plans, and team structures for the project. It is usually drafted by the project manager after feasibility studies and pilot studies have been completed or are underway.

PIR

Project Issue Register. A means by which issues can be identified and tracked throughout a project.

PLEST

Political, Legal, Economic, Social, Technological. Factors that affect the behavior of organizations and therefore have a bearing on the success of IS projects.

PRINCE

PRojects IN Controlled Environments. A structured method for project management. It is a de facto standard used extensively by the UK government and within the private sector.

Program

A group of projects managed in a co-ordinated way to obtain benefits not available from managing them individually.

Project coach

The project coach is accountable for supporting key members of a project team, giving them advice and guidance on project management, and helping them to perform beyond their own expectations

Project lifecycle
A sequence of defined stages through which the project progresses.

Project manager
The project manager is accountable to the project sponsor and is responsible for managing a set of tasks, which will deliver the required benefits and satisfy the stated business objectives.

Project organization
The structure adopted to support the people participating in a project.

Project plan
A document supporting the project definition section within a business case which details the schedule, resources, and costs for the project.

Project sponsor
The project sponsor is the business advocate and is responsible for ensuring that the conditions of satisfaction for the project are achieved (the realization of benefits) and for ensuring the overall viability of the project. The project sponsor is the owner of the business case and is the primary risk taker within a project.

PROMS
Performing Right Society On-line Membership System.

PSO
Project Support Office. A team providing administrative support to projects. One of the key tasks for a PSO will be to identify and distribute standards across the projects it supports.

QMS
Quality Management System. A system designed to support the quality management procedures within an organization.

Quality criteria
Criteria that a deliverable must meet in order to be accepted as fit for purpose.

Quality plan
A document defining the quality policies that will be applied on a project.

RAD

Rapid Application Development. An umbrella term used to describe various systems development tools and techniques integrated to achieve rapid information systems development.

Redundant backup

A standby system to which system tasks can be routed in the event that the main system is no longer able to operate normally.

Regression testing

Testing that must be performed after functional improvements or corrections have been made to the system to confirm that the changes have not created any unintended side effects.

RFP

Request For Proposal. A document produced by an organization requesting the services of an external supplier. An RFP should identify what is required by the customer and the terms under which that must be delivered.

Risk

An event that may jeopardize the success of the project. Risk is analyzed during the planning process and managed throughout the duration of the project.

RUP

Rational Unified Processes. A methodology used for object-oriented development, developed by the Rational Corporation. RUP advocates an iterative model of software development.

Schedule

A time-based representation of work activities, including the start and duration of activities and the relationship between them.

SDLC

Software Development Life cycle. The process of developing information systems involving analysis, design, construction, testing, implementation, and maintenance.

SEI

Software Engineering Institute. A federally funded research and development center sponsored by the US Department of Defense. The SEI's core purpose is to help others make measured improvements in their software engineering capabilities.

Sequential development

The traditional or "waterfall" approach to systems development. A linear approach to software development whereby each step of the process must be completed in a strict, sequential order. The next step cannot be completed until the previous step has been completed. Compare with *iterative development*.

Showstopper

An event within the lifecycle of a project which may seriously jeopardize its success, e.g. the withdrawal of funding.

SLA

Service Level Agreement. A commitment, usually in writing, between a service provider and a service user that specifies the scope of the service offered.

Soft systems methodology

A systems development methodology developed by Peter Checkland, which places emphasis on resolving 'soft' issues (such as politics, social issues and human behavior).

SQA

Software Quality Assurance. The process by which software quality can be assured through the use of techniques such as inspections, peer reviews, walkthroughs, and testing.

SSADM

Structured Systems Analysis and Design. A methodology covering the analysis and design stages of systems development.

Stakeholder

Any person or group who has an interest or involvement in the project.

Sub-project

A sub-project is a unit of work that has been sub-divided from a large project. It allows an activity to be managed more closely and is especially useful when contracting out specific tasks to external agencies.

SWOT analysis

A strategic decision-making technique, based on analyzing the potential Strengths, Weaknesses, Opportunities, and Threats inherent within different scenarios.

TickIT

A quality standard specifically aimed for software development, relating directly to the requirements set out in ISO 9001:2000.

TQM

Total Quality Management. A comprehensive approach to quality within an organization, based on the concept of continuous improvement.

UML

Unified Modeling Language. A modeling language developed for use in object-oriented development. UML is supported by the Object Management Group (OMG), which adopted it as a standard in 1997. Since then it has been actively reviewed and updated.

Waterfall model

The traditional approach to software development, where activities are performed in a strictly sequential basis.

WSDDM

World-wide Solution Design and Delivery Method. IBM's project management methodology developed to replace MITP. WSDDM is now largely superseded by WWPMM.

WWPMM

World-Wide Project Management Methodology. IBM's current project management methodology.

Index

Figures in **bold** indicate glossary entries.